Shakespeare's World
World
Background Readings in the
English Renaissance

SHAKESPEARE'S WORLD

Background Readings in the English Renaissance

Edited with Commentary and Notes by
GERALD M. PINCISS
and
ROGER LOCKYER

A Frederick Ungar Book

CONTINUUM · NEW YORK

1995

The Continuum Publishing Company
370 Lexington Avenue
New York, NY 10017

Printed in the United States of America

Library of Congress Cataloging-in-Publication Data

Shakespeare's world: background readings in the English Renaissance /
edited by Gerald M. Pinciss and Roger Lockyer.
p.   cm.
"A Frederick Ungar book."
Bibliography: p.
Includes index.
ISBN 0-8264-0451-0
1. Shakespeare, William, 1564–1616—Sources. 2. Renaissance—
England. 3. European literature—Renaissance, 1450–1600.
4. Shakespeare, William, 1564–1616—Knowledge and learning.
5. Great Britain—Civilization—16th century. I. Pinciss, G. M.
II. Lockyer, Roger.
PR2953.R4S53 1989
822.3'3—dc19   88-31229
                                                              CIP

Contents

Acknowledgments

This book could not have been written without the help and encouragement of many friends, colleagues, and students. Our mutual friends, Professors Emeriti Morton Cohen of the City University of New York and Richard Swift of New York University, brought us together and nurtured our efforts. Only their assistance combined with the unfailing generosity in listening time and advice of Dr. Lewis Falb of the New School for Social Research in New York and of Percy Steven of the Rose Bruford College in London prevented such a long-distance project from disappearing over the Atlantic. Our good friend and colleague Professor Marlies K. Danziger patiently read and improved our various drafts, offering intelligent criticism, wise advice, and continual support. This has become a far better work for her efforts; we acknowledge our debt to her with gratitude. Professor Calvin Edwards of Hunter College as well as Drs. Julian Chrysostomides and John Carter of Royal Holloway College kindly commented on sections of our manuscript, making most helpful recommendations. Hunter students who used portions of this material as a text also taught us invaluable lessons. Finally, we wish to express our thanks to our editor, Evander Lomke, for his skillful and experienced problem solving.

Gerald M. Pinciss, Hunter College,
City University of New York

Roger Lockyer, Royal Holloway
and Bedford New College,
University of London

Preface

This anthology of background readings in the English Renaissance is designed to meet the needs of students and general readers of both literature and history. The selections have been chosen to illustrate the ideas that most profoundly shaped the assumptions and practices of English men and women in the late sixteenth and early seventeenth centuries. Collectively, these readings provide an introduction to an especially complex age, one that first confronted many of the social, political, and moral problems that still trouble modern society. And since, as the New Historicist criticism has shown, the literature of a culture both reflects and shapes it, we have included many specific references to the works of major writers who imaginatively treat the subjects discussed in the extracts. William Shakespeare, Philip Sidney, Edmund Spenser, Christopher Marlowe, Ben Jonson, and Francis Bacon—to name only a few who are mentioned here—dealt in their works with the crucial questions of their age. By these citations we hope to demonstrate how literature assimilates the issues and ideas of the time and to suggest how, in turn, it affects the public's response to them. Many of the excerpts included here are of substantial length. All are reprinted in modern spelling. Introductions and headnotes discuss the intellectual contribution of each selection, tell the reader something about its author, and illustrate its impact on Shakespeare and his contemporaries by giving specific examples from Elizabethan and Jacobean literature. Texts that were written originally in Latin, French, and Italian are presented here in their Renaissance English translations.

We begin with "The Universe and the Human Condition," in which we examine works that offer metaphysical and philosophical responses to life. In the seldom-read but highly revealing A Discourse of the Preservation of the Sight, André DuLaurens sets forth the traditional view of an orderly universe. In this account, human nature is determined by the balance of the four elements that singly or in combination make up all of matter. As DuLaurens well knows, however, balance is not always attained, for humanity has fallen, and, with one or another element predominating, physical and mental illness ensue. Passion rules reason; and melancholy, one of the most common and debilitating maladies, results. Appropriately, DuLaurens concentrates on the causes and cures of this disease, for it was both the most prevalent and the most fashionable of the time.

DuLaurens speaks as a conservative medical authority, but a more personal and questioning response to the human condition is recorded in the *Essays* of Michel de Montaigne. Sensitive and intelligent, Montaigne found himself living in an ambiguous and uncertain world, a world in which conflicting and irreconcilable approaches to knowledge were being advocated everywhere. The skepticism that resulted was both a matter of personal disposition and a consequence of what he had seen of the corruption of the legal system and of the viciousness and cruelty that characterized the continual religious warfare in France. No wonder Montaigne preferred the peace and security of his tower. As he explains in his *Essays*, it is all but impossible to understand other people—though the attempt to do so is intriguing. Indeed, it is hardly possible to understand oneself—though the effort must be made. The human mind can never establish absolute truth or pierce to the very heart of things. As a consequence, belief in a higher wisdom must be taken on trust: Montaigne's fideism is a logical result.

In Part II we focus on the central topic of religion. We begin with excerpts from two Anglican homilies—sermons designed to be read in churches throughout the country. The homily "Against Disobedience" demonstrates how support of the monarchy was made a religious cause by describing rebellion in terms of its wickedness; and the homily "Of Matrimony" shows the way in which the church tried to influence patterns of private behavior.

Our next two selections cast light on the cloudy subject of predestination. The official Anglican position as defined in the *Thirty-nine Articles* is relatively positive, since it suggests that all humanity may hope for salvation. In contrast, the Calvinist view, expressed in the *Lambeth Articles*, claims that God has predestined only "the elect" to be saved and the rest to be damned eternally. Although Elizabeth personally prevented the adoption of the Lambeth Articles, we reprint them to illustrate an important aspect of continental Protestantism that was fervently embraced by many English men and women.

Our final reading in the section on "Religion" is taken from Richard Hooker's *Of The Laws of Ecclesiastical Polity*—a majestic defense of the Elizabethan ecclesiastical settlement. In masterly prose Hooker marshals his arguments with what has been properly described as "sweet reasonableness." His great work presents the Anglican Church not as a feeble and temporary compromise but as a firmly based and permanent institution combining the best elements of Roman Catholicism and continental Protestantism.

Part III deals with magic and the occult, and covers the topics of Hermeticism, witchcraft, fairylore, astrology, numerology, alchemy, and white magic. Although these beliefs were widespread and still attracted devoted adherents, many Elizabethans were gradually turning away from such irrational ideas. Our excerpts from *The Discovery of Witchcraft* demonstrate how a writer can use reason and irony to cast doubt on popular suprarational practices, for Reginald Scot was blessed with a mocking sense of humor. His efforts did not immediately convert all believers, but his book attests to the growing power of inductive reasoning, the basis of the scientific method. In this period of transition from one method of pursuing truth to another, many Elizabethans tried to hold onto opposing and even contradictory principles. John Dee, the best known Elizabethan alchemist and white magician, reveals in his preface to a translation of Euclid's *Geometry* that he well understood the practical applications of this discipline. Yet at the same time he thought that by applying Hermetic teaching to mathematics he could unlock the hidden secrets of the universe and its Creator. For Dee, the prospect is wondrous and dangerous, the attempt thrilling and threatening, as his excited prose reveals.

New and iconoclastic ideas were being expressed also in the field of political theory, as we demonstrate in Part IV. Niccolò Machiavelli, who had had considerable experience of Italian politics, came to the conclusion that metaphysical truth is a poor guide to the successful conduct of human affairs. Instead, in his influential little book, he stresses the need to look to history as well as the contemporary world before formulating a theory of politics. In contrast to the idealism of many of his predecessors, Machiavelli argues that political stability, imposed through the power of an autocratic ruler, offers the best hope of lasting peace and security on both an international and a civic level. Accordingly, his advice—shocking and pragmatic as it turned out to be—is directed to teaching a prince how to gain and hold political power while paying little more than lip service to conventional morality.

Whereas Machiavelli's experiences made him acutely aware of the dangers of weak government, the French Huguenot, Philippe Duplessis-Mornay, who witnessed the slaughter of his fellow Protestants in the St. Bartholomew's Day Massacre of 1572, was concerned to construct a defense against government that was too strong. In the *Vindiciae Contra Tyrannos* he develops a powerful argument that kings are merely God's deputies, and that if their rule turns into tyranny their subjects, under the guidance of the civil magistrates, have a duty to resist them.

Another Frenchman, Jean Bodin, combined Machiavelli's advocacy of absolute princely rule with more traditional assumptions. In *The Six Bookes of a Commonweale* Bodin asserts that God, who appoints sovereigns to their high place, requires subjects to give them total obedience. Kings are morally bound to govern in the best interests of their people, but they are accountable for their actions only to God, and not to any human institution.

As one might expect, these views were also expressed by the philosopher–King James I. In the *Basilicon Doron* James lists the moral qualities desirable in a ruler, and encourages his son to live an exemplary life and to follow God's instructions in order to govern well. In *The Trew Law of Free Monarchies* James puts the practice of kingship into its philosophical context. Expressing views that are remarkably similar to those of Bodin, James claims that the royal prerogative is God-given; that kings are above the law; and that since all monarchs, good and bad, are chosen by God, rebellion is never justifiable.

It should not be assumed that James's subjects shared his views about the overriding authority of the ruler, as we make plain in Part V on "Common Law and the English Constitution." Many, if not most, of Shakespeare's contemporaries believed that in England the authority of the law was more powerful than the will of the monarch. Chief Justice Sir John Fortescue, who wrote his *De Laudibus Legum Angliae* in the troubled years of the Wars of the Roses, makes the claim that the English monarchy was constitutional, not absolute, and that no king could "make any alteration or change in the laws of the realm without the consent of the subject." Fortescue effectively establishes the theoretical and legal basis for the English system of limited monarchy, and his work became a fundamental text for successive generations of jurists. One of the most famous lawyers in the late Tudor and early Stuart period was Sir Edward Coke. In the excerpts presented here from his *Reports*, Coke gives thanks to Elizabeth for her commitment to constitutional rule and utters a great paean of praise to the common law as the guardian of English liberties.

In Part VI, on "Social Graces—Conduct and Language," we turn from broad social questions to matters affecting the individual. Social conduct and the ways in which manners could hinder or promote a successful career are discussed in Baldassare Castiglione's *Book of the Courtier*—a work that established a pattern of behavior for all those who hoped for advancement in the service of a prince. Castiglione's account of the conversations at the ducal court of Urbino demonstrated by its style the essentials of elegant sophistication, while by its subject it made plain the qualities required for the perfect courtier—his manner, talents, and character, as well as his susceptibility to feminine beauty and to the glories of love.

Castiglione's influence was still profound during Elizabeth's reign. Even so didactic a work as Sir Thomas Wilson's *The Arte of Rhetorique* found encouragement from Castigilione for its encomium on the civilizing power of eloquence and the utility of rhetoric. The author of *The Arte of English Poesie* was another who turned to Castiglione for inspiration, arguing that elegancies of language—the schemes and tropes that ornament and give delight to our words—are like the courtier's refined and graceful behavior. Understanding how Elizabethan writers organized their efforts, and which literary devices they thought were appropriate for what effects, enables one to gain a deeper understanding of the literature of the period.

In Part VII, on "Education," we show how English writers were influenced by powerful new trends in countries both north and south of the Alps. Sir Thomas Elyot and Roger Ascham were concerned with the education of sons of the nobility and gentry, whose social position would give them a key role in the government of Tudor England. Both authors believed that a combination of Christian morality and classical learning would provide the most appropriate curriculum to equip young gentlemen for the service of the state. But they were not content with this. In their writings they also emphasize the need for a new attitude on the part of teachers, substituting kindness for severity and sympathetic encouragement for force-feeding.

Part VIII, on "England and Her History," is concerned with a subject that received new attention in the Renaissance. Humanists, who devoted themselves to a detailed examination of classical texts, came to understand that literary styles reflected the age in which they were used, and that the vocabulary of a writer could only be fully understood by setting his work in its historical context. This interest in ancient history and what it could reveal led in due course to the study of the history of England as a subject also worthy of attention. We have included selections from two books that attempted to provide for England what classical authors had already done for Greece and Rome. Sir Thomas Smith's *De Republica Anglorum* analyzes the English constitution and the organization of English society; William Camden's *Britannia* offers detailed and scholarly accounts of the topography and antiquities of England, Scotland, and Ireland. Both works bear witness to the growing national pride and self-consciousness of the inhabitants of Elizabethan England.

The final section, "Monarchy in Action" reprints the words of rulers and courtiers at critical moments in their lives. Included are excerpts from a late address of Queen Elizabeth I to a delegation from the House of Commons; an exchange of letters between Francis Bacon and his patron, the Earl of Essex, who was the Queen's favorite; the charges against Essex and his fellow peer, the Earl of Southampton, when they stood trial for high treason; and Essex's last speech before he met his death on the scaffold. These extracts illustrate the innate theatricality of the men and women who ruled Elizabethan England, their concern to create a public image that would justify their actions not only to their contemporaries but also to posterity.

No background reader can hope to include every important work or author, or refer to every literary example, but the material contained in these pages should provide voyagers venturing into unfamiliar waters with some essential aids to navigation. We wish these adventurers, in the words of Shakespeare's Prospero, "calm seas, auspicious gales" *(Tempest V.i.).*

The Universe
and the
Human Condition

The Elizabethans thought of the universe as comprised of co-herently ordered, parallel planes: a cosmic order involving the sun, planets, seasons, nature; a political/social order, involving the government, the courts, the army, and the family; and a personal order, involving one's physiological and psychological well-being. This divine plan worked by correspondences so that all three planes shared comparable elements and relationships. For example, the hierarchy of the state is reflected in the hierarchy of the sun and planets, and proper government in the state requires the same respect for authority as proper government in the home. The human body, too, reflects the same ordering as both of these planes, for it is a little world, a microcosm, that can replicate the macrocosm. In *King Lear* (1605) Shakespeare points up the interrelationship of natural events and human emotions: the fierceness of the thunder and lightning on the heath matches the fury of the king's anguish, though he "strives in his little world of man to out-storm / The to-and-fro conflicting wind and rain" (III.i.).

The belief that exact correspondences or analogies exist among the universal, political, and private spheres was certainly comforting; tidy and logical, this approach is undeniably appealing. God rules the heavens as the sun rules the sky, as the king rules the state, as the father rules the household, and as the mind rules the body. Yet other views of the universe were being heard ever more loudly, and these postulated nothing so permanent, rational, and optimistic. Fortune was ever fickle; change could be chaotic as well as orderly; humanity had fallen and all things beneath the moon were subject to decay. Eden was lost like the Golden Age of classical myth that was followed by an Age of Iron. The four elements might be held in balance, but they were always ready to resume their permanent opposition, fire with water and earth with air. These, according to some, were as irreconcilable as matter and spirit. The followers of Martin Luther and John Calvin described a God who was inscrutable and incomprehensible; and as for humanity, Calvin claims, "There is nothing at all in our nature but wretchedness and misery." According to Sir Philip Sidney, humanity has almost lost its ability to distinguish right from wrong; "erected wit" is hampered by an "infected will"—one is tempted by evil even when one knows it is evil. These factors together with the religious struggles between Catholics and Protestants and among the various Protestant sects; the new critical, objective study of nature promoted by such men as Galileo and Bacon; and the growing individualism and skepticism among the educated that were a consequence of these controversies and investigations all contributed to an increasingly negative view of life. On the private level, passion could sometimes rule reason; on the political level, rebellion could sometimes hold sway. For most Renaissance Englishmen, Sidney's terms perfectly described the moral dilemma of postlapsarian humanity and account for the astonishing combination of optimism and pessimism found in the literature of this period.

An elaborate example of the traditional Elizabethan belief in correspondences can be found in the way their worldview directly affected their explanation for human temperament and for a healthy psyche. Each of the four elements that were thought to compose the universe— earth, air, fire, and water—were described by simple, basic qualities: hot or cold and wet or dry. These same qualities of temperature and moisture were also believed to be characteristic of the four humors, or body liquids, that supposedly determine the temperament of an individual—melancholic, sanguinary (cheerful), choleric (irascible), and phlegmatic (dull and passionless). According to Elizabethan medical theory, each one of the four temperaments or "complexions" was a consequence of a particular body fluid that had the same qualities of temperature and moisture as one of the four elements. Moreover, each of the combinations of temperature and moisture resulted in a particular emotional state. For instance, coldness and dryness contracted the heart and aroused feelings associated with suffering, such as fear, sorrow, and despair; these were the cold and dry, or melancholy passions. Black bile or melancholic was the body fluid that caused coldness and dryness, the qualities shared by the earth.

Yet for the Elizabethans the correspondences between macrocosm and microcosm—the universe and the human body—were even more extensive and direct. For example, the cold and dry qualities of melancholy were shared by old age, the north wind, winter, the element earth, the planet Saturn, and the constellations Cancer, Scorpio, and Pisces; the hot and moist qualities of the sanguinary were shared by youth, spring, the south wind, air, the planet Jupiter, and the constellations Gemini, Libra, and Aquarius; the hot and dry qualities of the choleric complexion were found in infancy, summer, the west wind, fire, the planet Mars, and the constellations Aries, Leo, and Sagittarius; and, finally, the cold and moist qualities of the phlegmatic complexion were found among those in their declining years, autumn, the east wind, water, the moon, and the constellations Taurus, Virgo, and Capricorn. Each of these combinations of the signs of the zodiac that couple three constellations was called a "trigon." Because of his fiercely red face, Bardolph in *Henry IV, Part Two* (1597) is called "the fiery Trigon"—that is, Aries, Leo, and Sagittarius, joining forces, could account for the glowing color of his countenance. Everything related to everything else; everything had its analogue. For instance, many believed that to be born (or conceived) under Saturn's influence could contribute to one's melancholy nature. But in *King Lear*, Edmund, a skeptic and an atheist, ridicules this notion because he says that he would be as he is "had the maidenliest star in the firmament twinkled on my bastardizing."

These interconnections could be used to explain how the heavens might affect individual lives, acting as the agents of arbitrary chance or divine guidance. For example, using *King Lear* again as our example, both Gloucester and Kent, unlike Edmund, believe in the power of the stars; in fact, Kent thinks they alone can account for the difference between Cordelia and her sisters, all daughters of the same parents:

> *It is the stars,*
> *The stars above us, govern our conditions;*
> *Else one self mate and make could not beget*
> *Such different issues.*

> (IV.iii.)

According to Sir Walter Raleigh, the stars are not merely objects of beauty. They have "a peculiar virtue and operation" so that they function as "instruments and organs" of Providence.

The Elizabethans recognized that although the right proportion of the four humors created healthy individuals with perfectly balanced dispositions, such perfection was rare, and, depending on the religion and philosophy of the individual Elizabethan, not to be expected. To account for the human race's fallen and impaired condition, Renaissance medical theory postulated that, in actuality, human beings consisted of a mixture of the humors in which one predominated, establishing the personality. However, if the predominating humor should become overly strong, capable of causing an immoderate passion, it could prove pathological, damaging the body and even threatening the soul. Since people are all prone to sin and error, their affections could overwhelm their reason. In *Measure for Measure* (1604), the strength of Angelo's desire for Isabella and the weakness of his restraining intellect explain why he succumbs to temptation, for he is prompted "both in the heat of blood / And lack of temper'd judgment" (V.i.). According to the Elizabethans, the imagination, which is capable of distinguishing between pleasure and pain but not between right and wrong, could increase the power of the emotions, and together they could subordinate the ability of the mind to govern behavior. When passions control the rational faculties, they are the diseases of the soul, destroying one's moral being.

André DuLaurens,
A Discourse of the Preservation of the Sight; of Melancholic Diseases; of Rheums, and of Old Age.

Although each of the four possible human temperaments or complexions can turn into a disease, that caused by melancholy becomes an especially important topic toward the end of the sixteenth century. Those suffering from it are among the most interesting and complex figures in English Renaissance literature. The diseased state occurs when the black bile that produces melancholy is abnormal in quantity or when it becomes too cold or too hot. (Body temperature can be moved out of the normal range by an improper diet, a physiological disorder, or a powerful passion, for example.) When proper balance and control are lost, any immoderate emotion such as grief, anger, or joy can result in a pathological form of melancholy, and this state can even be caused by an intense preoccupation—melancholy is the occupational disease of scholars. But whatever forms it takes, melancholy, according to the medical tradition stemming from Galen, is a psychosis characterized by morbid depression and even hallucinations. Religious doubts may lead the melancholic to despair; and envy, distrust, and discontent may move him to criminal activity. In this view, melancholy results in a miserable mental condition.

But another and contrary view of the subject was also accepted in the Renaissance. According to Aristotle and the tradition that was derived from him, melancholy people are especially talented. The powerful intelligence and imagination typical of the melancholy may inspire them to produce works of genius. After all, the argument goes, all famous philosophers, politicians, poets, and artists were melancholy: Heracles, Ajax, and Bellerophon went mad, and Empedocles, Socrates, and Plato were atrabilious—that is, in them the excessive heat cooled to a mean temperature. Marsilio Ficino, the Florentine humanist, even argued that a scholar's mental powers are enhanced by melancholy; if properly adjusted, it will enable the fortunate individual to uncover the highest truths and raise him far above the level of common abilities where the secrets of nature will be revealed in mystic ecstasy.

The Renaissance reputations of Galen and Aristotle were so strong that these two opposing interpretations of melancholy were both given credence. With their high regard for authority, Renaissance writers accepted both views, little troubled by the inconsistencies, inadequacies, and contradictions involved. And in the end, although Galen dominated the medical literature of the period, Aristotle's view, making melancholy glamorous and attractive, ultimately shaped the popular and literary conception of this humor.

Since melancholy could be held responsible for a wide range of behavior patterns and emotional reactions, it was especially useful to writers. The vague sadness that tinges Antonio's life in *The Merchant of Venice* (1596) is a fairly harmless strain of melancholy, though it seems to render him passive and fatalistic. Other versions of the disease were more virulent, and a wide variety of melancholy humors became highly popular toward the end of the century. Nurtured particularly by aristocratic Italians—Ficino's praise had its consequences—the fashionable English traveler tended to return from the Continent with the symptoms of this disease. And in no time at all, even those who had never traveled caught the infection and acted as though they had just returned from Italy. In *As You Like It* (1599) Jaques has picked up "a most humorous sadness" abroad; Rosalind, however, is quick to point out the absurdity of his affectation: "I had rather have a fool to make me merry than experience to make me sad, and to travel for it too."

Unhappy with the way life has treated him, the discontented melancholic, often a scholar who cannot find a position he thinks worthy of his training and interests, becomes a bitter critic of the injustices of society. Like Shakespeare's Timon of Athens, when he is abandoned by those he thought were his friends, such malcontents, as they were called, are recognizable by their unsociable, morose, taciturn behavior—though occasionally their repressed anger gives way to condemnatory outbursts. These negative attributes—all found in Galen's discussion of the disease—may well conceal mental or artistic abilities of a high order, the positive qualities Aristotle describes as characteristic of the melancholy individual. In the end, the combination of high intelligence, fierce anger—almost to the point of madness—and unemployment frequently leads the malcontent to criminal activity. And because he is so clever, the malcontent may well practice a particularly ingenious and perverse brand of villainy. Cyril Tourneur's *The Revenger's Tragedy* (1606), George Chapman's *Bussy D'Ambois* (1604), and John Webster's *The Duchess of Malfi* (1614) all present characters of this sort, and John Marston likes to shock his audience with unexpected variations on the conventional malcontent.

As a final example of pathological melancholy, we can consider the lovesick lover. A comic example is Berowne in *Love's Labour's Lost* (1595), who, having just composed a sonnet to his mistress, acknowledges, "By heaven, I do love, and it hath taught me to rhyme, and to be melancholy." Erotic love—a hot and moist passion—is, as might be expected, usually found in those of sanguinary complexion. Othello, for example, claiming that Desdemona's hand is "hot, hot and moist," prescribes activities intended to lessen the amount of blood and reduce the danger of a potentially harmful emotion: strict living, "fasting and prayer, / Much castigation, [and] exercise devout." In fact, of course, the incident reveals how uncertain the Moor has become of his wife's fidelity. Frustrated love is dangerous because without consummation or medical assistance it cools and dries the body. The lover then becomes melancholic and experiences intense and conflicting emotions—hope, fear, joy, depression, elation, and especially jealousy and sorrow. Moreover, melancholy lovers are subject to mental derangement, manifesting anything from mild hysteria to utter madness, and may even be tempted to suicide. In his presentation of the lovers in *The Lover's Melancholy* (1628), *The Broken Heart* (1629), and *'Tis Pity She's a Whore* (1632), John Ford seems to be dramatizing many of the effects of love melancholy as they are described in the most extensive study of this disease ever compiled, Robert Burton's *The Anatomy of Melancholy* (1621).

But of all melancholic heroes, Shakespeare's Hamlet (1601) is surely the most fascinating and complex. A part of our fascination with this character comes from his astonishing range and comprehensiveness. Through him, Shakespeare demonstrates how thoroughly he understands the disordered melancholic personality by combining appropriate elements—external and internal, real and feigned—in his hero: he is a grieving son, frustrated lover, misogynist, political malcontent, madman, satirist, and scholar who rants hysterically, contemplates suicide, commits murder, appears in graveyards, and, when neither obstinately silent nor bitterly railing, talks to ghosts and converses with the skulls of dead men. What hero of melancholy complexion could do more and remain plausible?

Our excerpt on melancholy is taken from the work of the French Renaissance physician André DuLaurens (c. 1558–1609), A *Discourse of the Preservation of the Sight*. Among sixteenth-century writers, DuLaurens offers one of the clearest statements on the humors and on the effects of melancholy. The directness of his writing may be due to the fact that DuLaurens is addressing his patient, the Duchess of Uzes, to whom the book is dedicated. The Duchess suffered from three health problems: a cataract in her right eye, melancholy, and rheums. In this work, DuLaurens also included a fourth topic, "on old age," assuring the Duchess that, even though she is over fifty, she need not worry about it yet; that section, he hastens to add, was written "against the time to come." Through his friendship with her, DuLaurens received appointments at court, ultimately becoming premier physician to Marie de Médicis in 1603 and premier physician to Henry IV in 1606. Though not a great scientist, DuLaurens was a typical and influential doctor of the early seventeenth century: he knew his classical authorities thoroughly; he was familiar with the new discoveries of the age; and he was willing to modify his ideas in light of them.

A *Discourse of the Preservation of the Sight*, written in French, was first published in Paris in 1597; it was reprinted in France six times in the next ten years. Italian translations of the entire book appeared in Venice and Naples, and excerpts from it were also printed in Italy. In Munich, Augsburg, and Geneva, portions of it were published in Latin. Thomas Moundeford (1550–1630), the President of the College of Physicians, translated the section on melancholy into Latin; it was printed in London in 1599 by Felix Kingston. Richard Surphlet's English translation of Du Laurens's book was also issued in London in 1599 by Kingston. Surphlet, about whom little is known, attended Cambridge and acquired some reputation for his skill in curing cataracts.

From *A Discourse of the Preservation of the Sight*

The Four Humors

It is a thing most freely agreed upon in physic that there are four humors in our bodies: blood, phlegm, choler, and melancholy; and that all these are to be found at all times, in every age, and at all seasons to be mixed and mingled together within the veins, though not alike much of every one. For even as it is not possible to find the party in whom the four elements are equally mixed, and as there is not that temperament in the world in which the four contrary qualities are in the whole and every part equally compounded, but that of necessity there must be some one ever more which doth exceed the other. Even so it is not possible to see any perfect living creature in which the four humors are equally mixed; there is always some one which doth overrule the rest, and of it is the party's complexion named: if blood do abound, we call such a complexion sanguine; if phlegm, phlegmatic; if choler, choleric; and if melancholy, melancholic.

These four humors, if they do not too much abound, may very easily stand with the health of the party, for they do not sensibly hurt and hinder the actions of the body. It is most true that every constitution bringeth forth his different effects, which make the actions of the soul more quick and lively, or more dull and dead. Phlegmatic persons are for the most part blockish and lubberlike, having a slow judgment and all the noblest powers of the mind, as it were, asleep because the substance of their brain is too thick and the spirits labored therein too gross. These are no fit men for the undergoing of weighty affairs, neither apt to conceive of profound mysteries. A bed and a pot full of pottage is fitted for them.

The sanguine persons are born for to be sociable and lovers of company. They are, as it were, always in love; they love to laugh and be pleasant. This is the best complexion for health and long life because that it hath the two main pillars of life, which are natural heat and moisture, in greatest measure, and yet such folk are not the fittest for great exploits nor yet for high and hard attempts because they be impatient and cannot be long in doing about one thing, being for the most part drawn away either by their senses or else by their delights, whereto they are naturally addicted.

Choleric persons, being hot and dry, have a quick understanding, abounding with many slight inventions, for they seldom sound any deep and hidden secrets. It fitteth not their fist to grapple with such business as require continuance of time and pains of body. They cannot be at leisure; their bodies and spirits do let[1] them. Their spirits are soon spent by reason of their thinness and their weak bodies cannot endure much watching. I will add also that one thing which Aristotle mentioneth in his *Ethics* is that they love change of things and for this cause are not so fit for consultations of great importance.

The melancholic are accounted as most fit to undertake matters of weighty charge and high attempt. Aristotle in his *Problems* saith that the melancholic are most witty and ingenious. But we must look that we understand this place aright, for there are many sorts of melancholy. There is one that is altogether gross and earthy, cold and dry; there is another that is hot and adust (men call it *atrabilis*[2]); there is yet another which is mixed with some small quantity of blood and yet notwithstanding is more dry than moist. The first sort which is gross and earthy maketh men altogether gross and slack in all their actions both of body and mind, fearful, sluggish, and without understanding: it is commonly called Asse-like melancholy. The second sort, being hot and burnt, doth cause men to be outrageous and unfit to be employed in any charge. There is none [remaining] then but that which is mixed with a certain quantity of blood that maketh men witty and causeth them to excel others. The reasons hereof are very plain: the brain of such melancholic persons is neither too soft nor too hard and yet it is true that dryness doth bear the sway therein. But Heraclitus oftentimes said that a dry light did make the wisest mind. There are but small store of excrements[3] in their brain. Their spirits are most pure and are not easily wasted. They are hardly drawn from their purpose and meaning. Their conceit is very deep; their memory very fast; their body strong to endure labor. And when this humor groweth hot by the vapors of blood, it causeth, as it were, a kind of divine ravishment commonly called *Enthousiasma*, which stirreth men up to play the philosophers, poets, and also to prophesy in such manner as that it may seem to contain in it some divine parts. See here the effects of the four complexions, and how they may all four be within the bounds of health. It is not then of these sound melancholic persons that we speak in this treatise. We will intreat only of sick, and such as are pained with the grief which men call melancholy, which I am now about to describe.

---

1. *let*: prohibit, prevent, hinder.
2. *atrabilia* or *atrabilis*: a diseased humor, especially dangerous and difficult to treat, caused by the scorching or burning of normal humors by unnatural heat. Since the intense heat burns the humors into cinders or ashes, the condition that results may also be called "melancholy adust."
3. *excrement*: outgrowth, excrescence.

Chapter IV: The definition of melancholy and all the differences of it.

Diseases commonly take their names either from the place which they seize upon or of some irksome accident accompanying them, or of the cause which causeth them. Melancholy matcheth in his hindermost rank, for this name was given it because it springeth of a melancholic humor [which] we will define (as other good authors do) [as] a kind of dotage without any fever, having for his ordinary companions fear and sadness without any apparent occasion. . . . We call that dotage when some one of the principal faculties of the mind, as imagination or reason, is corrupted. All melancholic persons have their imagination troubled, for that they devise with themselves a thousand fantastical inventions and objects which in deed are not at all. They have also very oft their reason corrupted. Wherefore we cannot make any doubt whether melancholy be a dotage or no, but it is ordinarily without a fever because the humor is dry and hath these two qualities, coldness and dryness. . . .

Chapter V: Of melancholy which hath his proper seat in the brain, of all accidents which do accompany the same, and the causes of fear, sadness, watching, fearful dreams, and other symptoms.

That melancholy which cometh of the dry and cold distemperature of the brain is ordinarily accompanied with so manifold and tedious accidents that it should stir up everyone to be moved with pity and compassion, for the body is not only cast into a trance but the mind is yet a great deal more violently set on the rack. For here behold all the tyrannous executioners and tormentors of melancholy: fear keepeth company with it day by day, and now and then assaileth the party with such an astonishment as that he is made afraid and becometh a terror unto himself. Sadness doth never forsake him, suspicion doth secretly gall him, sighings, watchings, fearful dreams, silence, solitariness, bashfulness, and the abhorring of the sun are, as it were, inseparable accidents of this miserable passion.

[DuLaurens next explains why the melancholic has these reactions and elaborates on them.]

Chapter VI: Whence it cometh that melancholic persons have all of them their particular and altogether divers objects whereupon they dote.

[Melancholy] causes sundry and diverse effects, making some to laugh and some to weep; making some lumpish and drowsy, and othersome over-watchful and furious. Even so this humor affecteth the imagination after diverse sorts and fashions. This difference ariseth either from the disposition of the body, or from the manner of living, or from such studies as the parties do most apply themselves unto, or from some other secret and hidden causes.

Chapter VII: Histories of melancholic persons which have had strange imaginations.

[Examples of melancholic persons with strange imaginations are described. DuLaurens explains that one kind of] melancholy which hath his seat in the brain . . . is caused of a cold and dry distemperature either simple or mixed with matter. It followeth sometimes the hot sicknesses of the brain, as frenzies and burning fevers, and then the face appeareth red. Avicen[4] observeth that stammerers, and such as have rolling eyes, and such as are hairy and black, such also as have great veins and thick lips, are most incident to this kind of melancholy: sadness, fear, deep muses, the use of gross and melancholy meats do sometimes cause this disease.

Chapter VIII: An order of diet for such as have this melancholic disease in the brain.

[The proper air, diet, and activities for curing those who suffer from melancholy.]

Chapter IX: How we must cure such melancholic persons as have the disease growing in the brain.

I will set down in this chapter the most special remedies that I have been able to observe, together with the order how such melancholy persons must be handled.

[DuLaurens discusses bloodletting, purging, and potions—pills and decoctions.] All, both Greek and Arabian physicians, do appoint in such diseases of melancholy as are old and hardly removed, *Hellebor*[5] should be given. It is true indeed that we must in this case use discretion, and not to give it in substance, for the decoction or infusion thereof must be taken and choice made of that which is black and good. For the apothecaries do

---

4. Avicen: Avicenna (980–1037), Arab physician and philosopher.
5. Black hellebore was the most popular cure for melancholy. The medicine, in the form of a powder or extract, was made from the dried rhizome and root of an herb of the lily family (genus *Helleborus*).

oftentimes sell for black *Hellebor* a kind of *Aconitum*[6] which is very hurtful and pernicious; the white is not to be used at all in these cases. There must also diligent care be had not to mix anything with the *Hellebor* we use which hath any astringent or binding faculty, such as are *Mirabolanes*,[7] lest thereby it might be stayed too long in the stomach. The poets that have written long ago have acknowledged this property of *Hellebor* that it hath against melancholy diseases when as they send melancholic persons unto Antieyra, where the best Hellebor groweth. . . . Some there be which use Antimony[8] prepared, but all such forcible means must be prescribed advisedly and with discretion. I could like it better to use milder things and to reiterate them the oftener as a good magistral syrup or else some opiate.

[Inward and outward moistening is another method of altering the melancholic humor since it is caused by dryness. DuLaurens recognized the usefulness of chicken broth, a syrup of apples, bugloss (a kind of plant), hops, and violets macerated, or of baths and ointments. And, finally, methods of overcoming sleeplessness, or "overwatchfulness," by the use of opiates, potions, pills, powders, ointments, nosegays, horseleeches, lotions, etc., may also prove necessary.]

Chapter X: Of another kind of melancholy which cometh by the extremity of love.

There is another kind of melancholy very ordinary and common, which the Greek physicians call *Erotic* because it cometh of a fury and raging love. The Arabians called it *Iliscus*, and the common sort [called it] the divine passion, imputing the cause thereof to the petty god which the poets have made so great reports of. . . . I intend to manifest unto every man by the description of this melancholy how greatly a violent and extreme love may tyrannize in commanding both mind and body.

Love, therefore, having abused the eyes as the proper spies and porters of the mind,[9] maketh a way for itself smoothly to glance along through the conducting guides, and passing without any perseverance in this sort through the veins unto the liver, doth suddenly imprint a burning desire to obtain the thing which is or seemeth worthy to be beloved, setteth concupiscence on

6. *Aconitum*: an herb, such as monkshood or wolfsbane, used as a sedative.

7. An astringent plumlike fruit recommended as a cure for agues and melancholy. Ben Jonson's Lady Would-be recommends this to Volpone (III.iv) when he complains of fears, fevers, nightmares, and tremors—all of which are really caused by the incessant chatter of her visits.

8. Monksbane: as stibium or black antimony, it could be used as a poison or emetic.

9. The eyes, the windows to the soul, are the organ through which the feelings of love enter the body. As the song in *The Merchant of Venice* says, fancy or love "is engend'red in the eyes, / With gazing fed" (III.ii).

fire, and beginneth by this desire all the strife and contention. But fearing herself too weak to encounter with reason the principal part of the mind, she posteth in haste to the heart to surprise and win the same. Whereof when she is once sure, as of the strongest hold, she afterward assaileth and setteth upon reason and all the other principal powers of the mind so fiercely as that she subdueth them and maketh them her vassals and slaves. Then is all spoiled; the man is quite undone and cast away. The senses are wandering to and fro, up and down. Reason is confounded, the imagination corrupted, the talk fond and senseless, the silly loving worm cannot any more look upon anything but his idol. All the functions of the body are likewise perverted. He becometh pale, lean, swooning, without any stomach to his meat, hollow and sunk-eyed, and cannot (as the poet sayeth) see the night either with his eyes or breast. You shall find him weeping, sobbing, sighing, and redoubling his sighs, and in continual restlessness, avoiding company, loving solitariness, the better to feed and follow his foolish imaginations. Fear buffeteth him on the one side and oftentimes despair on the other. He is (as Plautus sayeth) there where indeed he is not. Sometimes he is as hot as fire, and upon the sudden he findeth himself as cold as ice. His heart doth always quake, and his pulse keepeth no true course. It is little, unequal, and beating thick, changing itself upon the sudden, not only at the sight but even at the very name of the object which he affecteth. . . . Let no man therefore hereafter call it a divine and sacred passion, if it be not only to signify the greatness thereof. . . . Neither let any man call it the sweet passion or affection, seeing of all other miseries this is the greatest misery, yea so great as that all the tortures which have been so exquisitely devised by the wit of tyrants will never be able to exceed the cruelty thereof. . . . Love corrupteth the imagination and may be the cause of melancholy or of madness. For in thus busying both the body and the mind, it so drieth the humors as that the whole frame of temperature especially that of the brain is overthrown and marred.

Chapter XI: The means to cure the love, foolish and melancholic.

Here are two ways to cure this amorous melancholy. The one is the enjoying of the thing beloved. The other resteth in the skill and pains of a good physician. As concerning the first, it is certain that the principal cause of the disease, which is this burning desire being taken away, the diseased party will find himself marvelously relieved, though notwithstanding there may remain behind some certain prints and scars in the body. . . . But this course of cure being such as neither ought nor can always be put in practice, as being contrary unto the laws of God and men, we must have recourse unto the other which dependeth upon the industry of the physician. If therefore it happen unto any physician to meet with some of these melancholy patients thus ravished of love, he must first of all assay to draw him with fair words from these fond and foolish imaginations, showing him the danger whereinto he doth cast himself headlong and setting before him the examples of such as have been overthrown thereby as not only losing their loves but their souls also. If all this do no good, we must by some other wile and by the setting a work of divers men strive to make him hate that which so tormenteth him, as in affirming the thing to be evil, in calling his mistress light, inconstant, foolish, devoted to variety, mocking and laughing to scorn this his grief and corrosive, disdainful as not acknowledging his deserts, and one which loveth better a base companion to glut her brutish lust than to entertain an honest and chaste love. And look how deeply you dispraise his lady, so highly shall you praise himself, declaring the excellence of his understanding, his worthiness and deserts. If words be not sufficient and able to cure his enchantment, as in very deed they can do very little in place where melancholic conceitedness hath taken root, we must bethink ourselves of some other course.

Removing—that is to say, the changing of the air—is one of the rarest remedies because that under color of that we may bestow him in some remote place and send him quite out of the country, for the sight of his mistress doth daily blow up the coals of his desire and the only reciting of her name serveth as a bait for his ardent affections to bite upon. It will be good for him to lodge in the fields, or in some pleasant house, to cause him to walk often, to keep him occupied every hour with one or other pleasant pastime, to bring into his mind a hundred and a hundred sundry things to the end he may have no leisure to think of his love, to carry him out a-hunting, to the fence-school, to hold him up sometimes with fine and grave stories, sometimes with pleasant tales, and therewith to have merry music. You must not feed him too full or daintily lest the blood, beginning to wax hot, should rouse up the flesh and thereby renew the old fire. Take away idleness, take away belly-cheer and quaffing of strong drinks, and without doubt lechery will fall stark lame. [DuLaurens suggests that the remedies, purges and gentle medicines recommended in the previous chapter for the melancholic may also be used with the amorous person, for in both instances the body has compelled the mind into a diseased state and the cure rests in restoring the proper degree of hot moisture.]

Michel de Montaigne:
Essays

Montaigne's musings on manners, morals, and human nature are as intriguing and provocative today as they were to their Renaissance readers. The essays arouse these reactions because they probe the hidden springs of action, the inconsistencies of behavior, and the ambiguities of motivation. The paradoxes of life become everywhere apparent, and the essayist proves the impossibility of establishing absolute certainty about anything but incertitude. Yet in his skepticism, Montaigne is never bitter or despondent. This curiosity about himself and others, this fascination with men and morals, this interest in turning the prism of experience over in his mind to delight in its unexpected shades and colors—all become valuable for what they reveal of life itself. And understanding ourselves and others, developing an awareness of who we are and how we live, were and are unquestionably important, vital concerns for Montaigne and his readers.

Despite the breadth and range of his interest in human nature and society, Michel de Montaigne (1533–92) did not bring an enormous variety of personal experiences to his writing—he neither traveled widely nor maintained a highly diverse circle of friends. In fact, he passed most of his life at his birthplace, the Chateau de Montaigne, about thirty miles west of Bordeaux. The son of one of the leading families of that city, blessed with "the best father there ever was," Michel was raised by a tutor in an environment where only Latin was spoken. As a consequence, he was fluent in that language before he could speak French. For his formal education he was sent to an excellent school in Bordeaux where, due to his extraordinary fluency in

Latin, he finished the twelve-year curriculum in seven years. His training was probably completed by legal studies at the University of Toulouse; there, in addition to learning Roman law, students relaxed by reading Sophocles, Aristophanes, Euripides, Demosthenes, Cicero, Virgil, and Horace.

Before he was twenty-five, Montaigne held a position as magistrate, hearing cases involving taxes, duties, and customs; shortly after he joined this legal office, the *Cour des Aides*, it became a part of the Bordeaux Parlement. For the next dozen years he served in various capacities in the regional government, often representing the interests of his peers at the court of France. No doubt his experiences as a councillor ripened his skepticism about our ability to uncover truth or determine what is just. He came to believe that human institutions are unreliable, that truth is relative and subjective, and that judgment is inconsistent. From the bickering, venality, and pedantry of his colleagues, Montaigne also discovered the injustice and unreliability of the courts, the limitations of the human mind to recognize reality, and the uselessness of attempting to legislate morals. His skepticism may well have been intensified by the religious controversy in Bordeaux at this time, for the attempt to give Protestants greater freedom of religion inflamed Catholics, and this, in turn, led to the danger of armed conflict between religious parties. At the age of thirty-seven, Montaigne withdrew from public office to live on his estate. Yet even after he resigned his position, Montaigne was recalled to the government: he was twice elected mayor of Bordeaux, and on several occasions he served as arbitrator between Catholic and Protestant factions.

A series of unhappy events, all of them pointing up the brevity and precariousness of the human condition, must have contributed to Montaigne's decision in 1571 to retire in search of "freedom, tranquility, and leisure": first, the sudden death at the age of thirty-three of Etienne de La Boétie, his dearest friend and colleague in the Parlement, in 1563; next, the death of his father in 1568; then, the shocking death of his twenty-seven-year-old brother Arnaud in late 1568 or early 1569 from a blow over the ear while playing court tennis; then, his own near death when about a year later he was knocked semiconscious by a dangerous fall from his horse; and, finally, in 1570, shortly after his marriage, the death of his first child at the age of two months.

When he was not occupied with problems involving the maintenance of his lands and the care of his laborers, Montaigne enjoyed spending his leisure time reading and writing in his library. This was his favorite room, located on the third floor of the tower over the entrance to his chateau; he liked it all the more "for being a little hard to reach and out of the way." Here, on the circular walls surrounding his table and chair, were five rows of shelves containing his books, which he claimed numbered more than one thousand, and windows offering views in three directions. For decoration and contemplation, the beams of this drafty library, sixteen paces in diameter, were inscribed with some fifty quotations from Greek and Latin writers as well as seventeen Pyrrhonian—that is, skeptical—maxims.

In this setting, browsing without aim first in one book and then another, musing, pacing back and forth—"My mind will not budge unless my legs move it"—Montaigne jotted down his thoughts. At first setting down little more than anecdotes with a moral point, he began to find his subject by writing, expanding and revising these, creating what he called simply "chapters": ultimately, fifty-seven in Book 1 of what he called his *Essays*, thirty-seven in Book 2 (both published in 1580), and thirteen in Book 3 (published with Books 1 and 2 in 1588). He coined the term "essays" to refer to the whole collection. This title is original with Montaigne, and it is appropriately chosen, for it suggests the tentative nature of his undertaking—a series of tests, trials, attempts, or samplings *(essais)*.

Although Montaigne was aware of works that were similar to his, especially Plutarch's *Moralia* and Machiavelli's *Discourses*, he must have realized that no earlier author had presented so intimate a discussion with himself as the subject: "I am myself the matter of my book." Through his self-analysis, Montaigne came to realize that he was representative of all humanity so that by submitting his self-portrait to his critical judgment, by analyzing his own behavior and mental processes, he could arrive at an understanding not only of himself but of mankind as well. In short, he showed how understanding oneself can lead to an understanding of human nature and an awareness of the ethical issues that confront us.

Since Montaigne's mind and reactions are his subject matter, the essays are not logical or orderly. Instead, they follow the movement of his thought, the spontaneous flow of his ideas, the associations that come to him by mixing experience and reading, observations of nature, and examples from the great writers of the past: "I do not portray being: I portray passing . . . from day to day, from minute to minute." As a consequence of the instability, irresolution, and contradictoriness of one's ideas, Montaigne argues, one's knowledge is partial, biased, and short-lived. Such a creature is hardly superior to the rest of creation, but is a prey to its own passions and weaknesses. With this as his outlook, Montaigne developed his own brand of skepticism. Yet Montaigne gradually came to think these limitations were not obstacles to one's happiness. With a knowledge of human nature, one can establish principles and rules of conduct. For example, if security leads to boredom, then "difficulty gives value to things" and being short-lived may be a necessary condition for happiness (as Shakespeare says in Sonnet 73, we love more strongly that which we "must leave ere long"). If man is so arbitrary that his sense impressions can alter things—the taste of wine is not the same to the sick as to the healthy—then one's response to experience depends on oneself alone (as Shakespeare says in Sonnet 138, "When my love swears that she is made of truth / I do believe her, though I know she lies").

We have no evidence that Shakespeare knew Montaigne's work when he wrote his sonnets (1592–94)—the English translation of the *Essays* appeared only in 1603—but the two men were certainly kindred spirits from the start. The two examples just cited suggest that Montaigne and Shakespeare expressed similar ideas and held comparable views of human nature. Indeed, the similarities are striking. Both delighted in considering life from different points of view—do I play with my cat, or does my cat play with me, Montaigne asked. Since this seemingly simple question is really unanswerable, Montaigne is actually raising a profound question about man's ability to determine the truth. His skepticism is all-pervasive. His attitude is, perhaps, expressed most memorably in the phrase "What do I know?" ("Que sais-je?"), which became his motto for a time. No such explicit statement can, of course, be found in Shakespeare, but he clearly shared Montaigne's fascination with unanswerable questions and multiple possibilities. Both men also enjoyed a deep curiosity about people, about customs, and about the springs of human conduct; and both were intrigued by the uniqueness of the individual personality. No wonder, then, that they were both avid readers of Plutarch, whose subtle and perceptive analysis of character and conduct could serve as a model: Montaigne wrote, men should be "spectators or observers of other men's lives and actions, that so they may the better judge and direct their own." Moreover, Shakespeare's skepticism like Montaigne's is fundamentally optimistic. Both men were fully sensitive to the beauty of nature, the richness of experience, and the need for generosity and understanding. Indeed, having looked hard at life, they came not only to accept it but to praise it as well. As Montaigne writes in "Of Experience":

> Our life is composed, like the harmony of the world, of contrary things, also of different tones, sweet and harsh, sharp and flat, soft and loud. If a musician liked only one kind, what would he have to say? He must know how to use them together and blend them. And so must we do with good and evil, which are consubstantial with our life. Our being is impossible without this mixture, and one element is no less necessary for it than the other.

At the end of his career, Shakespeare used a passage from Montaigne's essay "Of the cannibals" in *The Tempest* (II.i.) (1611). But even here the direct borrowing is less significant than the affinity in their general outlook. To cite only one example from this play, Miranda's remark, "How beauteous mankind is! O brave new world, / That has such people in't" is immediately followed by her father's, "'Tis new to thee." The juxtaposition of two different points of view, the innocent optimism of the one and the more experienced skepticism of the other, would have been appreciated by Montaigne. *Troilus and Cressida* (1603) is another play that considers many subjects from a point of view that Montaigne would have found sympathetic. For example, Shakespeare dramatizes Montaigne's thesis that "no proposition is seen which is not controversied and debated amongst us": Troilus argues the notion of relativity—"what's aught, but as 'tis valued" (II.ii.)—in the same way that Montaigne refused to grant superiority to the values of the European or the American savage. And Montaigne's point that subjectivity alters perception is demonstrated by Troilus's tormented view of Cressida's nature when his understanding is racked between his emotional attachment, the "credence in my heart," and his witnessing her lewd behavior, "th'attest of eyes and ears" (V.ii.).

To Jacobean playwrights the *Essays* were widely known—so much so that Jonson satirized their influence in *Volpone* (1606). In that play, the foolish and pretentious Lady Politic Would-be praises Montaigne and claims he is a major source for English writers, who "steal out" of his work. But unlike Shakespeare, Marston and Webster turned to the *Essays* to confirm their own pessimistic views of the human condition. They could find confirmation for their feelings of doubt and uncertainty in Montaigne's skepticism, his sense of man's limited powers and subordinate place in the universe.

Montaigne's words were turned into English by John Florio (1553–1625), the son of a pastor to an Italian congregation in London. Florio was born in England and completed his education at Magdalen College, Oxford, where he matriculated in 1581. The author of translations, books on the art of polite conversations, and dictionaries, Florio had the Earls of Southampton and Pembroke as his patrons and served two members of the royal family, becoming tutor to Prince Henry in French and Italian as well as Reader to Queen Anne in Italian. The translation of Montaigne was licensed for printing in 1599; the first edition appeared in 1603, a second, revised edition in 1613, and a third in 1632. In an age of great translation—Thomas North's *Plutarch's Lives*, Thomas Hoby's *Courtier*, and the *King James* Version of the Bible, for example—Florio's version of Montaigne is notable for its vigor, energy, and liveliness. Florio believed that "learning cannot be too common, and the commoner the better," but his impulse to educate never dulls his love of language or his inventiveness with words.

A copy of the first edition in the British Museum contains a Shakespeare signature that may be genuine.

Of the Cannibals

I find (as far as I have been informed), there is nothing in that nation [the natives of Brazil] that is either barbarous or savage unless men call that barbarism which is not common to them. As indeed, we have no other aim of truth and reason than the example and idea of the opinions and customs of the country we live in. There is ever perfect religion, perfect policy, perfect and complete use of all things. They are even savage as we call those fruits wild which nature of herself and of her ordinary progress hath produced. Whereas indeed, they are those which ourselves have altered by our artificial devices and diverted from their common order we should rather term savage. In those are the true and most profitable virtues and natural properties most lively and vigorous which in these we have bastardized, applying them to the pleasure of our corrupted taste. And if notwithstanding in divers fruits of those countries that were never tilled we shall find that in respect of ours they are most excellent and as delicate unto our taste, there is no reason art should gain the point of honor of our great and puissant mother nature. We have so much by our inventions surcharged the beauties and riches of her works that we have altogether overchoked her. Yet wherever her purity shineth, she makes our vain and frivolous enterprises wonderfully ashamed.

> Ivies spring better of their own accord,
> Unhaunted plots much fairer trees afford.
> Birds by no art much sweeter notes record. [1]

All our endeavor or wit cannot so much as reach to represent the nest of the least birdlet, its contexture, beauty, profit, and use; no, nor the web of a silly spider. All things, saith Plato, are produced either by nature, by fortune, or by art. The greatest and fairest by one or other of the two first, the least and imperfect by the last. [2] Those nations seem therefore so barbarous unto me because they have received very little fashion from human wit, and are yet near their original naturality. The laws of nature do yet command them which are but little bastardized by ours, and that with such purity as I am sometimes grieved the knowledge of it came no sooner to light, at what time there were men that better than we could have judged of it. I am sorry Lycurgus and Plato had it not, for me seemeth that what in those nations we see by experience doth not only exceed all the pictures wherewith licentious poesy hath proudly embellished the golden age, and all her quaint inventions to feign a happy condition of man, but also the conception and desire of philosophy. They could not imagine a genuity [3] so pure and simple as we see it by experience, nor ever believe our society might be maintained with so little art and human combination. It is a nation, would I answer Plato, that hath no kind of traffic, no knowledge of letters, no intelligence of numbers, no name of magistrate nor of politic superiority; no use of service, of riches, or of poverty; no contracts, no successions, no partitions, no occupation but idle; no respect of kindred, but common; no apparel but natural; no manuring of lands, no use of wine, corn, or metal. The very words that import lying, falsehood, treason, dissimulations, covetousness, envy, detraction, and pardon were never heard amongst them. [4] How dissonant would he find his imaginary commonwealth from this perfection?

---

1. Propertius, *Elegies*, 1.2.10.
2. Plato, *Laws*, X.
3. *genuity*: a breed.
4. In Shakespeare's *The Tempest*, Gonzalo's description of the ideal commonwealth (II.i.) is indebted to Montaigne's account. Specific verbal parallels occur in the passage, beginning "It is a nation" and concluding with "Never heard of amongst them."

Nature at first uprise,
These manners did devise. [5]

Furthermore, they live in a country of so exceeding pleasant and temperate situation that as my testimonies have told me, it is very rare to see a sick body amongst them. And they have further assured me they never saw any man there either shaking with the palsy, toothless, with eyes dropping, or crooked and stooping through age. They are seated along the sea coast . . . They have great abundance of fish and flesh that have no resemblance at all with ours and eat them without any sauces or skill of cookery, but plain boiled or broiled. . . .

They spend the whole day in dancing. Their young men go hunting after wild beasts with bows and arrows. Their women busy themselves therewhilst with warming of their drink, which is their chiefest office. Some of their old men in the morning before they go to eating, preach in common to all the household, walking from one end of the house to the other, repeating one selfsame sentence many times, till he have ended his turn—for their buildings are a hundred paces in length. He commends but two things unto his auditory. First, valor against their enemies, then lovingness unto their wives. They never miss (for their restraint) to put men in mind of this duty, that it is their wives which keep their drink lukewarm and well seasoned. . . .

They believe their souls to be eternal, and those that have deserved well of their gods to be placed in that part of heaven where the sun riseth, and the cursed toward the west in opposition. They have certain prophets and priests which commonly abide in the mountains and very seldom show themselves unto the people. But when they come down, there is a great feast prepared and a solemn assembly of many townships together—each grange, as I have described, maketh a village, and they are about a French league one from another. The prophet speaks to the people in public, exhorting them to embrace virtue and follow their duty. All their moral discipline containeth but these two articles: first an undismayed resolution to war, then an inviolable affection to their wives. He doth also prognosticate of things to come, and what success they shall hope for in their enterprises. He either persuadeth or dissuadeth them from war, but if he chance to miss of his divination and that it succeed otherwise than he foretold them, if he be taken, he is hewn in a thousand pieces and condemned for a false prophet. And therefore he that hath once misreckoned himself is never seen again.

5. Virgil, *Georgics*, 2.20.

Divination is the gift of God, the abusing whereof should be a punishable imposture. . . .

They war against the nations that lie beyond their mountains. . . . Every victor brings home the head of the enemy he hath slain as a trophy of his victory and fasteneth the same at the entrance of his dwelling place. After they have long time used and entreated their prisoners well, and with all commodities they can devise, he that is the master of them summoning a great assembly of his acquaintance . . . [together with] the dearest friend he hath and both in the presence of all the assembly kill him with swords. Which done, they roast and then eat him in common and send some slices of him to such of their friends as are absent. It is not as some imagine to nourish themselves with it (as anciently the Scythians wont to do) but to represent an extreme and inexpiable revenge. Which we prove thus: some of them perceiving the Portuguese . . . to use another kind of death, when they took them prisoners, which was to bury them up to the middle and against the upper part of the body to shoot arrows and then being almost dead to hang them up. They supposed that these people of the world (as they who had sowed the knowledge of many vices amongst their neighbors, and were much more cunning in all kinds of evils and mischief than they) undertook not this manner of revenge without cause, and that consequently it was more smartful and cruel than theirs, and therefore began to leave their old fashion to follow this. I am not sorry we note the barbarous horror of such an action, but grieved that prying so narrowly into their faults we are so blinded in ours. I think there is more barbarism in eating men alive than to feed upon them being dead, to mangle by tortures and torments a body full of lively sense, to roast him in pieces, to make dogs and swine to gnaw and tear him in mammocks[6] (as we have not only read, but seen very lately, yea and in our own memory, not amongst ancient enemies, but our neighbors and fellow citizens; and which is worse, under pretense of piety and religion) than to roast and eat him after he is dead.[7]

. . . They are yet in that happy estate as they desire no more than what their natural necessities direct them. Whatsoever is beyond is to them superfluous. Those that are much about one age do generally enter-call[8] one another [as] brethren, and such as are younger and they call children, and the aged are esteemed as fathers to all the rest. These leave this full possession of goods in common and without division to their heirs, without other claim

---

6. *mammocks:*, fragments.
7. Montaigne has in mind the cruelty French Catholics and Protestants inflicted on each other.
8. *enter-call:* address.

or title, but that which nature doth plainly impart unto all creatures even as she brings them into the world. . . .

Their men have many wives, and by how much more they are reputed valiant, so much the greater is their number. The manner and beauty in their marriages is wondrous strange and remarkable. For, the same jealousy our wives have to keep us from the love and affection of other women, the same have theirs to procure it. Being more careful for their husband's honor and content than of anything else, they endeavor and apply all their industry to have as many rivals as possibly they can, forasmuch as it is a testimony of their husband's virtue. Our women would count it a wonder, but it is not so. It is virtue properly matrimonial, but of the highest kind. . . .

Three of that nation, ignorant how dear the knowledge of our corruptions will one day cost their repose, security, and happiness, and how their ruin shall proceed from this commerce, which I imagine is already well advanced—miserable as they are to have suffered themselves to be so cozened by a desire of new-fangled novelties and to have quit the calmness of their climate to come and see ours—were at Rouen in the time of our late King Charles IX, who talked with them a great while. . . .[9] I talked a good while with one of them, but I had so bad an interpreter and who did so ill apprehend my meaning and who through his foolishness was so troubled to conceive my imaginations that I could draw no great matter from him. Touching that point, wherein I demanded of him, what good he received by the superiority he had amongst his countrymen, for he was a captain and our mariners called him king, he told me, it was to march foremost in any charge of war. Further I asked him how many men did follow him. He showed me a distance of place to signify they were as many as might be contained in so much ground, which I guessed to be about four or five thousand men. Moreover, I demanded if when wars were ended all his authority expired; he answered that he had only this left him which was that when he went on progress and visited the villages depending on him, the inhabitants prepared paths and highways athwart the hedges of their woods for him to pass through at ease. All that is not very ill—but what of that? They wear no kind of breeches nor hose![10]

---

9. In 1562.

10. By showing that the natives in Brazil know how to live happily in nature, Montaigne raises the question whether art, a product of education and civilization, is superior to nature in a pure state. This issue is also discussed by Puttenham, who considers "in what cases the artificial is more commended than the natural, and contrariwise." (See pages 186–89.)

An Apology of Raymond Sebond

At his father's request, Montaigne translated from the Latin Raymond Sebond's *Book of Creatures, or Natural Theology,* nearly one thousand pages long. Although written in 1434–36, this work became popular in France years later as a defense of Catholicism against Protestantism and atheism. Montaigne's French version was first published in 1568; a second edition appeared in 1581.

Montaigne's "Apology" was written several years after the translation, at a period when his own ideas were changing, and in all likelihood it is comprised of material that was initially intended for other purposes. This may explain why, although Montaigne's defense of Sebond is by far the longest of the chapters in the *Essays,* less than one-tenth of it deals with Sebond at all. And when it discusses Sebond's position, it presents a very weak defense. Praising Sebond as well-intentioned, devout, and possibly helpful in this time of religious controversy, Montaigne disagrees with the fundamental premise of the book—that human reason can prove the truth of the tenets of Catholicism. Instead, he argues "that Christians do themselves harm in trying to support their belief by human reasons, since it is conceived by faith and by a particular inspiration of divine grace." Montaigne's faith in God is based on his skepticism that human reason can determine truth and on his reliance on divine grace. (We should keep in mind that Montaigne uses "reason" to refer to two different mental activities: theoretical reason, something he always considers dangerous, and practical reason, something he always presents as good.)

In "An Apology" Montaigne is critical of three groups: the Protestants, whom Sebond also attacked; classical dogmatic philosophers; and the followers of Stoic humanism. According to Montaigne, Protestants are presumptuous for placing a higher value on their own reason than on the wisdom of the Church; dogmatists are vainglorious, for they can never come to discover the truth; and, finally, the Stoic humanists, who ignore the nature and condition of humanity, fail to realize that people cannot improve by their own efforts but need God's grace to acquire true knowledge. Ultimately, Montaigne suggests that skepticism is the philosophy that best provides a basis for Christianity. Since people are a part of the flux and since their responses are conditioned by the external world, they can never attain perfect knowledge without God's grace. The discussion here provides the fullest expression of Montaigne's doubt, his conviction that human reason is impotent unless aided by a higher power.

From *An Apology of Raymond Sebond*

We lend nothing unto devotion but the offices that flatter our passions. There is no hostility so excellent as that which is absolutely Christian. Our zeal worketh wonders whenever it secondeth our inclination toward hatred, cruelty, ambition, avarice, detraction, or rebellion. Towards goodness, benignity, or temperance it goeth but slowly and against the hair, except miraculously some rare complexion lead him unto it, it neither runs nor flieth to it. Our religion was ordained to root out vices, but it shroudeth, fostereth, and provoketh them. As commonly we say, "We must not make a fool of God." Did we believe in him, I say not through faith but with a simple belief, . . . we should then love him above all other things by reason of the infinite goodness and unspeakable beauty that is and shines in him. Had he but the same place in our affections that riches, pleasures, glory, and our friends have. The best of us doth not so much fear to wrong him as he doth to injure his neighbor, his kinsman, or his master.

. . . All of which is a most evident token that we receive our religion but according to our fashion and by our own hands and no otherwise than other religions are received. We are placed in the country where it was in use, where we regard her antiquity or the authority of those who have maintained her, where we fear the menaces wherewith she threateneth all misbelievers, or follow her promises. The considerations ought to be applied and employed to our belief but as subsidiaries—they be human bonds. Another country, other testimonies, equal promises, alike menaces might semblably imprint a clean contrary religion in us. We are Christians by the same title as we are either Perigordins or Germans. . . .

Let us now but consider man alone without other help, armed but with his own weapons and unprovided of the grace and knowledge of God, which is all his honor, all his strength, and all the ground of his being. Let us see what holdfast or freehold he hath in this gorgeous and goodly equipage. Let him with the utmost power of his discourse make me understand upon what foundation he hath built those great advantages and odds he supposeth to have over other creatures. Who hath persuaded him that this admirable moving of heaven's vaults, that the eternal light of these lamps so fiercely rolling over his head, that the horror-moving and continual motion of this infinite vast ocean were established and continue so many ages for his commodity and service? Is it possible to imagine anything so ridiculous as this miserable and wretched creature which is not so much as master of himself exposed, and subject to offenses of all things, and yet dareth call himself master and emperor of this universe? In whose power it is not to know the least part of it, much less to command the same. And the privilege which he so fondly challengeth to be the only absolute creature in this huge world's frame, perfectly able to know the absolute beauty and several parts thereof, and that he is only of power to yield the great Architect thereof due thanks for it and to keep account both of the receipts and layings out of the world—who hath sealed him this patent? Let him show us his letters of privilege for so noble and so great a charge. Have they been granted only in favor of the wise? Then concern they but a few. Are the foolish and wicked worthy of so extraordinary a favor, who, being the worst part of the world, should they be preferred before the rest?[11]

Presumption is our natural and original infirmity. Of all creatures man is the most miserable and frail, and therewithal the proudest and disdainfullest. Who perceiveth and seeth himself placed here amidst the filth and mire of the world, fast tied and nailed to the worst, most senseless, and drooping part of the world in the vilest corner of the house and farthest from heaven's cope with those creatures that are the worst of the three conditions[12] and yet dareth imaginarily place himself above the circle of the moon and reduce heaven under his feet. It is through the vanity of the same imagination that he dare equal himself to God, that he ascribeth divine conditions unto himself, that he selecteth and separateth himself from out the rank of other creatures; to which his fellow brethren and compeers, he cuts out and shareth their parts and allotteth them what portions of means or forces he thinks good. How knoweth he by the virtue of his understanding the inward and secret motions of beasts? By what comparison from them to us doth he conclude the brutishness he ascribeth unto them? When I am playing with my cat, who knows whether she have more sport in dallying with me than I have in gaming with her? We entertain one another with mutual apish tricks. . . .

. . . When all is said and done, whatsoever is not as we are is not of any worth. And God to be esteemed of us must (as we will show anon) draw somewhat near it. Whereby it appeareth that it is not long of a true discourse but of a foolish hardiness and self-presuming obstinacy we prefer ourselves before other creatures and sequester ourselves from their condition and society. But to return to our purpose, we have for our part inconstancy;

11. Cicero, *On the Nature of the Gods*, 1.9.
12. That is, of the air, water, and the earth.

irresolution; uncertainty; sorrow; superstition; carefulness for future things (yea after our life); ambition; covetousness; jealousy; envy; inordinate, mad, and untamed appetites; war; falsehood; disloyalty; detraction; and curiosity. Surely we have strangely overpaid this worthy discourse whereof we so much glory and this readiness to judge or capacity to know if we have purchased the same with the price of so infinite passions to which we are incessantly enthralled. . . .

Learning hath a place amongst things necessary for man's life, as glory, nobleness, dignity, or at most as riches and such other qualities which indeed stead the same, but afar off and more in concept than by nature. We have not much more need of offices, of rules and laws how to live in our commonwealth, than the cranes and ants have in theirs. Which notwithstanding, we see how orderly and without instruction they maintain themselves. If man were wise he would value everything according to its worth, and as it is either more profitable or more necessary for life. He that shall number us by our actions and proceedings shall doubtless find many more excellent ones amongst the ignorant than among the wiser sort. I mean in all kind of virtues. My opinion is that ancient Rome brought forth many men of much more valor and sufficiency both for peace and war than this late learned Rome, which with all her wisdom hath overthrown her erst-flourishing estate. If all the rest were alike, then should honesty and innocence at least belong to the ancient, for she was exceedingly well placed with simplicity. But I will shorten this discourse which haply would draw me further than I would willingly follow. Yet thus much I will say more, that only humility and submission is able to make a perfect honest man. Everyone must not have the knowledge of his duty referred to his own judgment, but ought rather to have it prescribed unto him, and not be allowed to choose it at his pleasure and free will. Otherwise, according to the imbecility of our reasons and infinite variety of our opinions, we might peradventure forge and devise such duties unto ourselves as would induce us (as Epicurus saith) to endeavor to destroy and devour one another.[13] The first law that ever God gave unto man was a law of pure obedience. . . .

Now can nothing of ours, in what manner soever, be either compared or referred unto divine nature that doth not blemish or defile the same with as much imperfection. How can this infinite beauty, power, and goodness admit any correspondence or similitude with a thing so base and abject as we are without extreme interest and manifest derogation from his divine greatness? . . .

For us to go according to nature is but to follow according to our

13. Plutarch, *Against the epicurean Colotes*, XIV.

understanding as far as it can follow and as much as we can perceive in it. Whatsoever is beyond it is monstrous and disordered. By this account all shall then be monstrous to the wisest and most sufficient, for even to such, human reason hath persuaded that she had neither ground nor footing, no not so much as to warrant snow to be white. And Anaxagoras said it was black. . . .[14]

Now if on our part we receive anything without alteration, if man's holdfasts were capable and sufficiently powerful by our proper means to seize on truth, those means being common to all, this truth would successively remove itself from one to another. And of so many things as are in the world at least one should be found that by an universal consent should be believed of all. But that no proposition is seen which is not controversied and debated amongst us, or that may not be, declareth plainly that our judgment doth not absolutely and clearly seize on that which it seizeth, for my judgment cannot make my fellow's judgment to receive the same, which is a sign that I have seized upon it by some other means than by a natural power in me or other men. Leave we apart this infinite confusion of opinions which is seen amongst philosophers themselves, and this universal and perpetual disputation in and concerning the knowledge of things.

For it is most truly presupposed that men—I mean the wisest, the best born, yea and the most sufficient—do never agree. No, not so much that heaven is over our heads. For they who doubt of all do also doubt of this, and such as affirm that we cannot conceive anything say we have not conceived whether heaven be over our heads, which two opinions are in number (without any comparison) the most forcible. . . .

Who shall be a competent judge in these differences? As we said in controversies of religion, that we must have a judge inclined to neither party and free from partiality or affection, which is hardly to be had among Christians, so happeneth it in this. For if he be old, he cannot judge of age's sense, himself being a party in this controversy; and so, if he be young, healthy, sick, sleeping or waking, it is all one. We had need of somebody void and exempted from all these qualities that without any preoccupation of judgment might judge of these propositions as indifferent unto him. By which account we should have a judge that were no man.[15] To judge of the appearances that we receive of subjects, we had need have a judicatory instrument; to verify this instrument we should have demonstration; and to approve demonstration, an instrument. Thus are we ever turning round. Since the senses cannot determine our disputation, themselves being so full

14. Cicero, *Academics*, 2: 23 & 31.
15. Sextus Empiricus, *Hypotyposes*, 1:14.

of uncertainty, it must then be reason. And no reason can be established without another reason. Then are we ever going back unto infinity. . . .

In few, [16] there is no constant existence, neither of our being, nor of our objects. And we and our judgments and all mortal things else do incessantly roll, turn, and pass away. Thus can nothing be certainly established, nor of the one nor of the other; both the judging and the judged being in continual alteration and motion. We have no communication with being, for [17] every human nature is ever in the middle between being born and dying, giving nothing of itself but an obscure appearance and shadow, and an uncertain and weak opinion. And if perhaps you fix your thought to take its being, it would be even as if one should go about to grasp the water, for how much the more he shall close and press that, which by its own nature is ever gliding, so much the more he shall lose what he would hold and fasten. Thus, seeing all things subject to pass from one change to another, reason, which therein seeketh a real subsistence, finds herself deceived as unable to apprehend anything subsistent and permanent. . . .

And nothing remaineth or ever continueth in one state. For to prove it, if we should ever continue one and the same, how is it then that now we rejoice at one thing and now at another? How comes it to pass we love things contrary or we hate them, or we love them or we blame them? How is it that we have different affections, holding no more the same sense in the same thought? For it is not likely that without alteration we should take other passions, and what admitteth alterations continueth not the same. And if it be not one selfsame, then is it not. But rather with being all one, the simple being doth also change, ever becoming other from other. And by consequence, Nature's senses are deceived and lie falsely, taking what appeareth for what is, for want of truly knowing what it is that is. But then what is it, that is indeed? That which is eternal, that is to say that which never had birth nor ever shall have end and to which no time can bring change or cause alteration. For time is a fleeting thing and which appeareth as in a shadow with the matter ever gliding, always fluent without ever being stable or permanent. . . .

Wherefore we must conclude that only God is, not according to any measure of time, but according to an immovable and immutable eternity, not measured by time nor subject to any declination, before whom nothing is, nor nothing shall be after, nor more new, nor more recent, but one really being which by one only now or present filleth the Ever, and there is nothing

16. *In few*: in short, in few words.
17. What follows to "and sans ending" was taken by Montaigne from Amyot's translation of Plutarch's *Moral Essays*, "On the Meaning of ει," Book 12.

that truly is but He alone. Without saying He hath been or He shall be, without beginning and sans ending. To this so religious conclusion of a heathen man, I will only add this word, taken from a testimony of the same condition for an end of this long and tedious discourse which might well furnish me with endless matter: "Oh, what a vile and abject thing is man," saith [Seneca], "unless he raise himself above humanity."[18] Observe here a notable speech and a profitable desire, but likewise absurd. For to make the handful greater than the hand, and the embraced greater than the arm, and to hope to straddle more than our leg's length is impossible and monstrous. Nor that man should mount over and above himself or humanity, for he cannot see but with his own eyes nor take hold but with his own arms. He shall raise himself up, if it please God extraordinarily to lend him His helping hand. He may elevate himself by forsaking and renouncing his own means, and suffering himself to be elevated and raised by mere heavenly means. It is for our Christian faith, not for his stoic virtue to pretend or aspire to this divine metamorphosis or miraculous transmutation.

18. Seneca, preface to *Natural Questions*, book 1.

Religion

The Tudor period witnessed a transformation in English religious life greater than anything that had been seen since the original conversion of the country to Christianity nearly a thousand years earlier. The process began with Henry VIII, whose determination to divorce his wife, Catherine of Aragon, and marry Anne Boleyn, led him to break with Rome. The Church in England, which had hitherto been part of the international Catholic community, now became the Church of England, and control over it passed from the Papacy to the crown. In matters of doctrine, Henry was generally conservative, but the breach with Rome coincided with the appearance of Protestantism, under the stimulus first of Luther and subsequently of Ulrich Zwingli, Martin Bucer, and Calvin. Even without the divorce proceedings England would have had to come to terms with the spiritual revolution that was shaking the whole of Christendom. Henry did what he could to limit the degree and pace of change, but the Protestants came to power with the accession of his son, Edward VI, in 1547. However, their triumph was short-lived, for Edward's death in 1553 opened the way to the rule of Henry's eldest daughter, Mary Tudor, who was a devout Catholic. With the assistance of her cousin, Cardinal Pole, she restored England not only to the old faith but also to communion with Rome, and the future course of events would have been very different if she had been granted a long reign. As it happened, however, she only ruled for five years, and at her death in 1558 the throne passed to her Protestant half sister Elizabeth, the daughter of Henry and Anne Boleyn.

Henry VIII had declared himself to be "Supreme Head" of the newly created Church of England. Elizabeth was content with the more ambiguous title of "Supreme Governor," but she was no less determined than her father to mould the religious destiny of her people. Control over the Church was of enormous advantage to the crown, for regular attendance at Sunday services had been made compulsory by statute, and by prescribing forms of prayer and instructing the parish priests what to say from the pulpit, the government could address the people directly. The Church, in short, was the Tudor equivalent of a propaganda machine, the best available means of mass communication.

The Homilies

The religious upheavals that marked the middle years of the sixteenth century had caused a marked decline in the quality of the clergy. Only a minority were licensed to preach, and even those who fulfilled this function were often uncertain about what to say, for the boundary between orthodoxy and heterodoxy was constantly being redrawn. To give some guidance in the period of uncertainty following Henry VIII's death the government published *Certain Sermons or Homilies appointed by the King's Majesty to be declared and read by all Parsons, Vicars and Curates, every Sunday.*

The twelve sermons in the first edition of 1547 avoided abstract theological issues. Some dealt with specific topics, such as the reading of Holy Scripture, obedience, the misery of mankind, the salvation of mankind, and Christian love and charity. Others fulminated against such vices as swearing and perjury, whoredom and adultery, strife and contention. A second series of homilies appeared in 1562–63. These likewise were concerned with a wide range of religious and moral issues, such as fell within the purview of the Church courts that remained a fully functioning part of the Reformation state in England.

In 1571, a homily *Against Disobedience and Wilful Rebellion* was printed separately. Subsequently it was included in all editions of the *Homilies.* It was a direct response to the Northern Rebellion of 1569, which was an attempt to restore Catholic worship in England. The rebellion was quickly crushed, but it prompted the Pope to issue a bull in February 1570 formally excommunicating the heretic Queen Elizabeth and absolving her subjects from obedience to her commands.

In substance, *Against Disobedience and Wilful Rebellion* restates positions set out in earlier homilies. It argues that princes are ordained by God, subjects are hardly qualified to determine who is a just or unjust ruler, and evil princes may be God's means of punishing the people's wickedness. It even repeats the same Old and New Testament examples from other homilies to make its case—David tolerating Saul and Jesus submitting to Pilate. But the new homily specifically describes the horrors of revolution, especially civil war, and stresses the sinfulness and futility of rebellion. Each section ends with the congregation joining in prayer. The sixth and last part concludes with an attack on Catholicism for hiding the word of God in Latin and oppressing England to profit Rome.

Many of the ideas expressed in the homilies are repeated in the plays of Shakespeare and his contemporaries. The scene in which the rebel lords are discovered in *Henry V* (II.ii) (1599) recalls the words of the 1571 homily *Against Disobedience*. In *Richard II* (1595), John of Gaunt's reasons for passive obedience (I.ii.), the king's claim that his person is sacrosanct (III.ii), and the Bishop of Carlisle's picture of the kingdom wasted by civil war (IV.i.) are all restatements of positions taken in the homilies. In addition, something of the homily *Against Disobedience* is presented in Shakespeare's *King John* (1595) when it describes the wicked practices of the papacy against England. And the homily's warning that in civil wars sons kill their fathers and fathers their sons is actually dramatized in *Henry VI, Part Three* (II.v.) (1591). The description of those who lead rebellions and uprisings as among "the most rash and hare-brained men, the most greatest unthrifts, that have most lewdly wasted their own goods and lands" is a model for Jack Cade, the rebel leader in *Henry VI, Part Two* (IV.ii, vii, viii, x) (1591).

The idea most frequently repeated in the literature of this period that finds support in the homilies is the doctrine of a coherently planned universe and the absolute need to preserve its order. In the *Four Hymns* (1596), Spenser's "Hymn of Love" describes how the "contrary forces" of the four elements—earth, air, fire, and water—became tempered through "loved means." Moreover, since order is both a spiritual and political desideratum, achieved through the divinely appointed ruler who is head of both church and state, it becomes a subject of importance for theologians such as Thomas Hooker as well as for political commentators such as Thomas Elyot. For Shakespeare it is a pervasive theme: in *Midsummer Night's Dream* (II.i.) (1595) the quarrel between Titania and Oberon has devastating effects on the fertility of the land—an example of the harmful effects of disorder; in *Macbeth* (IV.iii.) (1606) Malcolm and Macduff discuss the suffering in Scotland under the evil rule of Macbeth and contrast this with the happiness of England under

a saintly king. And the positive effects of order are described fully in
Henry V (I.ii.) (1599) and in the famous passage on degree in *Troilus
and Cressida* (I.iii.).

Books 1 and 2 of the *Homilies* were frequently reprinted in the
sixteenth and seventeenth centuries, and they were reissued regularly
even in the nineteenth century.

Against Disobedience and Wilful Rebellion

The First Part

As God the creator and lord of all things appointed His angels and
heavenly creatures in all obedience to serve and to honor His majesty, so was
it His will that man, His chief creature upon the earth, should live under the
obedience of His creator and lord. . . . And as God would have man to be
His obedient subject, so did He make all earthly creatures subject unto man,
who kept their due obedience unto man so long as man remained in his
obedience unto God, in the which obedience if man had continued still,
there had been no poverty, no diseases, no sickness, no death nor other
miseries wherewith mankind is now infinitely and most miserably afflicted
and oppressed. . . . The first author of rebellion, the root of all vices and
mother of all mischiefs, was Lucifer. . . . Thus you do see that neither
heaven nor paradise could suffer any rebellion in them, neither be places for
any rebels to remain in. . . .

After this breach of obedience to God and rebellion against His majesty
. . . God forthwith, by laws given unto mankind, repaired again the rule and
order of obedience thus by rebellion overthrown; and, besides the obedience
due unto His majesty, He not only ordained that in families and households
the wife should be obedient unto her husband, the children unto their
parents, the servants unto their masters, but also, when mankind increased
and spread itself more largely over the world, He by His holy word did
constitute and ordain in cities and countries several and special governors
and rulers unto whom the residue of His people should be obedient. . . .

What shall subjects do then? Shall they obey valiant, stout, wise, and good
princes, and condemn, disobey, and rebel against children being their
princes, or against indiscreet and evil governors? God forbid. For first, what a
perilous thing were it to commit unto subjects the judgment which prince is
wise and godly and his government good, and which is otherwise—as though

the foot must judge of the head, an enterprise very heinous and must needs breed rebellion. For who else be they that are most inclined to rebellion but such haughty spirits? From whom springeth such foul ruin of realms? Is not rebellion the greatest of all mischiefs? And who are most ready to the greatest mischiefs but the worst men? Rebels, therefore, the worst of all subjects, are most ready to rebellion as being the worst of all vices and furthest from the duty of a good subject; as, on the contrary part, the best subjects are most firm and constant in obedience, as in the special and peculiar virtue of good subjects. What an unworthy matter were it then to make the naughtiest subjects, and most inclined to rebellion and all evil, judges over their princes, over their government, and over their counsellors. . . .

. . . If we will have an evil prince (when God shall send such a one) taken away, and a good in his place, let us take away our wickedness, which provoketh God to place such a one over us, and God will either displace him, or of an evil prince make him a good prince, so that we first will change our evil into good. . . .

[The second part of this homily discusses examples from the Old and New Testament "of the obedience of subjects not only unto their good and gracious governors but also unto their evil and unkind princes"—David before King Saul and Christ before Pontius Pilate.]

[The third part describes "what an abominable sin against God and man rebellion is, and how dreadfully the wrath of God is kindled and inflamed against all rebels, and what horrible plagues, punishments, and deaths, and finally eternal damnation doth hang over their heads; as how, on the contrary part, good and obedient subjects are in God's favor and be partakers of peace, quietness, and security, with other God's manifold blessings in this world."]

How horrible a sin against God and man rebellion is cannot possibly be expressed according unto the greatness thereof. For he that nameth rebellion nameth not a singular or one only sin as is theft, robbery, murder, and such like; but he nameth the whole puddle and sink of all sins against God and man, against his prince, his country, his countrymen, his parents, his children, his kinsfolks, his friends, and against all men universally; all sins, I say, against God and all men heaped together, nameth he that nameth rebellion.

The Fourth Part

And as the holy Scriptures do show, so doth daily experience prove, that the counsels, conspiracies, and attempts of rebels never took effect, neither came to good but to most horrible end. For though God do oftentimes prosper just and lawful enemies, which be no subjects, against their foreign enemies, yet did he never long prosper rebellious subjects against their prince, were they never so great in authority or so many in number. . . .

And whoso looketh, on the one part, upon the persons and government of the Queen's most honorable counselors, by the experiment of so many years proved honorable to her majesty and most profitable and beneficial unto our country and countrymen; and, on the other part, considereth the persons, state, and conditions of the rebels themselves, the reformers, as they take upon them of the present government, he shall find that the most rash and harebrained men, the most greatest unthrifts that have most lewdly wasted their own goods and lands, those that are over the ears in debt, and such as for thefts, robberies, and murders dare not in any well-governed common-wealth, where good laws are in force, show their faces, such as are of most lewd and wicked behavior and life, and all such as will not or cannot live in peace are always most ready to move rebellion or to take part with rebels. And are not these meet men, trow you, to restore the commonwealth decayed, who have so spoiled and consumed all their own wealth and thrift? And very like to mend other men's manners who have so vile vices and abominable conditions themselves?

[The fifth part addresses the high "ambition and desire of dominion" of those in spiritual places who should follow Christ's example and humble themselves.]

The Bishop of Rome "did by intolerable ambition challenge not only to be the head of all the church dispersed throughout the world, but also to be lord of all the kingdoms of the world, as is expressly set forth in the book of his own canon laws. . . . He became at once the spoiler and destroyer both of the church, which is the kingdom of our savior Christ, and of the Christian empire, and all Christian kingdoms, as an universal tyrant over all."

[The sixth part explains how the Roman church acquired political power and retained control over its followers.]

You shall understand that by ignorance of God's word, wherein they kept all men, especially the common people, they wrought and brought to pass all these things, making them believe that all they said was true, all that they did was good and godly, and that to hold with them in all things against father, mother, prince, country, and all men was most meritorious. And indeed what mischief will not blind ignorance lead simple men unto?

. . . And to use one example of our own country, the Bishop of Rome did pick a quarrel to King John of England about the election of Stephen

Langton to the bishopric of Canterbury, wherein the king had ancient right. . . . Now had Englishmen at that time known their duty to their prince set forth in God's word, would a great many of the nobles and other Englishmen . . . have rebelled against their sovereign lord the king? . . . Would Englishmen have brought their sovereign lord and natural country into this thralldom and subjection to a false usurper, had they known and had any understanding in God's word at all? Out of the which most lamentable case, and most miserable tyranny, raveny, and spoil of the most greedy Romish wolves ensuing hereupon, the kings and realm of England could not rid themselves of the space of many years after, the Bishop of Rome by his ministers continually not only spoiling the realm and kings of England of infinite treasure but also with the same money hiring and maintaining foreign enemies against the realm and kings of England to keep them in such his subjection. . . .

. . . And to join unto the reports of history matters of later memory, could the Bishop of Rome have raised the late rebellions in the north and west countries in the times of King Henry [VIII] and King Edward [VI], our gracious sovereign's father and brother, but by abusing of the ignorant people? . . . Or who seeth not that upon like confidence yet more lately he hath likewise procured the breach of the public peace in England . . . by the ministry of his disguised chaplains, creeping in laymen's apparel into the houses and whispering in the ears of certain northern borderers, being men most ignorant of their duty to God and their prince of all people of the realm. . . .

[Marginal notes point out the many Old and New Testament references. In the last section, citations are given for papal decrees, and the names of those involved in the quarrel with King John are supplied. This portion ends with "A Thanksgiving for the Suppression of the Last Rebellion."]

On the State of Matrimony

This homily sets forth the received notion of the ideal relationship between husband and wife in marriage. Its position on two issues is particularly significant: first, that husband's command and wives must obey; and second, that wife beating is never permissible. These injunctions are qualified by such arguments as that the husband should "yield something to the woman" since she is "not endued with like strength and constancy of mind"; that wives should control and command the children and family [i.e., administer household matters], but they "should acknowledge the authority of the husband, and refer to him the honor of obedience." And finally, that the unfortunate spouse of a shrewish wife or a violent husband should suppose "that thereby is laid up no small reward hereafter, and in this life no small commendation to thee, if thou canst be quiet." The words of Saints Peter and Paul as well as the Old Testament story of Abraham and Sarah and a reference to Socrates and Xanthippe are recalled to strengthen this line of reasoning.

In practice, it appears that Elizabethan marriages operated according to a very wide spectrum of possibilities. In part, the Protestant movement seems to have encouraged contradictory impulses. On the one hand, it emphasized a wife's submission and docility—Luther said she should run the house and raise the children. There were those clergymen who recited the doggerel: "A spaniel, a woman, and a walnut tree, / The more they are beaten, the better they be." Yet on the other hand, some Protestants stressed the individual's spiritual independence and material rights. In any case, we are perhaps wisest to conclude that, the party line notwithstanding, variations are an inevitable consequence of the characters of the particular husband and wife, joined in the closest and most intimate of all adult relationships.

In *The Taming of the Shrew* (1594) Shakespeare dramatizes the courtship and marriage of shrew and shrew-tamer. We are allowed to watch the machinations of Petruchio and Katherina as they bicker, strive to dominate, and, finally, reach an ambiguous but happy and loving accommodation: is she merely allowing him to think he has the upper hand, does he really rule the roost, or do they play public roles that are very different from their own private entente cordiale?

From *The State of Matrimony*

Married persons must apply their minds in most earliest wise to concord, and must crave continually of God the help of His holy Spirit, so to rule their hearts and to knit their minds together that they be not dissevered by any division of discord. This necessity of prayer must be oft in the practice and using of married persons, that ofttimes the one should pray for the other, lest hate and debate do arise betwixt them. And because few do consider this thing, but more few do perform it (I say, to pray diligently), we see how wonderful the devil deludeth and scorneth this state, how few matrimonies there be without chidings, brawlings, tauntings, repentings, bitter cursings, and fightings.

St. Peter giveth this precept, saying, "You husbands, deal with your wives according to knowledge, giving honor to the wife as unto the weaker vessel, and as unto them that are heirs also of the grace of life, that your prayers be not hindered." This precept doth particularly pertain to the husband, for he ought to be the leader and author of love, in cherishing and increasing concord, which then shall take place if he will use moderation and not tyranny, and if he yield something to the woman. For the woman is a weak creature, not endued with like strength and constancy of mind; therefore they be the sooner disquieted and they be the more prone to all weak affections and dispositions of mind more than men be, and lighter they be and more vain in their phantasies and opinions. These things must be considered of the man, that he be not too stiff, so that he ought to wink at some things and must gently expound all things and to forbear. Howbeit the common sort of men doth judge . . . that it is a man's part to fume in anger, to fight with fist and staff. Howbeit, howsoever they imagine, undoubtedly St. Peter doth better judge what should be seeming to a man and what he should most reasonably perform. For he saith, "Reasoning should be used, and not fighting." Yea, he saith more, "that the woman ought to have a certain honor attributed to her."

. . . Now as concerning the wife's duty. What shall become her? Shall she abuse the gentleness and humanity of her husband, and, at her pleasure, turn all things upside down? No, surely, for that is far repugnant against God's commandment; for thus doth St. Peter preach to them: "Ye wives, be ye in subjection to obey your husbands." To obey is another thing than to control or command, which yet they may do to their children and to their family; but as for their husbands, them must they obey and cease from commanding and perform subjection. . . .

When I take in hand to admonish thy husband to love thee, and to cherish thee, yet will I not cease to set out the law that is appointed for the woman as well as I would require of the man what is written for his law. Go thou, therefore, about such things as becometh thee only and show thyself tractable to thy husband. . . . He that loveth his friend seemeth to do no great thing; but he that honoreth him that is hurtful and hateful to him, this man is worthy most commendation. Even so, think you, if thou canst suffer an extreme husband, thou shalt have a great reward therefore, but if thou lovest him only because he is gentle and courteous, what reward will God give thee therefore? Yet I speak not these things that I would wish the husbands to be sharp towards their wives, but I exhort the women that they would patiently bear the sharpness of their husbands.

Whensoever any displeasant matter riseth at home, if thy wife hath done aught amiss, comfort her and increase not the heaviness. For though thou shouldst be grieved with never so many things, yet shalt thou find nothing more grievous than to want the benevolence of thy wife at home. . . . For if she be poor, upbraid her not; if she be simple, taunt her not, but be the more courteous; for she is thy body, and made one flesh with thee. But thou peradventure wilt say that she is a wrathful woman, a drunkard, and beastly without wit and reason. For this cause bewail her the more. Chafe not in anger, but pray unto almighty God. Let her be admonished and helped with good counsel. . . . But if thou shouldst beat her, thou shalt increase her evil affections, for frowardness [i.e., perverseness] and sharpness is not amended with frowardness, but with softness and gentleness. Furthermore, consider what reward thou shalt have at God's hand, for where thou mightst beat her and yet, for the respect of the fear of God, thou wilt abstain and bear patiently her great offenses, the rather in respect of that law which forbiddeth that a man should cast out his wife what fault soever she be cumbered with, thou shalt have a very great reward, and before the receipt of that reward, thou shalt feel many commodities. For by this means she shall be made the more obedient, and thou for her sake shalt be made the more meek.

My counsel is that, first and before all things, a man do his best endeavor to get him a good wife, endued with all honesty and virtue. But if it so chance that he is deceived, that he hath chosen such a wife as is neither good nor tolerable, then let the husband . . . instruct his wife in every condition and never lay these matters to sight, . . . that we may have the fellowship of our wives, which is the factor of all our doings at home in great quiet and rest. And by these means all things shall prosper quietly, and so shall we pass through the dangers of the troublous sea of this world.

Puritans and Predestination

The Church of England, as it was finally established by the Acts of Supremacy and Uniformity in 1559, did not satisfy the spiritual needs of all English Protestants. Among the most vociferous of its critics were those referred to as Puritans, who wished it to adopt more of the practices associated with the Calvinist churches on the Continent. Many of these people had taken refuge in Germany and Switzerland during the reign of the Catholic Mary Tudor (1553–58), and had experienced Calvinism at firsthand. When they returned home at Elizabeth's accession they took with them an antagonism towards "popish" survivals, such as ritual and vestments, and a distrust of the institution of episcopacy—that is, church government by bishops—which the Continental reformed churches had abandoned. This brought them into conflict with Elizabeth, the Supreme Governor of the Church of England, who stood out against further change. The Queen believed that any move towards the Calvinist system, in which the clergy were elected by the congregation and administration was placed in the hands of "presbyteries" of ministers and laymen, would undermine her own authority as monarch and tend towards re-publicanism. James I took the same view and declared that a Presbyterian system, which he had endured in Scotland, "as well agreeth with monarchy as God and the Devil."

One of the most controversial religious issues in Elizabethan England was that of predestination. For all Christians, it was a basic assumption that those who believed in God were enabled, through the sacrifice of Jesus Christ, to attain eternal life. But this assumption poses a fundamental problem: since God is, by definition, all-powerful, He must be the generating source of this saving faith. Moreover, since God is all-

44

knowing, He must have selected those who, on account of the belief He has infused into them, are be saved. By the same logic He has also condemned the rest to damnation. Yet the idea of God creating human beings merely in order to condemn them is not simply repugnant; it is also contrary to another basic Christian assumption, namely that God is a merciful and loving Father, who has endowed His children with free will in order that they may work out their own salvation.

The Church of England dealt with this paradox by emphasising the positive aspect of predestination. Its formal position was defined by the seventeenth of the Thirty-nine Articles which were approved by the Queen and Parliament in 1571 and given statutory authority. This begins by affirming that the purpose of God is to save, and although it subsequently refers to the unhappy condition of those who are "lacking the spirit of Christ" it carefully refrains from delineating the parameters within which human free will operates. In other words, the article assumes that Christ died for all men, and leaves open the possibility that all men are therefore eligible for salvation.

This relatively optimistic view of the human condition was in accord with one strand of Christian tradition. However, there was another, more pessimistic strand, which had been given powerful expression by St. Augustine in the fourth century and was restated in even more uncompromising terms by the Protestant reformer, John Calvin, in his book *De Predestinatione*, published in 1552. Calvin argued that Christ died not for all men but only for those whom God had singled out for salvation. This immutable decree, issued by God and taking no account of individual aspirations and endeavors, was a guarantee of eternal life and blessedness for those whom He had "elected to grace." But by the same token it was a sentence of eternal suffering on those whom He had "reprobated to damnation."

There were many Calvinists in Elizabethan England. The more committed and hard-line ones were often referred to as Puritans, but in fact the Church as a whole had moved in a Calvinist direction as far as dogma was concerned. When, in the 1590s, a number of Cambridge theologians challenged this Calvinist consensus and affirmed that the Seventeenth Article was capable of quite another interpretation, they caused a furore. The conservative heads of colleges appealed for support to the Archbishop of Canterbury, John Whitgift, and at Lambeth Palace, his official London residence, he gave his approval to a series of supplementary articles designed to complement the Thirty-Nine and give them an unequivocally Calvinist orientation. As Archbishop of Canterbury, Whitgift was the senior cleric in the Church of England, but its Supreme Governor, under the terms of the Act of Supremacy of 1559, was Queen Elizabeth. She was not a Calvinist, nor did she have any intention of allowing her Church to be taken over by the Puritan element within it. She therefore intervened to prevent formal adoption of the Lambeth Articles, as they were called, and they remained thereafter in a state of limbo. Yet there seems little reason to doubt that very many of the Queen's subjects, quite possibly a majority, held views on predestination that were closer to the Lambeth Articles than to the official position. This was one way in which the English could assert their uncompromising Protestantism at a time when the Pope and his ally, the King of Spain, were the major threats not only to their religion but to their sense of national identity.

Since religious beliefs were so controversial, most Elizabethan dramatists shied away from treating them directly. Even in alluding to them, the playwrights tended to remain ambiguous. For instance, in Marlowe's *Doctor Faustus* (1592), perhaps the most dramatic and explicit treatment of these issues in the theater, the tragic hero—a great scholar from Luther's own city of Wittenberg—tries to find his way through the maze of teachings on such subjects as despair, repentance, faith, and salvation. Although forgiveness for his pact with Lucifer is always theoretically possible, Faustus, as a fallen man, is incapable of initiating this repentance and of sustaining trust in God. When he pleads for mercy and forgiveness, he finds a God of "heavy wrath" who "bends His ireful brows." But whether Faustus's damnation is a consequence of predestination or of his own personal inadequacy is never completely resolved.

In Shakespeare's *Othello* (1604), the drunken Cassio affirms his belief that "God's above all, and there be souls that must be saved, and there be souls must not be saved" (II.iii.). But his opinion on the doctrine of predestination cannot be taken at face value, since it is uttered when he is totally inebriated. In *Hamlet*, some speeches that bear on these questions are delivered more seriously. Hamlet himself—another student from Wittenberg—expresses views that are to some extent in conformity with Calvin's doctrines but do not unequivocally acknowledge predestination. Such observations as "There's special providence in the fall of a sparrow," and "If it be not now, yet it will come. The readiness is all" (V.ii.) may attest not only to a belief that everything that happens is foreordained but also to a conviction that resignation, humility, and a form of Christian stoicism are the best responses to the trials and tribulations of human existence.

⚜

The Thirty-Nine Articles of the Church of England, 1571

Article Seventeen: Of Predestination and Election

Predestination to life is the everlasting purpose of God, whereby (before the foundations of the world were laid) He hath constantly decreed, by His counsel secret to us, to deliver from curse and damnation those whom He hath chosen in Christ out of mankind, and to bring them by Christ to everlasting salvation, as vessels made to honor. Wherefore, they which be endued with so excellent a benefit of God be called according to God's purpose by His spirit working in due season; they through grace obey the calling; they be justified freely; they be made sons of God by adoption; they be made like the image of His only-begotten son Jesus Christ; they walk religiously in good works; and at length, by God's mercy, they attain to everlasting felicity.

As the godly consideration of predestination, and our election in Christ, is full of sweet, pleasant, and unspeakable comfort to godly persons and such as feel in themselves the working of the spirit of Christ, mortifying the works of the flesh and their earthly members and drawing up their mind to high and heavenly things, as well because it doth greatly establish and confirm their faith of eternal salvation to be enjoyed through Christ, as because it doth fervently kindle their love towards God: so, for curious and carnal persons, lacking the spirit of Christ, to have continually before their eyes the sentence of God's predestination, is a most dangerous downfall, whereby the Devil doth thrust them either into desperation, or into wretchlessness of most unclean living, no less perilous than desperation.

Furthermore, we must receive God's promises in such wise, as they be generally set forth to us in holy scripture; and, in our doings, that will of God is to be followed which we have expressly declared unto us in the word of God.

The Lambeth Articles, 1595

1. God from eternity hath predestinated some to life. Some He hath predestinated to death.
2. The moving or efficient cause of predestination to life is not the prevision of faith, or of perseverance, or of good works, or of anything which may

be in the persons predestinated, but only the will of the good pleasure of God.

3. Of the predestinated there is a fore-limited and certain number which can neither be diminished nor increased.

4. They who are not predestinated to salvation will be necessarily condemned on account of their sins.

5. A true, living and justifying faith, and the spirit of God sanctifying, is not extinguished, does not fall away, does not vanish in the elect either totally or finally.

6. A truly faithful man—that is, one endowed with justifying faith—is certain by the full assurance of faith of the remission of his sins and his eternal salvation through Christ.

7. Saving grace is not given, is not communicated, is not granted to all men, by which they might be saved if they would.

8. No man can come to Christ except it be given to him, and unless the Father draw him. And all men are not drawn by the Father that they may come unto the Son.

9. It is not placed in the will or power of every man to be saved.

Richard Hooker:
Of the Laws of Ecclesiastical Polity

Puritan attacks upon the Church of England provoked a number of its adherents to come out in print in defense of it. The classic statement of this position was produced by Richard Hooker, who had experienced Puritan criticism at firsthand. He had been plucked from the tranquillity of Oxford University, where he had won a reputation for learning and godliness, to be Master of the Temple, the collegiate institution in London that was the center of legal studies and a hotbed of Puritanism. The agent of this change was his patron Edwin Sandys, at that time Bishop of London, who knew from his own experience how much the Church needed defenders, theologians of formidable ability who could meet the Puritans on their own ground and refute their arguments point by point. This was why he persuaded Hooker to accept the Mastership of the Temple, which involved regular preaching to the students and members of the Inns of Court.

The lawyers of the Temple had already chosen a prominent Puritan, Walter Travers, to give a series of afternoon lectures, and as a consequence "the pulpit," in Thomas Fuller's words, "spake pure Canterbury in the morning, and Geneva in the afternoon, until Travers was silenced." Travers was expelled after the intervention of the Archbishop of Canterbury, John Whitgift, but Puritan sentiment remained strong among the lawyers of the Temple, as throughout the country as a whole, and Hooker recognized the need for the Anglican Church to acquire a solid intellectual foundation, a theological bedrock upon which its doctrines and its discipline could be firmly based. It already had something of the sort in John Jewel's *Apologia pro Ecclesia Anglicana*, with which Hooker was very familiar. Indeed it was only through Jewel's patronage that he had been enabled to go to Oxford. Jewel died in 1571, when Hooker was eighteen, but Hooker kept his memory green and took the *Apology* as his starting point when he embarked upon his own great work.

Hooker was convinced, as was Elizabeth herself, that the Anglican Church set up by parliamentary statute in 1559, shortly after the Queen's accession, was as close to perfection—at least in its broad outlines—as any merely human institution could hope to become. It retained, in his view, all that was best of the historic Roman Catholic church of which it was the legitimate descendant, having purged itself of the superstition, corruption, and worldliness that he believed disfigured the papal church of his own day. Likewise it had adopted the best features of the Protestant churches—Lutheran, Zwinglian, and Calvinist—but had not followed them in denying its Catholic origins or adopting extreme theological positions.

Hooker retired from the turbulence of the Temple to a country living so that he could pursue his studies in peace and quiet, and 1594 saw the publication of the first four books of the *Laws of Ecclesiastical Polity.* Book 5, with an appropriate dedication to Archbishop Whitgift— himself a learned and formidable controversialist and a passionate defender of the established Church—appeared in 1597, at which time Hooker was settled in the Kentish countryside, not far from Canterbury. He died in 1600, leaving the three final books of the *Ecclesiastical Polity* in a more or less finished state. However, his wife and son-in-law treated these with scant respect, and they disappeared from sight. All that survived were Hooker's voluminous notes, but these were carefully preserved by the ecclesiastical authorities and used to reconstruct the missing sections of his work. Books 6 and 8 were eventually published fifty years after Hooker's death, at a time when the Church of England that he had loved and labored to defend was in eclipse—proscribed and driven underground by the republican government set up by the Puritans after their victory in the Civil War. Book 7 made its appearance only in 1662, by which time both the English monarchy and the Anglican Church had been restored.

In Hooker's day the Church of England was, at any rate in theory, the church of all the English people, and at its head stood the sovereign. Henry V, in Shakespeare's play of that name, broods upon the "hard condition" of his kingly office and comforts himself with the reflection that his responsibility to those over whom he rules is limited: "Every subject's duty is the King's, but every subject's soul is his own" (IV.i.). Elizabeth I, however, could take no such comfort, for by virtue of her dual role as Queen and Supreme Governor she was responsible for the spiritual as well as the physical wellbeing of her people. Seen in this light, the expansion of royal authority under the Tudors was a source of weakness, for many individuals who were happy to acknowledge their subjection to Elizabeth in the secular sphere were conscious of a primary allegiance to God where religion was concerned. An Elizabethan member of Parliament noted in his diary the main points of a sermon he had heard that obviously impressed him: "The magistrate is the minister of God and must submit himself to His word as a rule to direct him in all his government. The magistrate must command in the Lord. The subject must obey in the Lord. . . . Obedience, what it is: it is due unto the Lord only."[1]

The fusion of temporal and spiritual power in the person of the monarch meant that when Hooker set out on his philosophical quest to establish the bases of the Church's authority, he had to deal with the major political issues of his day—issues that were not purely English but were agitating and frequently convulsing all the states of post–Reformation Europe. How and why had political communities come into existence? By what sanction did monarchs exercise their authority? How could this authority be reconciled with the liberties of their subjects? And if a ruler abused his authority, did his subjects have any right to rebel against him, or was he responsible only to God? These are themes that are frequently touched upon by Shakespeare, and not only in the histories. He had to tread carefully—as, indeed, did Hooker—for in an age of political and religious upheavals the Queen's government kept a close watch over all publications and did not permit the open expression of heterodox opinions. Yet the burning issues of the day were a matter of passionate concern to writers of all sorts and conditions, and although they might be forced to approach them obliquely, they approached them nonetheless.

The Law of Nature

Machiavelli's amoral view of politics became notorious in the Renaissance period, but it was by no means universally accepted, nor did it

---

1. Quoted by Patrick Collinson in "The Monarchical Republic of Queen Elizabeth I," *Bulletin of the John Rylands University Library of Manchester*, vol. 69 (1987): 409.

drive out older and more conventional interpretations. The scholastic tradition, which derived from St. Thomas Aquinas's fusion of Aristotle and theology in the thirteenth century, was never eclipsed, despite the humanists' avowed contempt for it. Indeed, the beginning of the sixteenth century saw a revival of scholasticism centered on the Sorbonne, the University of Paris, which was to be enormously influential. The Sorbonnists taught that the universe was God's creation and therefore a work of reason. It was governed by a hierarchy of laws, of which the most relevant from the human point of view was the *lex naturalis*, the law of nature, since all men were born with an instinctive awareness of it.

The Puritans in England adhered to the alternative tradition that derived from St. Augustine and had been given a powerful restatement by the Protestant reformers in the sixteenth century. The Puritans believed that fallen man was so corrupt in his nature that he was bound hand and foot by the chains of sin, incapable of bettering his condition unless God chose to implant the seed of regeneration in him. They discounted reason and took a profoundly pessimistic view of human nature.

Shakespeare was familiar with the concepts of a law of nature and a law of nations, for in *Troilus and Cressida* he refers to both. But in this play he dramatizes a view of human nature that is close to that of the Puritans, for the Trojan hero, Hector, while recognizing what is right and just, is unwilling (or, as the Puritans would have put it, unable) to make this his goal. Instead he advocates a course of action that he knows to be wrong:

> *There is a law in each well-order'd nation*
> *To curb those raging appetites that are*
> *Most disobedient and refractory.*
> *If Helen then be wife to Sparta's king,*
> *As it is known she is, these moral laws*
> *Of nature and of nations speak aloud*
> *To have her back return'd. Thus to persist*
> *In doing wrong extenuates not wrong,*
> *But makes it much more heavy. Hector's opinion*
> *Is this in way of truth; yet ne'ertheless,*
> *My spritely brethren, I propend to you*
> *In resolution to keep Helen still.*

> (II.ii.)

As the following extracts show, Hooker stood firmly within the scholastic tradition. Not only did he accept the Thomists' view of the cardinal importance of natural law; he also followed them in insisting that men could deepen their knowledge and understanding of it by using their God-given faculty of reason. In short, he was an optimist, convinced that man, even in his fallen state, was capable of apprehending truth and goodness.

Of that law which God from before the beginning hath set for Himself to do all things by [Book 1. 2.]

All things that are have some operation not violent or casual. Neither doth anything ever begin to exercise the same without some fore-conceived end for which it worketh. And the end which it worketh for is not obtained unless the work be also fit to obtain by it. For unto every end every operation will not serve. That which doth assign unto each thing the kind, that which doth moderate the force and power, that which doth appoint the form and measure, of working, the same we term a *Law*. So that no certain end could ever be attained unless the actions whereby it is attained were regular; that is to say, made suitable, fit, and correspondent unto their end by some canon, rule or law. Which thing doth first take place in the works even of God Himself.

The Law which natural agents have given them to observe, and their necessary manner of keeping it [Book 1. 3.]

This world's first creation, and the preservation since of things created, what is it but only so far forth a manifestation by execution what the eternal law of God is concerning things natural? And as it cometh to pass in a kingdom rightly ordered that after a law is once published it presently takes effect far and wide, all states framing themselves thereunto; even so let us think it fareth in the natural course of the world. Since the time that God did first proclaim the edicts of His law upon it, heaven and earth have hearkened unto His voice, and their labor hath been to do His will. He "made a law for the rain";[2] He gave His "decree unto the sea, that the waters should not pass His commandment."[3]

2. Job 28:26.
3. Jeremiah 5:22.

Now if nature should intermit her course and leave altogether, though it were but for a while, the observation of her own laws; if those principal and mother elements of the world, whereof all things in this lower world are made, should lose the qualities which now they have; if the frame of that heavenly arch erected over our heads should loosen and dissolve itself; if celestial spheres should forget their wonted motions, and by irregular volubility turn themselves any way as it might happen; if the prince of lights of heaven, which now as a giant doth run his unwearied course, should as it were through a languishing faintness begin to stand and to rest himself; if the moon should wander from her beaten way, the times and seasons of the year blend themselves by disordered and confused mixture, the winds breathe out their last gasp, the clouds yield no rain, the earth be defeated of heavenly influence, the fruits of the earth pine away as children at the withered breasts of their mother no longer able to yield them relief: what would become of man himself, whom these things now do all serve? See we not plainly that obedience of creatures unto the law of nature is the stay of the whole world?

Of the natural way of finding out laws by reason to guide the will unto that which is good [Book 1. 8.]

Laws of reason have these marks to be known by. Such as keep them resemble most lively in their voluntary actions that very manner of working which nature herself doth necessarily observe in the course of the whole world. The works of nature are all behoveful, beautiful, without superfluity or defect; even so theirs, if they be framed according to that which the law of reason teacheth. Secondly, those laws are investigable by reason without the help of revelation, supernatural and divine. Finally, in such sort they are investigable that the knowledge of them is general, the world hath always been acquainted with them. . . . Law rational, therefore, which men commonly use to call the law of nature—meaning thereby the law which human nature knoweth itself in reason universally bound unto, which also for that cause may be termed most fitly the law of reason—this law, I say, comprehendeth all those things which men by the light of their natural understanding evidently know, or at leastwise may know, to be beseeming or unbeseeming, virtuous or vicious, good or evil for them to do.

"Some Kind of Regiment the Law of Nature Doth Require"

The revived scholasticism which had such a powerful influence on Hooker's thought is nowhere more apparent than in his discussion of the origins of political communities. The Sorbonnists argued that in the prelapsarian state (before the fall of man) there was no need for coercive authority, for Adam and Eve lived in instinctive harmony with natural law. However, their fall from grace had left the way open for evil to infiltrate into the world, and such were its seductive ways that although men and women had an instinctive knowledge of the good, they all too often chose the bad instead. This meant that as the number of inhabitants of the earth multiplied, so too did "envy, strife, contention and violence." Fortunately, God had given men the capacity to construct a form of organization that could preserve them from the worst effects of these evils, and so, in the search for self-preservation and a more peaceful existence, they agreed to give up their right to freedom—since in practice such freedom seemed only to lead to anarchy—and to subordinate themselves to the rule of a single person. In this way political communities were created.

As will be seen in the extracts that follow, Hooker entirely accepted this interpretation. He also followed the Sorbonnists in his attitude towards the communities so created. The rule of a single person, he argued, was preferable to anarchy and the ever-present threat of sudden death, but arbitrary government provided no long-term solution to the problem of organizing human societies, for a single ruler, either out of wickedness or incapacity, might well prove to be almost as intolerable as no ruler at all. Hooker describes how, in order to prevent such a situation from arising, the various communities drew up laws, and it was these products of human reason that henceforth defined the relationship between the ruler and his subjects. All rightful rulers were bound to observe these laws, and if, instead, they imposed their own will on their people, or made themselves, and not the community as a whole, the source of law, they degenerated into tyrants.

How reason doth lead men unto the making of human laws
whereby politic societies are governed; and to agreement about laws
whereby the fellowship or communion of independent societies
standeth [Book 1. 10]

All men desire to lead in this world a happy life. . . . But neither that which we learn of ourselves nor that which others teach us can prevail where wickedness and malice have taken deep root. If therefore when there was but as yet one family in the world, no means of instruction human or divine could prevent effusion of blood, how could it be chosen but that when families were multiplied and increased upon earth, after separation each providing for itself, envy, strife, contention and violence must grow amongst them? . . .

To take away all such mutual grievances, injuries, and wrongs there was no way but only by growing unto composition and agreement amongst themselves, by ordaining some kind of government public, and by yielding themselves subject thereunto; that unto whom they granted authority to rule and govern, by them the peace, tranquillity, and happy estate of the rest might be procured. Men always knew . . . that strifes and troubles would be endless, except they gave their common consent all to be ordered by some whom they should agree upon: without which consent there were no reason that one man should take upon him to be lord or judge over another; because although there be according to the opinion of some very great and judicious men a kind of natural right in the noble, wise and virtuous to govern them which are of servile disposition, nevertheless, for manifestation of this their right, and men's more peaceable contentment on both sides, the assent of them who are to be governed seemeth necessary.

To fathers within their private families nature hath given a supreme power; for which cause we see throughout the world, even from the foundation thereof, all men have ever been taken as lords and lawful kings in their own houses. Howbeit, over a whole grand multitude having no such dependency upon any one, and consisting of so many families as every politic society in the world doth, impossible it is that any should have complete lawful power but by consent of men or immediate appointment of God; because not having the natural superiority of fathers, their power must needs be either usurped, and then unlawful, or, if lawful, then either granted or consented unto by them over whom they exercise the same, or else given extraordinarily from God, unto whom all the world is subject. . . . So that, in a word, all public regiment of what kind soever seemeth evidently to have risen from deliberate advice, consultation, and composition between men, judging it convenient and behoveful; there being no impossibility in nature, considered by itself, but that men might have lived without any public regiment. Howbeit, the corruption of our nature being presupposed, we may not deny but that the law of nature doth now require, of necessity, some kind of regiment; so that to bring things unto the first course they were in, and utterly to take away all kind of public government in the world, were apparently to overturn the whole world.

The case of man's nature standing therefore as it doth, some kind of regiment the law of nature doth require. Yet the kinds thereof being many, nature tieth not to any one, but leaveth the choice as a thing arbitrary. At the first, when some certain kind of regiment was once approved, it may be that nothing was then further thought upon for the manner of governing, but all permitted unto their wisdom and discretion which were to rule; till, by experience, they found this for all parts very inconvenient, so as the thing which they had devised for a remedy did indeed but increase the sore which it should have cured. They saw that to live by one man's will became the cause of all men's misery. This constrained them to come unto laws, wherein all men might see their duties beforehand, and know the penalties of transgressing them. . . .

The lawful power of making laws to command whole politic societies of men belongeth so properly unto the same entire societies, that for any prince or potentate of what kind soever upon earth to exercise the same of himself, and not either by express commission immediately and personally received from God, or else by authority derived at the first from their consent upon whose persons they impose laws, it is not better than mere tyranny. . . .

Of this point therefore we are to note, that since men naturally have no full and perfect power to command whole politic multitudes of men, therefore utterly without our consent we could in such sort be at no man's commandment living. And to be commanded we do consent when that society whereof we are part hath at any time before consented, without revoking the same after by the like universal agreement. Wherefore as any man's deed past is good as long as himself continueth, so the act of a public society of men done five hundred years since standeth as theirs who presently are of the same societies, because corporations are immortal; we were then alive in our predecessors, and they in their successors do live still. Laws therefore human, of what kind soever, are available by consent.

"Kingly Regiment"

Hooker lived in a world in which monarchy was the norm, and although he was careful to state that such a form of government, while in conformity with natural law, was not specifically and exclusively prescribed by it, he also emphasized that once a sovereign authority had been created, it acquired divine sanction: in the words of St. Paul "the powers that be are ordained of God" (Romans 13:1). Yet Hooker remained convinced that kings, like all other rulers, existed for the benefit of their people, and although they had been granted power, they were under an obligation to use it responsibly. In a striking phrase that is also found in the *Vindiciae Contra Tyrannos* [see below], Hooker insists that the king is *major singulis, universis minor*—greater than any individual but less than the community as a whole.

This, of course, raised the difficult and dangerous question of whether the community could withdraw its allegiance from a ruler who was abusing it; in other words, whether rebellion was justified. Hooker was careful not to commit himself on this point. The logic of his position might well have led him to conclude that rebellion could be justified in certain circumstances. If the ruler acted as a tyrant, he broke the conditions of the grant that had given him power, and his subjects— or so it might be assumed—were thereby set at liberty to transfer their allegiance. Shakespeare's Richmond, for instance, leading his army against Richard III, whom he condemned as a "bloody tyrant," assured his followers that "God will, in justice, ward you as his soldiers; / If you do sweat to put a tyrant down, / You sleep in peace, the tyrant being slain" (*Richard III* V.iii.) (1592). However, Hooker showed his realism when he pointed out that unless the ruler voluntarily agreed to surrender his power, there was no obvious means by which his people could take it from him.

It is conceivable that in dealing with the thorny topic of rebellion, Hooker to some extent concealed his true views. But as the defender of an established Church against the assault of potentially rebellious Puritans, his sympathies were with the "powers that be." Moreover, as an Englishman he could afford to take a detached view of such matters, because England—unlike France, the Netherlands, and parts of Germany—had not been torn asunder by civil war, nor had its traditional constitution been abrogated. Like Fortescue before him, and Coke after him, Hooker derived comfort and pride from the survival in England of a system of government that seemed to secure both the authority of the sovereign and the liberties of the subject.

What the power of dominion is [Book 8.2]

Unto kings by human right, honor by very divine right is due. Man's ordinances are many times presupposed as grounds in the statutes of God. And therefore, of what kind soever the means be whereby governors are lawfully advanced unto their seats, as we by the law of God stand bound meekly to acknowledge them for God's lieutenants, and to confess their power His, so they, by the same law, are both authorized and required to use that power, as far as it may be in any sort available, to His honor. . . . That the Christian world should be ordered by kingly regiment, the law of God doth not anywhere command. And yet the law of God doth give them right, which once are exalted to that estate, to exact at the hands of their subjects general obediences in whatsoever affairs their power may serve to command. So God doth ratify the works of that sovereign authority which kings have received by men.

This is therefore the right whereby kings do hold their power. But yet in what sort the same doth rest and abide in them, it somewhat further behoveth to search. Wherein, that we be not enforced to make overlarge discourses about the different conditions of sovereign or supreme power, that which we speak of kings shall be with respect to the state . . . where the people are in no subjection but such as willingly themselves have condescended unto, for their own most behoof and security. In kingdoms therefore of this quality the highest governor hath indeed universal dominion, but with dependence upon that whole entire body over the several parts whereof he hath dominion; so that it standeth for an axiom in this case, the king is *major singulis, universis minor.*

The king's dependency we do not construe as some have done, who are of opinion that no man's birth can make him a king, but every particular person advanced unto such authority hath at his entrance into his reign the same bestowed upon him, as an estate in condition, by the voluntary deed of the people, in whom it doth lie to put by anyone and to prefer some other before him better liked of, or judged fitter for the place. . . . Which strange, untrue and unnatural conceits, set abroad by seedsmen of rebellion only to animate unquiet spirits and to feed them with a possibility of aspiring unto thrones and scepters if they can win the hearts of the people (what hereditary title soever any other before them may have)—I say these unjust and insolent positions I would not mention, were it not thereby to make the countenance of truth more orient. For unless we will openly proclaim defiance unto all law, equity, and reason, we must (there is no remedy) acknowledge that, in kingdoms hereditary, birth giveth right unto sovereign dominion. . . .

The case thus standing, albeit we judge it a thing most true that kings, even inheritors, do hold their right to the power of dominion with dependency upon the whole entire body politic over which they rule as kings, yet . . . the cause of dependency is in that first original conveyance when power was derived by the whole into one, to pass from them unto him . . . Neither can any man with reason think but that the first institution of kings is a sufficient consideration wherefore their power should always depend on that from which it did then flow. Original influence of power from the body into the king is cause of the king's dependency in power upon the body. . . .

May then a body politic at all times withdraw, in whole or in part, that influence of dominion which passeth from it, if inconvenience doth grow thereby? It must be presumed that supreme governors will not in such case oppose themselves, and be stiff in detaining that, the use whereof is with public detriment. But surely without their consent I see not how the body should be able, by any just means, to help itself, saving when dominion doth escheat. Such things therefore must be thought upon beforehand, that power may be limited ere it be granted; which is the next thing we are to consider.

In power of dominion, all kings have not an equal latitude. Kings by conquest make their own charter; so that how large their power, either civil or spiritual, is, we cannot with any certainty define, further than only to set them in general the law of God and nature for bounds. . . . Touching kings which were first instituted by agreement and composition made with them over whom they reign, how far their power may lawfully extend the articles of compact between them must show: not the articles only of compact at the first beginning, which for the most part are either clean worn out of knowledge or else known unto very few, but whatsoever hath been after, in free and voluntary manner, condescended unto, whether by express consent (whereof positive laws are witness) or else by silent allowance, famously notified through custom reaching beyond the memory of man. By which means of after-agreement it cometh many times to pass in kingdoms that they whose ancient predecessors were by violence and force made subject do grow even by little and little into that most sweet form of kingly government, which philosophers define to be "regency willingly sustained and endured, with chiefty of power in the greatest things. . . ."[4]

Happier that people whose law is their king in the greatest things, than that whose king is himself their law. Where the king doth guide the state, and the law the king, that commonwealth is like a harp or melodious instrument, the strings whereof are tuned and handled all by one, following as laws the rules and canons of musical science. . . . In which respect I cannot choose but commend highly their wisdom by whom the foundations of this commonwealth have been laid. Wherein, though no manner person or cause be unsubject to the king's power, yet so is the power of the king over all and in all limited, that unto all his proceedings the law itself is a rule. . . . Our kings, therefore, when they take possession of the room [office] they are called unto, have it painted [pointed] out before their eyes, even by the very solemnities and rites of their inauguration, to what affairs, by the said law, their supreme authority and power reacheth. Crowned we see they are, and enthronized, and anointed: the crown a sign of military, the throne of sedentary or judicial, the oil of religious or sacred, power.

4. Aristotle, *Politics* 1, Book 3, cap 1.

"Temporal Blessings"

While Hooker stood firmly in the scholastic tradition when he analyzed the origins and nature of political societies, he showed his humanist affiliations when he came to consider man as an individual. Aquinas had dismissed the pursuit of worldly honor and glory as a distraction from love of God and the contemplation of eternity, but the Italian humanists, inspired by Petrarch, believed that it was not only virtuous in itself but the best way in which to develop human potential. By Shakespeare's day this assumption was being questioned—as Falstaff shows in his comment that honor is not much use when it comes to mending limbs that are broken in the attempt to win it—but Hooker still rates honor highly. He also displays the humanists' contempt for wealth as such, and their insistence that true virtue resides in interior qualities rather than external display. In recommending a balanced approach to life's varying fortunes, he shows his debt to Aristotle and the Stoics, but what comes through most clearly in the following passage is the serenity of his Christian faith and the conviction that true happiness is not to be found in this world.

Of the nature of that ministry which serveth for performance of divine duties in the Church of God; and how happiness, not eternal only but also temporal, doth depend upon it [Book 5.76]

Of earthly blessings the meanest is wealth; reputation the chiefest. For which cause we esteem the gain of honor an ample recompense for the loss of all other worldly benefits. . . . Riches, to him which hath and doth nothing with them, they are a contumely. Honor is commonly presumed a sign of more than ordinary virtue and merit, by means whereof when ambitious minds thirst after it, their endeavors are testimonies how much it is in the eye of nature to possess that body, the very shadow whereof is set at so high a rate. . . .

If any think that iniquity and peace, sin and prosperity, can dwell together, they err, because they distinguish not aright between the matter and that which giveth it the form of happiness; between possession and fruition; between the having and the enjoying of good things. The impious cannot enjoy that they have, partly because they receive it not as at God's hands—which only consideration maketh temporal blessings comfortable—and partly because, through error, placing it above things of far more price and worth, they turn that to poison which might be food; they make their prosperity their own snare; in the nest of their highest growth they lay foolishly those eggs out of which their woeful overthrow is afterwards hatched. Hereby it cometh to pass that wise and judicious men, observing the vain behaviors of such as are risen to unwonted greatness, have thereby been able to prognosticate their ruin. So that in very truth no impious or wicked man doth prosper on earth but either sooner or later the world may perceive easily how at such time as others thought them most fortunate they had but only the good estate which fat oxen have above lean: when they appeared to grow, their climbing was towards ruin.

The gross and bestial conceit of them which want understanding is only that the fullest bellies are happiest. Therefore the greatest felicity they wish to the commonwealth wherein they live is that it may but abound and stand; that they which are riotous may have to pour out without stint; that the poor may sleep and the rich feed them; that nothing unpleasant may be commanded, nothing forbidden men which themselves have a lust to follow; that kings may provide for the ease of their subjects; that wantonness, excess, and lewdness of life may be left free; and that no fault may be capital besides dislike of things settled in so good terms. But be it far from the just to dwell either in or near to the tents of these so miserable felicities. . . .

By reason of man's imbecility of mind, too high a flow of prosperity is dangerous; too low an ebb again as dangerous, for that the virtue of patience is rare, and the hand of necessity stronger than ordinary virtue is able to withstand. Solomon's discreet and moderate desire we all know: "Give me, O Lord, neither riches nor penury."[5] Men overhigh exalted either in honor or in power or in nobility or in wealth; they likewise that are as much on the contrary hand sunk either with beggary or through dejection or by baseness, do not easily give ear to reason; but the one exceeding apt unto outrages, and the other unto petty mischiefs. For greatness delighteth to show itself by effects of power, and baseness to help itself with shifts of malice. For which cause a moderate, indifferent temper between fulness of bread and emptiness hath been evermore thought and found (all circumstances duly considered) the safest and happiest for all estates, even for kings and princes themselves.

Again, we are not to look that these things should always concur—no, not in them which are accounted happy—neither that the course of men's lives or of public affairs should continually be drawn out as an even thread (for that the nature of things will not suffer). But a just survey being made, as those particular men are worthily reputed good whose virtues be great and their faults tolerable, so him we may register for a man fortunate, and that for

5. Proverbs 30:8.

a prosperous or happy state, which, having flourished, doth not afterwards feel any tragical alteration such as might cause them to be a spectacle of misery to others. . . . No misery is reckoned more than common or human if God so dispose that we pass through it and come safe to shore; even as, contrariwise, men do not use to think those flourishing days happy which do end with tears.

"Somewhat above Capacity of Reason"

Hooker's debt to Aristotle is shown by his assumption that political society, though the product of violence, creates the conditions in which men can develop their potential. Yet as a Christian he also believed that there could be no ultimate fulfillment in this life, and that whatever satisfaction human beings might derive from the pursuit of earthly felicity, they would always be seeking something beyond it.

Wherefore God hath by scripture further made known such supernatural laws as do serve for men's direction [Book 1. 11]

Man doth seek a triple perfection. First a sensual, consisting in those things which very life itself requireth, either as necessary supplements or as beauties and ornaments thereof. Then an intellectual, consisting in those things which none underneath man is either capable of or acquainted with. Lastly a spiritual and divine, consisting in those things whereunto we tend by supernatural means here, but cannot here attain unto them.

They that make the first of these three the scope of their whole life are said by the Apostle to have no God but only their belly;[6] to be earthly minded men. Unto the second they bend themselves who seek especially to excel in all such knowledge and virtue as doth most commend men. To this branch belongeth the law of moral and civil perfection. That there is somewhat higher than either of these two, no other proof doth need than the very process of man's desire, which, being natural, should be frustrate if there were not some farther thing wherein it might rest at the length contented, which in the former it cannot do. For man doth not seem to rest satisfied either with fruition of that wherewith his life is preserved, or with performance of such actions as advance him most deservedly in estimation; but doth further covet—yea oftentimes manifestly pursue with great sedulity and earnestness—that which cannot stand him in any stead for vital use; that which exceedeth the reach of sense, yea somewhat above capacity of reason;

6. Philippians 3:19.

somewhat divine and heavenly which with hidden exultation it rather surmiseth than conceiveth. Somewhat it seeketh, and what that is directly it knoweth not. Yet very intentive desire thereof doth so incite it that all other known delights and pleasures are laid aside. They give place to the search of this but-only-suspected desire.

If the soul of man did serve only to give him being in this life, then things appertaining unto this life would content him, as we see they do other creatures. Which creatures, enjoying what they live by, seek no further, but in this contentation do show a kind of acknowledgment that there is no higher good which doth any way belong unto them. With us it is otherwise. For although the beauties, riches, honors, sciences, virtues and perfections of all men living were in the present possession of one; yet somewhat beyond and above all this there would still be sought and earnestly thirsted for. So that nature even in this life doth plainly claim and call for a more divine perfection than either of these two that have been mentioned.

"Musical Harmony"

Puritans were inclined to distrust the senses. Indeed, Sir Toby Belch, in *Twelfth Night* (1601), accuses Malvolio of being a Puritan because he denies himself the enjoyment of life: "Dost thou think because thou art virtuous there shall be no more cakes and ale?" (II.iii). In keeping with this attitude, the Puritans preferred their churches bare and devoid of ceremony. They were suspicious of music—unless it was the straightforward reciting of psalms—and associated harmony with popery. For Hooker, on the contrary, music offered a glimpse of the divine, opening up man's spiritual faculties in a way that nothing else could do. Here he was at one with Plato, who thought that music was an essential part of education, and had the power to transform stubborn human nature. This exalted view of music was characteristic of Renaissance thought, and finds expression in Shakespeare's plays, as when Lorenzo tells Jessica in *The Merchant of Venice*:

> The man that hath no music in himself,
> Nor is not moved with concord of sweet sounds,
> Is fit for treasons, stratagems, and spoils,
> The motions of his spirits are dull as night,
> And his affections dark as Erebus:
> Let no such man be trusted.

(V.i.)

Of Music with Psalms [Book 5. 38]

Touching musical harmony, whether by instrument or voice . . . such notwithstanding is the force thereof, and so pleasing effects it hath in that very part of man which is most divine, that some have been thereby induced to think that the soul itself by nature is or hath in it harmony. A thing which delighteth all ages and beseemeth all states; a thing as seasonable in grief as in joy; as decent being added unto actions of greatest weight and solemnity as being used when men most sequester themselves from action. The reason hereof is an admirable facility which music hath to express and represent to the mind, more inwardly than any other sensible mean, the very standing, rising and falling, the very steps and inflections every way, the turns and varieties of all passions whereunto the mind is subject; yea so to imitate them that whether it resemble unto us the same state wherein our minds already are, or a clean contrary, we are not more contentedly by the one confirmed than changed and led away by the other. In harmony the very image and character even of virtue and vice is perceived, the mind delighted with their resemblances, and brought, by having them often iterated, into a love of the things themselves; for which cause there is nothing more contagious and pestilent than some kinds of harmony; than some, nothing more strong and potent unto good.

And that there is such a difference of one kind from another, we need no proof but our own experience. Inasmuch as we are at the hearing of some, more inclined unto sorrow and heaviness; of some, more mollified and softened in mind: one kind apter to stay and settle us; another to move and stir our affections. There is that draweth to a marvelous grave and sober mediocrity; there is also that carrieth, as it were, into ecstasies, filling the mind with a heavenly joy and for the time in a manner severing it from the body. So that although we lay altogether aside the consideration of ditty or matter, the very harmony of sound, being framed in due sort and carried from the ear to the spiritual faculties of our souls, is by a native puissance and efficacy greatly available to bring to a perfect temper whatsoever is there troubled; apt as well to quicken the spirits as to allay that which is too eager; sovereign against melancholy and despair; forcible to draw forth tears of devotion if the mind be such as can yield them; able both to move and moderate all affections.

Science
and the Occult

I n their attempt to understand the world around them, Renaissance thinkers could bring to bear at least three different modes of reasoning. Some, turning to Aristotle, used the deductive method. Postulating a teleological or purposeful universe, they argued that all action was the result of one of four causes; that identifying the cause enabled one to know what effect it would have; and that change did not alter the fundamental unity existing between matter and form. In this view, change transforms matter into what it is capable of becoming, and the cause of the change determines the result. In contrast to this process of reasoning, which goes from broad principles to specific cases, men such as Francis Bacon, claiming that final causes are unknowable, argued for the validity of exactly the opposite approach. Rather than begin "by establishing certain abstract and useless generalities," Bacon argued in his treatise the *Novum Organum* (1620) that we should use the inductive approach to acquire knowledge, that only a series of controlled, verifiable experiments could establish the truth of a proposition. Bacon went on to explain that his procedure "derives axioms from the senses and particulars [i.e., observation and experiment], rising by gradual and unbroken ascent, so that it arrives at the most general axioms last of all." In effect, Bacon was describing what today is called the "scientific method."

Still other thinkers, who would not accept these two possibilities, followed what they thought was an even more powerful means of uncovering truth. They invoked the help of occult and mystical powers, forces that, they believed, animated the universe by means of the spirit or hidden virtues God sends to physical objects through the stars. According to their thinking, the energy of the divinity fills the universe He has created so that all things have a spiritual aspect; in this view, matter is thought to be almost alive, imbued with the divine.

Renaissance belief in the validity of the occult for understanding and gaining power over nature was generally popularized by the Italian Neoplatonists, who derived this view of life from newly discovered manuscripts. Known as the *Corpus Hermeticum*, or the wisdom of Hermes, these recently found writings were studied with enthusiasm and curiosity. In part, the great interest in them was due to the claims of some scholars that the manuscripts were older than Mosaic law—in fact, that the ideas in the *Hermetica* had been expressed first in the hieroglyphs of the ancient Egyptians. The great scholar, Marsilio Ficino, wrongly thought that Plato had traveled to Egypt, had become acquainted with the *Hermetica* there, and had been influenced by its ideas. So excited was Cosimo de' Medici by these papers that, as patron of the academy for classical studies in Florence, he directed Ficino in 1463 to set aside his translation of Plato in order to work on this material. In 1471, Ficino published his translation; by the end of the sixteenth century, sixteen editions had appeared and disciples of the work studied it throughout the Continent.

In actual fact, the *Hermetica* do not set forth a coherent or consistent philosophy; their lessons are often confused and contradictory. In the tracts, the Greek Hermes is identified with the Egyptian god Thoth, known as Hermes Trismegistus, or Hermes the Thrice-greatest. Hermes, who always appears as the central figure, teaches his followers how to develop a mystic sympathy with the world and mankind. In this way, they can come to discover the divine within themselves, acquiring special spiritual and intuitive knowledge as well as assuring their salvation. Students are to learn how to use heavenly inspiration and revelation as a means toward either accepting the universe as holy and uniting with it, or rising above matter and, through piety and asceticism, rejecting the world and the flesh.

According to the Hermetic tracts the seven planets and the stars are controlled by demons or spirits—those governing the planets are especially strong—and these forces rule the lower world. Through the mystic wisdom of Hermes, one can engage the powers of the celestial world for mastery over the physical. With this knowledge, such a person, a magus, could make use of the secret strength of such occult means as astrological and cabalistic signs, symbols, fetishes, names, and numbers.

In practice, then, the Hermetic revelations were joined with other approaches to knowledge and power—astrology, alchemy, numerology, mystical geometry, music, the cabala, the micro-macrocosm relationship, and various schools of occult mysticism. A magus could combine many of these in his effort to understand nature and advance his interests. Such men as Cornelius Agrippa (1486–1535) and Paracelsus (1493–1541), each with his own particular method, claimed that his results revealed the deepest secrets of nature.

Actually, such a combination of occult practices was consistent with the real origin of the Hermetic writings, since they were a compilation of disparate materials hardly as ancient as the Neoplatonists believed. Indeed, in 1614 Isaac Casaubon (1559–1614) proved that the texts were composed in the years between A.D. 100–300, probably by Alexandrian Greeks who combined Platonism and Stoicism with some Jewish and Persian ideas. Casaubon's dating effectively discredited the works.

As we might expect, Renaissance application of the different reasoning processes of Aristotle, Bacon, or Neoplatonic mysticism yielded very different and incompatible interpretations of the mysteries of nature. In Aristotelian thinking, an endless cycle of heat, cold, moisture, and dryness affected the four elements (earth, air, fire, and water) that compose matter (see above, pages 1–4); in Bacon's approach, the empirical method determined truth; and in mysticism, matter was thought to be animated from within. As a consequence, the answers and explanations of one school of thought generally had little influence on either of the others. Yet many thinkers in the Renaissance continued to believe in the validity of more than one of these processes. Even those we might consider the most modern defied logic, sustaining contradictory and conflicting ideas at the same time: Johannes Kepler, the astronomer, practiced astrology and cast horoscopes; Francis Bacon himself sometimes blurred the distinction between the animate and inanimate; and even Isaac Newton (1642–1727), the physicist and mathematician, spent thirty years pursuing alchemical studies. Indeed, in private Newton expressed the belief that universal gravitation was the will of God operating in the universe.

Nevertheless, despite the fact that some basically scientific thinkers attempted to maintain a kind of mental coexistence with these other methodologies, the effort became increasingly difficult in the course of the seventeenth century. For example, the differences between the occult and the empirical ways of acquiring knowledge remained both numerous and fundamental. The occult disciplines—astrology, alchemy, numerology, and magic—used symbolic or metaphoric language for finding answers, and then interpreted these symbols and metaphors literally to learn what would happen in the future. In practice, the believer in the occult was most often concerned with an individual's well-being. In effect, nature was not studied in itself but only as it could reveal another system capable of telling us what will happen in our lives. Objects were assigned qualities—masculine/feminine, pure/impure—and given a symbolic representation. Then these symbols, which could be properly understood only by the initiated, were treated as equivalent to realities. Knowledge was expressed in metaphoric language that was often made more complicated by secret or hidden elements—using exotic foreign words or omitting essential ingredients. And the experiments that verified this knowledge were personal and could not be replicated.

In contrast, the scientific method was also being formulated with a very different goal: the disinterested study of nature by direct observation. It set out to describe controlled experiments in nonmetaphoric language; it was impersonal, public, and repeatable. Moreover, unlike the methodology of the occult, which had a protective attitude toward established notions, the scientific approach tried to test generalized hypotheses and to eliminate those that proved deficient (e.g., the geocentric universe, the circular movement of the planets, the phlogiston theory of combustion).[1] In other words, the scientific method, then as now, was continuously evolving and open; the occult system was static or closed, holding on to hypotheses that could not be challenged or tested. As a final mark of their differences, we might note that the practitioner of the occult considered the past a golden age from which civilization has been declining; the scientist, on the other hand, would tend to think of the golden age as a possible future accomplishment.

Such occult practices as magic, astrology, numerology, and alchemy are all mutually reinforcing yet self-contained systems; each has its own special area of concern and uses its own imagery. Moreover, Renaissance curiosity in the occult was strengthened and enriched by both classical and biblical references. From reading Latin writers, students would have learned that pagans believed in augury or divination through birds; worshiped Hecate, the goddess of sorcery and witchcraft;

1. *phlogiston:* a hypothetical substance thought to exist in all combustible matter that was released in the process of burning.

and predicted that the ides of March would prove fatal to Caesar. These instances were supplemented by others from the Old and New Testament: Saul and the witch of Endor, the words of the prophets, or the mystical interpretations offered especially of the Book of Revelation. Such examples legitimatized interest in dark powers and suprarational forces. Since many literary references draw on the techniques and specialized vocabulary of particular occult practices, a brief explanation of the most significant ones will prove helpful to readers and students of Renaissance literature.

Reginald Scot:
The Discovery of Witchcraft

The most comprehensive and probably the most influential book on the subject of the supernatural is Reginald Scot's *Discovery of Witchcraft* (1584). Scot takes up not only "the lewd dealing of witches" but also such matters as "the knavery of conjurers," "the curiosity of figure-casters," "the beggarly art of alchemystry," and "the virtue and power of natural magic." Yet Scot's study is notable as much for its attitude as for its range. Although he did not doubt that witches might exist, he questioned whether "they can do such miraculous works as are imputed unto them." In his view, the evidence accepted at witch trials was largely hearsay and inconclusive. Moreover, natural causes could be found for many of the misfortunes blamed on the often elderly, poor, and ignorant women who were accused of being witches by the superstitious. In fact, his work was probably undertaken in reaction to a witch-hunt in 1582 in Essex, England, when some thirteen to eighteen people were tried and executed. Scot wrote his book to encourage a more humane, reasoned, and even skeptical attitude among his readers.

Born in 1538, Scot was educated at Oxford and trained in the law. He served as both a justice of the peace and a member of Parliament until he died in 1599. In his community Scot was regarded as something of a scholar—indeed, the *Discovery* cites 224 foreign and 23 English authorities, all of which he seems to have read. But the quality of his writing is inconsistent: at times it is racy and amusing, but it can also prove rambling, repetitive, and tiresome. His thorough explanations for some of the more popularly practiced card tricks, legerdemain, and juggling were undoubtedly an added attraction for his readers, who could learn how to delight friends with their newly acquired skill.

The skepticism and detail of *The Discovery* did not please everyone. To refute it, King James of Scotland wrote his little dialogue, *Daemonologie* (1597); and when he became king of England, James ordered Scot's book burned. It was, however, reprinted twice in the seventeenth century, in 1651 and 1665.

Who They Be That Are Called Witches

Witches, sorcerers, and evil angels are mentioned in both the Old and New Testaments. These references gave strong support to the Renaissance belief that the devil was always and everywhere ready to enter a pact with a human being, granting extraordinary powers to a black magician in exchange for his soul after death. Witches were thought to conjure up demons, copulate with incubi and succubi, and fly through the air to their witches' Sabbaths. As a consequence of the general fear and horror associated with the evil of witchcraft, opinion and belief were readily substituted for evidence and proof. Corroboration, should it be required, could be found in the scholarly writings of authorities who reported untested assertions as fact, and in the accusations of the malicious, superstitious, or hysterical. Finally, by the use of sufficient torture, a confession and admission of guilt could usually be extracted.

Most often, those who were accused of practicing black magic were women, ignorant, old, and often poor. Some of them acted in secret, attempting to punish those who had hurt them or denied them charity. Misfortunes having no obvious explanation—such as sterility, sickness, disease, injury, death, failure of crops, or unusual weather—could all be blamed on witches who supposedly caused harm by using curses, charms, potions, or sympathetic magic (e.g., thinking they could inflict pain by mutilating images of their victims, or cause rainstorms by beating a stream of water).

The increasingly skeptical outlook of the seventeenth century, encouraged by the impulse to subject assertions to empirical testing, led to a reduction in the accusations of witchcraft. The fear of witchcraft and the belief in its power were diminished by a growing doubt that human beings possessed invisible and intangible powers over nature or that everyday disasters could be blamed on diabolic intervention.

Still, a subject that intrigued its audience and that could be thrilling on the stage naturally found its way into many Renaissance plays.

According to one count, more than seventy Elizabethan and Jacobean dramas involve the supernatural—witches practicing their black arts, and ghosts, of classical or demonic origin, calling for revenge or tormenting the conscience of the guilty. In some cases, for instance the anonymous *Clyomon and Clamydes* (1570) or George Peele's *Old Wives' Tale* (1590), the sorcerers and enchanters are more comic than frightening; their schemes lead to high adventures and ultimately the plays end happily. In other works, such as Robert Greene's *Friar Bacon and Friar Bungay* (1589), the necromancer breaks his glass, abjures his magic, and repents. He tells himself that although he "must be damned / For using devils to countervail his God. / Yet, Bacon, cheer thee; drown not in despair. / Sins have their salves. Repentance can do much" (Scene xiii). In contrast, in Marlowe's *Dr. Faustus* the hero cannot believe that he can be forgiven for his pact with the devil; his despair negates the value of his repentance, and he is damned. In *Henry VI, Part One* (1592), Shakespeare presents Joan of Arc as a witch who uses "spells and periapts [amulets]," and in *Part Two* of this trilogy (1591), the witch Margery Jourdain conjures up a spirit to reveal the future. But Shakespeare's most famous witches are undoubtedly the three evil sisters in *Macbeth*, who deceive the hero by their riddling, ambiguous answers. Finally, as examples of still-other presentations of witches in the drama, Jonson's *Masque of Queens* (1609) calls for an antimasque of twelve women "in the habit of hags or witches, sustaining the persons of Ignorance, Suspicion, Credulity, etc., the opposites to good Fame," and John Ford, William Rowley, and Thomas Dekker in their tragicomedy *The Witch of Edmonton* (1621) created a surprisingly sympathetic treatment of an old woman who makes a pact with the devil in self-defense.

Ghosts in the drama might be the devil, who could appear in the body of someone recently deceased, or they could be figments of a troubled conscience, visible only to the guilty party. Moreover, when they call for vengeance in ranting speeches filled with mythological allusions, they reveal their debt to Seneca's tragedies. The ghost that appears twice to Hamlet seems at first (I.iv–v.) to be Senecan and possibly demonic: he seeks revenge and his presence is confirmed by others who are with the prince. But when the ghost reappears in the Queen's bedroom (III.iv.) he is seen only by Hamlet and speaks as the voice of Hamlet's conscience. No doubt, Shakespeare is exploiting the ambiguity about the possible nature of the ghost for dramatic effect. Unlike this example, however, the lineage of most stage spirits is usually easy to determine. In Thomas Kyd's *The Spanish Tragedy* (1587), the ghost of Andrea, who describes a classical underworld and who is accompanied by the spirit of Revenge, is clearly derived from Senecan ancestry, but the appearance of Banquo's ghost at Macbeth's feast is an example of the power of a guilty conscience.

Book I. Chapter III: Who they be that are called witches, with a manifest declaration of the cause that moveth men so commonly to think and witches themselves to believe that they can hurt children, cattle, etc. with words and imaginations; and of cozening witches.

One sort of such as are said to be witches are women which be commonly old, lame, blear-eyed, pale, foul, and full of wrinkles; poor, sullen, superstitious, and papists, or such as know no religion, in whose drowsy minds the devil hath got a fine seat, so as what mischief, mischance, calamity or slaughter is brought to pass, they are easily persuaded the same is done by themselves, imprinting in their minds an earnest and constant imagination hereof. They are lean and deformed, showing melancholy in their faces, to the horror of all that see them. They are doting scolds, mad, devilish, and not much differing from them that are thought to be possessed with spirits. So firm and steadfast in their opinions as whosoever shall only have respect to the constancy of their words uttered would easily believe they were true indeed.

These miserable wretches are so odious unto all their neighbors and so feared as few dare offend them or deny them anything they ask, whereby they take upon them, yea and sometimes think, that they can do such things as are beyond the ability of human nature. These go from house to house and from door to door for a pot full of milk, yeast, drink, pottage, or some such relief, without the which they could hardly live. Neither obtaining for their service and pains nor by their art, nor yet at the devil's hands (with whom they are said to make a perfect and visible bargain) either beauty, money, promotion, wealth, worship, pleasure, honor, knowledge, learning, or any other benefit whatsoever.[2]

It falleth out many times that neither their necessities nor their expectation is answered or served in those places where they beg or borrow, but rather their lewdness is by their neighbors reproved. And further, in tract of time the witch waxeth odious and tedious to her neighbors, and they again are

---

2. Scot points out that those who claim they are witches seem to get very little for giving their souls to the devil, so that such individuals are rather mad and fantasizing than bewitched.

despised and despited of her, so as sometimes she curseth one and sometimes another, and that from the master of the house, his wife, children, cattle, &c., to the little pig that lieth in the sty. Thus in process of time they have all displeased her, and she hath wished evil luck unto them all, perhaps with curses and imprecations made in form. Doubtless (at length) some of her neighbors die, or fall sick, or some of their children are visited with diseases that vex them strangely, as apoplexies, epilepsies, convulsions, hot fevers, worms, &c., which by ignorant parents are supposed to be the vengeance of witches. Yea and their opinions and conceits are confirmed and maintained by unskillful physicians, according to the common saying: *Inscitiae pallium maleficium et incantatio*, "Witchcraft and enchantment is the cloak of ignorance"—whereas indeed evil humors and not strange words, witches, or spirits are the causes of such disease. Also some of their cattle perish, either by disease or mischance. Then they, upon whom such adversities fall, weighing the fame that goeth upon this woman (her words, displeasure, and curses meeting so justly with their misfortunes) do not only conceive but also are resolved that all their mishaps are brought to pass by her only means.

The witch, on the other side, expecting her neighbor's mischances and seeing things come to pass according to her wishes, curses, and incantations (for Bodin[3] himself confesseth that not above two in a hundred of their witchings or wishings take effect) being called before a justice, by due examination of the circumstances is driven to see her imprecations and desires and her neighbor's harms and losses to concur and as it were to take effect and so confesseth that she (as a goddess) hath brought such things to pass. Wherein, not only she but the accuser and also the justice are foully deceived and abused as being through her confession and other circumstances persuaded (to the injury of God's glory) that she hath done or can do that which is proper only to God himself.

Another sort of witches there are which be absolutely cozeners.[4] These take upon them either for glory, fame, or gain to do anything which God or the devil can do, either for foretelling of things to come, betraying of secrets, curing of maladies, or working of miracles. But of these I will talk more at large hereafter.

---

3. Jean Bodin (1530–96), a sixteenth-century French philosopher best known for his political views: see entry from his *Six Bookes of a Commonweale*. Scot refers to him because Bodin claimed in his *Demonomanie des Sorciers* that witchcraft had been factually proven.

4. *cozeners*: con artists.

*Book III. Chapter VIII: What folly it were for witches to enter into
such desperate peril and to endure such intolerable tortures for no
gain or commodity, and how it comes to pass that witches are
overthrown by their confessions.*

Alas! If they were so subtle, as witchmongers make them[selves out] to be,
they would espy that it were mere folly for them not only to make a bargain
with the devil to throw their souls into hellfire, but their bodies to the
tortures of temporal fire and death for the accomplishment of nothing that
might benefit themselves at all. But they would at the leastwise indent[5] with
the devil both to enrich them and also to ennoble them and finally to endue
them with all worldly felicity and pleasure which is furthest from them of all
other. Yea, if they were sensible they would say to the devil: "Why should I
hearken to you, when you will deceive me? Did you not promise my
neighbor Mother Dutton to save and rescue her, and yet lo she is hanged?"
. . . But these old women being daunted with authority, circumvented
with guile, constrained by force, compelled by fear, induced by error, and
deceived by ignorance, do fall into such rash credulity, and so are brought
unto these absurd confessions. Whose error of mind and blindness of will
dependeth upon the disease and infirmity of nature. And therefore their
actions in that case are the more to be born withal, because they, being
destitute of reason, can have no consent. For, *Delictum sine consensu non
potest committi, neque injuria sine animinjuriandi*: that is, "There can be no
sin without consent, nor injury committed without a mind to do wrong." Yet
the law saith further that a purpose retained in mind doth nothing to the
private or public hurt of any man; and much more that an impossible
purpose is unpunishable. *Sanae mentis voluntas, voluntas rei possibilis est*:
"A sound mind willeth nothing but that which is possible."

*Chapter IX: How melancholy abuseth old women and of the effects
thereof by sundry examples.*

If any man advisedly mark their words, actions, cogitations, and gestures,
he shall perceive that melancholy abounding in their head and occupying
their brain hath deprived or rather depraved their judgments and all their
senses. I mean not of cozening witches, but of poor melancholy women
which are themselves deceived. For you shall understand that the force
which melancholy hath and the effects that it worketh in the body of a man

5. *indent:* sign an agreement between two or more parties, as in a contract by which an
apprentice is bound to a master; to agree to an indenture.

or rather a woman are almost incredible. For as some of these melancholic persons imagine they are witches and by witchcraft can work wonders and do what they list, so do other, troubled with this disease, imagine many strange, incredible, and impossible things.

. . . But if they may imagine that they can transform their own bodies, which nevertheless remaineth in the former shape, how much more credible is it that they may falsely suppose they can hurt and enfeeble other men's bodies, or which is less, hinder the coming of butter?

. . . If you read the executions done upon witches either in times past in other countries or lately in this land, you shall see such impossibilities confessed as none having his right wits will believe. Among other like false confessions, we read that there was a witch confessed at the time of her death or execution that she had raised all the tempests and procured all the frosts and hard weather that happened in the winter [of] 1565, and that many grave and wise men believed her.

Chapter XI: The strange and divers effects of melancholy, and how the same humor abounding in witches, or rather old women, filleth them full of marvelous imaginations, and that their confessions are not to be credited.

But in truth, this melancholic humor (as the best physicians affirm) is the cause of all their strange, impossible, and incredible confessions, which are so fond that I wonder how any man can be abused thereby. Howbeit, these affections, though they appear in the mind of man, yet are they bred in the body and proceed from this humor, which is the very dregs of blood, nourishing and feeding those places from whence proceed fears, cogitations, superstitions, fastings, labors, and such like. . . .

But why should there be more credit given to witches when they say they have made a real bargain with the devil, killed a cow, bewitched butter, enfeebled a child, forespoken her neighbor, &c., then when she confesseth that she transubstantiateth herself, maketh it rain or hail, flieth in the air, goeth invisible. . . But I say, both with the divines and philosophers, that that which is imagined of witchcraft hath no truth of action; or being besides their imagination, the which (for the most part) is occupied in false causes.

On Fairylore

Since they were believed capable of malicious behavior, fairies and other creatures of English folklore were thought by some to be closely related to the demonic or the damned, such spirits as hobgoblins and the ghosts of the dead. Indeed, devout Puritans believed all these creatures were devils. But for their most serious crime, the fairies were frequently charged not with causing damnation but with stealing a healthy baby and substituting a deformed one, a changeling child, in its place. Their other supposed offenses against human beings were generally more in the nature of mischievous tricks or practical jokes. And many of these were connected with the rural origin of the fairies, for they functioned in part as nature spirits, concerned with the fertility of the land and its inhabitants. Countryfolk seem to have felt they had little to fear from them. In fact, some fairies were thought not only to aid those who practiced husbandry but even to reward those who kept neat and tidy dairies, kitchens, and barns.

Beliefs in fairylore varied from region to region. For example, residents of Scotland and the northern counties believed in a closer connection between fairies and witches than did those in the rest of England, who postulated a more gentle variety. And according to regional beliefs, fairies could differ both in disposition and in size. Some were thought to be larger-than-life; others, such as the flower fairies, were believed to be as tiny as ants; and still others could take on whatever shape or size they pleased, even becoming invisible. Such a broad range of opinion about the behavior and size of fairies no doubt strengthened the skepticism of the educated who doubted the existence of these spirits.

In the June eclogue of his *Shepherdes Calendar* (1579), Spenser opposes "elvish ghosts" with "friendly Faeries . . . / And lightfote Nymphes." In the theater, John Lyly, no doubt capitalizing on the size and appearance of his actors, the child choristers of St. Paul's, has fairies appear in two of his plays: in *Gallathea* (1585) their "fair faces" are seen "dancing and playing" in the woods, and in *Endymion* (1588) they are described as "fair fiends" who protect Endymion by pinching those who disturb him "black and blue." The very same punishment can be inflicted by the "goblins, elves and sprites" mentioned by Shakespeare in *The Comedy of Errors* (1592); and in *The Merry Wives of Windsor* (1600) he presents children, disguised as fairies, who pinch and torment a frightened Falstaff.

Perhaps the most varied and influential dramatization of this invisible world occurs in Shakespeare's *Midsummer Night's Dream.* Oberon and his kind are benevolent fairies, "of another sort" from wandering ghosts or "damned spirits." As traditional English fairies, they are of average human height or slightly shorter, for Titania says to Bottom, "I will wind thee in my arms." In contrast, Puck is a "shrewd and knavish sprite." Also known as Robin Goodfellow, he is impish and boisterous, but harmless: "Those that 'Hobgoblin' call you, and Sweet 'Puck,' / You do their work, and they shall have good luck." An earthy and gross 'lob' with his coarse laughter and practical jokes, he is the opposite of the fairies Shakespeare named Peaseblossom, Cobweb, and Mustardseed, who courteously scratch Bottom's itches and sweetly bring him honey. Diminutive and shy, they may have been the predecessors in size and disposition of the fairies in the anonymous play *The Maid's Metamorphosis* (1600) and in Michael Drayton's poem *Nymphidia* (1627). Finally, in *L'Allegro* (ca. 1631), Milton describes some of the mischievous activities of Robin Goodfellow and Queen Mab, wife of the fairy king.

Book VII. Chapter XV: Of vain apparitions, how people have been brought to fear bugs, which is partly reformed by preaching of the Gospel, the true effect of Christ's miracles.

But certainly, some one knave in a white sheet hath cozened and abused many thousands that way, specially when Robin Goodfellow kept such a coil in the country. But you shall understand that these bugs specially are spied and feared of sick folk, children, women, and cowards which through weakness of mind and body are shaken with vain dreams and continual fear. The Scythians, being a stout and warlike nation (as divers writers report), never see any vain sights or spirits. It is a common saying, a lion feareth no bugs. But in our childhood our mother's maids have so terrified us with an ugly devil having horns on his head, fire in his mouth, and a tail in his breech, eyes like a basin, fangs like a dog, claws like a bear, a skin like a Niger, and a voice roaring like a lion, whereby we start and are afraid when we hear one cry, "Boo"; and they have so affrayed us with bull beggars, spirits, witches, urchins, elves, hags, fairies, satyrs, pans, fauns, silens,[6] kit-with-a-canstick,[7] tritons, centaurs, dwarfs, giants, imps, calcars,[8] conjurers, nymphs, changelings, incubus, Robin Goodfellow, the spoorne,[9] the mare, the man in the oak, the hell wain, the firedrake, the puckle,[10] Tom Thumb, hobgoblin, Tom Tumbler, boneless, and such other bugs, that we are afraid

6. *silens*: Silenus, a wood god, the foster father of Bacchus, a leader of the satyrs.
7. *kit-with-a-canstick*: jack-o'-lantern.
8. *calcars*: calculators of nativities, astrologers, magicians, or conjurers.
9. the *spoorne*: a special kind of specter or phantom.
10. the *puckle*: kind of bugbear.

of our own shadows. In so much as some never fear the devil but in a dark night, and then a polled[11] sheep is a perilous beast and many times is taken for our father's soul, specially in a churchyard, where a right hardy man heretofore scant durst pass by night but his hair would stand upright. . . . Well, thanks be to God, this wretched and cowardly infidelity since the preaching of the Gospel is in part forgotten, and doubtless the rest of those illusions will in short time (by God's grace) be detected and vanish away.

On Astrology

Astrology, which still has its adherents today, interprets how the planets and stars affect life on earth. In application, astrology was divided into two branches, natural and judicial. Natural astrology, considered a legitimate field of inquiry, was concerned with the ways that weather, oceans, plant life, and human health could be influenced by celestial bodies. In general, Elizabethans agreed that the stars and the planets governed not only such things as the tide but also the body humors, which determined the well-being of an individual. Since diseases were treated by controlling the humors, doctors had to know something about this kind of astrology.

Judicial astrology claimed the power to foretell the events of a life from birth to death. In order to predict the events of an entire lifetime, the judicial astrologer had to compute not simply the movements of the sun and moon but also the motions of planets, constellations, fixed stars, the signs of the zodiac, and all the accompanying lore of planetary aspects, influences, and the so-called houses, the sign of the zodiac indicating the seat of a planet in the heavens. So complex is the theory, so manifold the number of possible combinations, and so intricate the mathematics that accuracy seemed unattainable. As the predicting attempted to become more specific, the calculations grew more fantastic.

In addition, the notion that an individual's life was predetermined to such a great degree denied a belief in free will or in the possibility of divine intervention in human affairs. On these grounds it was obviously a threat to Christianity, and so clergymen opposed it. Still, some astronomers, natural philosophers, and physicians, extending their belief in astrological medicine to include astrological prediction, defended judicial astrology to varying degrees.

Ultimately, the practice of judicial astrology was unacceptable both to

11. *polled*: shorn, clipped.

the religious and to those of a skeptical turn of mind. Unable to demonstrate that it could foretell the future with any degree of success, it disappeared as a belief in the seventeenth century.

Literary references to the possible shaping influence of heavenly bodies either on an individual's personality or on human conduct are frequent. In Shakespeare's *Julius Caesar* (1599), Cassius first argues: "Men at some time are masters of their fates" and the cause of our faults "is not in our stars, / But in ourselves." Yet by the last act of the play, he has somewhat altered his view: "Now I change my mind, / And partly credit things that do presage." Othello, too, thinks the heavens can affect us irresistibly: "The moon comes more near the earth than she was wont and drives men mad." And in Webster's *The Duchess of Malfi*, Bosola discovers a paper casting the future life of the Duchess's newborn son based on the time and day of his birth (II. iii.); by astrological prediction the writer foresees a "short life" and "a violent death." Actually, the prediction proves ironic, for the boy is the only member of his family to survive.

Book IX. Chapter III: That certain observations are indifferent, certain ridiculous, and certain impious. . . .

I know not whether to disallow or discommend the curious observation used by our elders who conjectured upon nativities: so as if Saturn and Mercury were opposite in any brute sign, a man then born should be dumb or stammer much; whereas it is daily seen that children naturally imitate their parents' conditions in that behalf. Also, they have noted that one born in the spring of the moon shall be healthy; in that time of the wane, when the moon is utterly decayed, the child then born cannot live, and in the conjunction[12] it cannot long continue. . . . Furthermore, to play the cold prophet as to recount it good or bad luck when salt or wine falleth on the table, or is shed, &c.; or to prognosticate that guests approach to your house upon the chattering of pies or haggisters,[13] whereof there can be yielded no probable reason, is altogether vanity and superstition. . . But to make simple people believe that a man or woman can foretell good or evil fortune is mere witchcraft or cozenage. For God is the only searcher of the heart, and delivereth not His counsel to so lewd reprobates.

12. *conjunction:* in this instance, a year in which the astrological signs and planets under which the child was born and the waning of the moon occur simultaneously.
13. *pies* or *haggisters:* magpies.

On the Significance of Numbers

Interpretation of the significance of numbers or of combinations of numbers is known as numerology. Belief in the importance of numbers in the universal scheme of things is based primarily on their permanence, since permanence is taken as an attribute of perfection. This notion that permanence is a sign of perfection is in accordance with the Ptolemaic, or earth-centered, account of the cosmos. According to Ptolemaic cosmography, all elements below the moon are subject to constant change, to decline and regeneration. Under the impetus of the upper spheres and the warmth of the sun, a constant cycle transforms fire into air, air into water, water into earth, and so on. But above the moon all is perfect, permanent until the Last Judgment. In increasing distance from the earth, the moon, Mercury, Venus, the sun, Mars, Jupiter, and Saturn, are each held within a solid sphere. Beyond these are the spheres of the fixed stars, the crystalline heaven, and, last, the primum mobile, the outer limit of the universe, the final boundary of time and space. And so the numerologist, combining a Pythagorean interest in mathematics, harmonics, and proportion with a Neoplatonic emphasis on the mystic power of numbers, was able to prove that the Ptolemaic universe was based on mathematical principles and that, as a consequence, numbers contained hidden power and meaning.

Aided by Pythagorean theories of proportion and harmonics and enriched by the addition of a strain of Neoplatonic mysticism, some Elizabethans believed geometry and arithmetic could ultimately solve the mysteries of the universe. Through numbers they hoped to conjure angels or control material forces. And through mathematics they hoped to attain a profound understanding of the Deity, for God could be regarded as a geometrician, a logician who measures, numbers, and weighs. The Bible, especially the Book of Revelation, could be interpreted through numerology, and astrological computations were thought to be a means of determining the age of the world or the coming of the Last Judgment.

As might be expected, the importance of numerological interpretation declined with the loss of belief both in the Ptolemaic universe and in the Neoplatonic and cabalistic texts that claimed greatness for this method.

Renaissance critics of literature, such as Sir Philip Sidney, believed that the power of poetry was derived in part from its use of meter, rhythm, and harmony—all of which can be measured or explained through numbers. This close connection of poetry and numbers helped account for poetry's "divine force" and prophetic nature. In addition, the permanence and perfection of numbers gave them great symbolic and even mystic value to poets. Dante's *The Divine Comedy* (ca. 1300) demonstrated the intricate and hidden ways by which poets incorporated mystic or symbolic significance into their works; his writing provided a pattern for later Renaissance writers in England who used the number of lines, syllables, or sections of their verses as a means of conveying both their commitment to art and their religious belief.

For example, in the envoi to his *Shepherdes Calendar*, Spenser used the number twelve, symbolic of constancy, to symbolize his hope for enduring fame as a poet. Each of the twelve lines that make up this closing stanza is composed of twelve syllables, reflecting the number of months in the year—the *Calendar*, after all, offers a separate poem for each month. The emphasis on twelve is to suggest that Spenser's verse, though celebrating the cycle of the year, will outlast the changing nature of time. In the *Epithalamion* (1595), Spenser's poem celebrating his marriage, he uses an even more intricate number symbolism. To name just a few of its elements: the twenty-four stanzas represent the number of hours in a day; the 365 long lines represent the number of days in a year; the sixteen positive and eight negative refrains reflect the number of daylight and nighttime hours at the time of year when the wedding was held; and since June 11, the actual day of the marriage, is the 103rd day of the year (reckoning the year as beginning on March 1), Spenser has the marriage ceremony completed with the 103rd long line of his poem.

Book XI. Chapter X: The cozening art of sortilege or lottery, practiced especially by Egyptian vagabonds, of allowed lots, of Pythagoras his lot, &c.

The counterfeit *Egyptians*, which were indeed cozening vagabonds, practising the art called *Sortilegium*, had no small credit among the multitude: howbeit their divinations were as was their fast and loose, and as the witches' cures and hurts, and as the soothsayers' answers, and as the conjurers' raising up of spirits, and as Apollo's or the Rood of grace's oracles, and as the jugglers' knacks of legerdemain, and as the papists' exorcisms, and as the witches' charms, and as the counterfeit[s'] visions, and as the cozeners' knaveries. . . .

There is a lot also called *Pythagoras'* lot, which (some say) Aristotle believed: and that is where the characters of letters have certain proper numbers whereby they divine (through the proper names of men) so as the numbers of each letter being gathered in a sum and put together give victory to them whose sum is the greater—whether the question be of war, life, matrimony, victory, &c.—even as the unequal number of vowels in proper names portendeth lack of sight, halting, &c. which the godfathers and godmothers might easily prevent if the case stood so.

Chapter XXI: That figure-casters are witches, the uncertainty of their art, and of their contradictions, Cornelius Agrippa's sentence against judicial astrology.

These casters of figures may be numbered among the cozening witches, whose practice is above their reach, their purpose to gain, their knowledge stolen from poets, their art uncertain and full of vanity, more plainly derided in the Scriptures than any other folly. And thereupon many other trifling vanities are rooted and grounded, as physiognomy, palmestry, interpreting of dreams, monsters, auguries, &c., the professors whereof confess this to be the necessary key to open the knowledge of all their secrets. For these fellows erect a figure of the heavens by the exposition whereof (together with the conjectures of similitudes and signs) they seek to find out the meaning of the significators, attributing to them the ends of all things, contrary to truth, reason, and divinity; their rules being so inconstant that few writers agree in the very principles thereof.

On Alchemy

Alchemy can be defined as the process of attempting to transform baser metals into gold. In theory the steps were fairly straightforward: mercury was most often chosen to practice on because of its similarity to silver, the metal thought nearest to gold, and because of its liquidity, suggesting that it is readily changeable. Once its fluidity (i.e., the element of water), volatility (i.e., the element of air), and grossness (i.e., the element of earth) were removed, the purified mercury was yellowed by the addition of sulphur and "fixed" by the addition of salt. Gold was supposed to be the result. According to the particular school and the alchemist, other substances—antimony, for example—could be substituted for mercury, and variant laboratory procedures could be applied. Like other occult practices, these operations were described in metaphoric language: metals could "marry," "copulate," "die," and become "resurrected."

Although the theory may sound simple, its application was intricate and obscure. The actual procedure was slow, laborious, and expensive, involving years of effort, the help of assistants, and the purchase of fuel, furnaces, equipment, and materials. In addition, to succeed in his endeavor the alchemist in charge had to be devout and spiritually pure. Without such purity of mind and heart, either God Himself would prevent the alchemist's success, or the spiritual aspect of matter, capable of detecting a moral lapse even in the subconscious of the alchemist, would frustrate his work.

To the Elizabethan clergy the alchemist was somewhat too closely linked to the practitioner of black magic, and in his efforts to alter matter he was rivaling a power that belonged only to God. Despite these reservations, the Church expressed less animosity toward alchemy than it had toward astrology. Yet even with the less-energetic opposition of the Church and the occasional encouragement of a ruler such as Elizabeth in England or the Holy Roman Emperor Rudolph II (1552–1612) in Prague, the growing skeptical and empirical attitude of the seventeenth century ultimately denied validity to alchemy. Alchemists themselves continually failed to prove the worth of their methods—even when they were jailed; their texts, including the *Hermetica*, were discovered to be less ancient and divine than they claimed; and according to the new chemistry of such men as Robert Boyle (1627–1691), elements cannot be divided into other substances.

In literature the subject was treated both literally and metaphorically. In *The Alchemist* (1610) Ben Jonson created the best known and most extensive satire on those who claimed to practice this "mystery" and on those who subsidized it. Such humorous and satiric presentations of this topic have a long history: for example, Jonson's immediate predecessor was John Lyly, whose play *Gallathea* presents both an alchemist and an astrologer as comic butts. But Lyly is without doubt consciously indebted to the earliest English mocker of alchemists, for he makes use of the technical language in Chaucer's *Canon's Yeoman's Tale*; in this installment of *The Canterbury Tales* (ca. 1386) the clever fraud and deceit of an alchemist–con artist are revealed by his assistant. As a metaphor for transforming baser elements into precious metal, Shakespeare in *King John* describes the sun as an "alchemist / Turning with splendor of his precious eye / The meagre cloddy earth to glittering gold" (III.i.), and in his masque *Mercury Vindicated from the Al-*

chemists at Court (1616), Jonson uses the language and some of the elements of alchemy as a comic metaphor for praising King James and his courtiers.

Book XIV. Chapter I: Of the art of Alcumystrie [Alchemy], of their words of art and devices to blear men's eyes, and to procure credit to their profession.

Here I thought it not impertinent to say somewhat of the art or rather the craft of alchemy. . . .

. . . Because the practicers hereof would be thought wise, learned, cunning, and their craft's masters, they have devised words of art, sentences, and epithets obscure and confections so innumerable . . . as confound the capacities of them that are either set on work herein or be brought to behold or expect their conclusions. For what plain man would not believe that they are learned and jolly fellows that have in such readiness so many mystical terms of art as (for a taste), their subliming, amalgaming, engluting, imbibing, incorporating, cementing, ritrination, terminations, mollifications, and indurations of bodies, matters combust and coagulate, ingots, tests, &c.? Or who is able to conceive . . . the operation and mystery of their stuff and workmanship? For these things and many more are of necessity to be prepared and used in the execution of this endeavor, namely orpiment, sublimed mercury, iron squames, mercury crude, groundly large, bole armoniac, verdigris, borace, boles, gall, arsenic, sal armoniac, brimstone, salt, paper, burnt bones, unslaked lime, clay, saltpeter, vitrial, salt tartar, alcaly, sal preparat, clay made with horse dung, man's hair, oil of tartar, allum, glass. . . . And because they will not seem to want any point of cozenage to astonish the simple or to move admiration to their enterprises, they have (as they affirm) four spirits to work withal. . . . Then have they seven celestial bodies . . . to whom they apply seven terrestrial bodies . . . attributing unto these the operation of the other, specially if the terrestrial bodies be qualified, tempered, and wrought in the hour and day according to the feats of the celestial bodies—with more like vanity.

On The Magus
and White Magic

One who claimed to have special power over nature and who had not endangered his soul in acquiring this power was called a white magician or a magus. Turning to nature as his object of study, the white magician tried to learn the qualities and effects of the four elements, the powers of herbs, the techniques of medicine, and the properties of minerals. He was, moreover, regarded as a perfect philosopher, mathematician, numerologist, and astrologer. His knowledge, when combined with an understanding of those mystical, Neoplatonic texts that reveal the occult virtues of things, gave him the power to perform what seemed to be miracles. But these wonders were not to be thought miraculous, only the consequences of natural effects achieved when, to use the language of a practitioner, earthly things were subdued to the heavenly or when inferior things were made subject to their superiors. According to the Hermetic view no part of the world lacks consciousness; the entire universe is animated partly through a world soul and partly through ministering angels or daemons, intermediate between men and gods. Through their help a white magician, a magus, could gain further power, control, and understanding over life. Because the white magician signed no pact with the devil and called upon no demonic powers, his labors did not place his immortal soul in jeopardy. But he could use rituals, charms, cabalistic names, signs, and symbols, and he could invoke the Holy Trinity or other deities through whom God's will might be done. White magic, in effect, operated in an area bound by natural science on the one hand and religion on the other.

For the Puritans, the age of miracles was past, and they denied that the church service possessed any special inherent magic power, just as they argued that what might seem to be the supernatural effects of wizards or white magicians were either illusions or the work of the devil. But the simplicity of the Protestant service and the reliance on individual communion with God characteristic of the Reformation stripped away much of the color, mystique, and mystery of the old religion— auricular confession was abolished, belief in transubstantiation was denied, clergymen could now marry, their powers of exorcism were gone, and their ability to bless or consecrate was reduced. The new directness and self-reliance of this religion, with its emphasis on the word in the Scriptures or from the pulpit, left a taste for mystery and magic that could only be satisfied by the local wizard, cunning man, or white magician. And so those who claimed to be knowledgeable in occult practices continued to flourish until the emphasis placed by the Reformation on self-help and direct prayer, aided by the application of hard work, generated an attitude among the population that rejected magic not only because its sources were questionable but also because it was too easy.

Shakespearean drama makes several references to white magic and those who know how to practice it. In her disguise as Ganymede, Rosalind in *As You Like It* claims she can "do strange things": "I have since I was three year old conversed with a magician, most profound in his art and yet not damnable." Her claim to these beneficial powers is perhaps not completely a fabrication, for the multiple weddings that conclude the play are celebrated by "mirth in heaven" and by the blessing of Hymen, the god of marriage. Shakespeare's Cerimon, the doctor in *Pericles* (1608) who restores Thaisa to life, is a magus who knows "the blest infusions / That dwells in vegetives, in metals, stones; / And can speak of the disturbances that / Nature works, and of her cures." Indeed, since he is familiar with Egyptian examples of bringing the dead to life, he may even have been a follower of Hermes Trismegistus. Prospero, the wonder-working magus of *The Tempest*, is another figure who has learned the secrets of nature, for he has "call'd forth the mutinous winds," "rifted Jove's stout oak / With his own bolt," and, like Cerimon, claims "graves at my command / Have wak'd their sleepers, op'd, and let 'em forth / By my so potent art."

From *The Mathematicall Praeface* to Henry Billingsley's English translation of Euclid's Geometry

In his preface to Henry Billingsley's *English Translation of Euclid* (1570), Dr. John Dee (1527–1608), whose learning gained him an international reputation, extolled mathematics as an instrument of both applied and pure science. He considered it essential for acquiring practical knowledge in such fields as surveying, navigation, cosmography, and hydrography. In addition, Dee praised mathematics as a tool for searching out the hidden secrets of God and nature. Dee was a positive influence on the most important explorers, geographers, astronomers, and scientists of his day. At the same time, his conversations with Neoplatonic angelic spirits—conducted through his medium, a younger man named Edward Kelley—and his séances with a crystal were not to lead to such positive results, even though Dee thought these activities were of the greatest importance. By concentrating his efforts on gaining spiritual rather than earthly wisdom, Dee encountered increasing antagonism with the general public and the court in the closing years of the sixteenth century. In fact, he was accused of sorcery as well as of conjuring with the help of demons and evil spirits. Dee died in poverty in 1608.

How immaterial and free from all matter Number is, who doth not perceive? Yea, who doth not wonderfully wonder at it. . . . O ravishing persuasion, to deal with a science whose subject is so ancient, so pure, so excellent, so surmounting all creatures, so used of the Almighty and incomprehensible wisdom of the Creator in the distinct creation of all creatures, in all their distinct parts, properties, natures, and virtues by order and most absolute number, brought from nothing to the formality of their being and state. By numbers properly therefore of us by all possible means (to the perfection of science) learned, we may both wind and draw ourselves into the inward and deep search and view of all creatures' distinct virtues, natures, properties, and forms. And also, farther arise, climb, ascend, and mount up (with speculative wings) in spirit to behold in the glass of creation the form of forms, the exemplar number of all things numerable both visible and invisible, mortal and immortal, corporal and spiritual. Part of this profound and divine science had Joachim the Prophet[14] attained unto by numbers, formal, natural, and rational foreseeing, concluding, and foreshowing great particular events long before their coming. His books yet remaining hereof are good profit. And the noble Earl of Mirandola,[15] besides that a sufficient witness that Joachim in his prophecies proceeded by no other way than by numbers formal.

14. Joachim the Prophet: St. John, the supposed author of the Book of Revelation.
15. Earl of Mirandola: Pico della Mirandola, who with Marsilio Ficino was a member of Cosimo de' Medici's Neoplatonic academy responsible for translating the Hermetic documents.

. . . But well you may perceive by Euclid's *Elements* that more ample is our science than how to measure plains, and [yet] nothing less therein is taught of purpose than how to measure land. Another name, therefore, must needs be had for our mathematical science of magnitudes, which regardeth neither clod nor turf, neither hill nor dale, neither earth nor heaven, but is absolute Megethologia:[16] not creeping on ground and dazzling the eye with pole, perch, rod, or line but lifting the heart above the heavens by invisible lines and immortal beams meeteth with the reflections of the light incomprehensible and so procureth joy and perfection unspeakable. . . .

. . . And for us Christian men, a thousand, thousand more occasions are to have need of the help of Megethological contemplations whereby to train our imaginations and minds, by little and little, to forsake and abandon the gross and corruptible objects of our outward senses and to apprehend by sure doctrine demonstrative things mathematical. And by them readily to be helped and conducted to conceive, discourse, and conclude of things intellectual, spiritual, eternal, and such as concern our bliss everlasting which otherwise (without special privilege of illumination or revelation from heaven) no mortal man's wit (naturally) is able to reach unto or to compass. And verily by my small talent (from above), I am able to prove and testify that the literal text and order of our divine law, oracles, and mysteries require more skill in numbers and magnitudes than commonly the expositors have uttered.

. . . And for these and suchlike marvelous acts and feats, naturally, mathematically, and mechanically wrought and contrived, ought any honest student and modest Christian philosopher be counted and called a conjurer? Shall the folly of idiots and the malice of the scornful so much prevail that he who seeketh no worldly gain or glory at their hands but only of God, the treasure of heavenly wisdom and knowledge of pure verity, shall he (I say) in the mean space be robbed and spoiled of his honest name and fame? He that seeketh (by Saint Paul's advertisement) in the creatures, properties, and wonderful virtues to find just cause to glorify the eternal and almighty Creator by, shall that man be (in hugger-mugger)[17] condemned as a companion of hellhounds and a caller and conjurer of wicked and damned spirits? . . . Surely for my part, somewhat to say herein, I have not learned to make so brutish and so wicked a bargain. Should I, for my twenty or twenty-five years study, for two or three thousand marks spending, seven or eight thousand miles going and traveling only for good learning's sake, and that in all manner of weathers, in all manner of ways and passages both early and

16. *Megethologia*: greater subject of study.
17. *hugger-mugger*: concealment, secrecy.

late, in danger of violence by man, in danger of destruction by wild beasts, in hunger, in thirst, in perilous heats by day with toil on foot, in dangerous damps of cold by night almost bereaving life (as God knows) with lodgings ofttimes to small ease and sometime to less security.[18] And for much more than all this done and suffered for learning and attaining wisdom should I (I pray you) for all this no otherwise, nor more warily, or (by God's mercifulness) no more luckily have fished with so large and costly a net so long time in drawing (and that with the help and advice of Lady Philosophy and Queen Theology) but at length to have catched and drawn up a frog, nay a devil? For so doth the common peevish prattler imagine and jangle. And so doth the malicious scorner secretly wish and bravely and boldly face down behind my back. Ah, what a miserable thing is this kind of men. How great is the blindness and boldness of the multitude in things above their capacity. What a land; what a people; what manners; what times are these?[19]

. . . And to conclude, most of all let them be ashamed of man and afraid of the dreadful and just Judge both foolishly or maliciously to devise and then devilishly to father their new fond[20] monsters on me, innocent in hand and heart, for trespassing either against the law of God or man in any [of] my studies or exercises philosophical or mathematical, as in due time, I hope, will be more manifest.

18. Dee studied at Cambridge, Louvain, and Paris and made several journeys on the Continent, living in Poland and Bohemia from 1583 to 1589.

19. These words were to prove painfully true: shortly after Dee left London for Poland (September 21, 1583), his house at Mortlake was ransacked by a mob that destroyed his great library—holding, according to Dee, over three thousand printed books and over one thousand manuscripts—his instruments, and his three chemical laboratories.

20. *fond*: foolish, silly.

Political Theory

I t was not by coincidence that the nature of political authority and obligation became one of the most hotly debated topics in sixteenth-century Europe. As the Middle Ages drew to a close, natural disasters such as plague, and man-made ones, of which the worst was incessant warfare, shook the foundations of states both large and small, and threatened their stability. Princes had to struggle to maintain or reassert their authority, and as they did so they swept aside many of the traditions and assumptions that had hitherto structured the relationship between rulers and subjects. While the princes continued to pay lip service to morality, their actions were determined by the pursuit of power rather than of justice, and they defined the general good in terms of their own self-interest.

Niccolò Machiavelli:
The Prince

In *The Prince* Machiavelli attempted to bring political theory and practice closer together. Writing a handbook of advice for a ruler was a long and well-established literary practice. Plato's *Republic* was an obvious source of inspiration, but Machiavelli was also familiar with the works of Xenophon, Aristotle, and Cicero, and he drew on historical studies by Herodian, Herodotus, Livy, Plutarch, Sallust, Tacitus, and Thucydides. However, *The Prince* differs from its predecessors in important ways. First of all, it was intended only for the eyes of the ruler, and not for a general readership. Furthermore, it neither offers a theory of government nor assumes a belief in natural law. Indeed, Machiavelli's treatise is not concerned with questions of justice, with the distinction between power and right, or with the legal limitations on the actions of sovereigns. Writing in the belief that only a strong ruler could achieve stability in Italy and free the country from foreign domination, Machiavelli separated political ethics—what is right or wrong for states and princes—from social and personal ethics—what is right or wrong for people or individuals. What mattered, in his view, was not the intention of an action or its conformity (or otherwise) to generally accepted codes of conduct, but its consequence. If it strengthened the power of the ruler and thereby contributed to the stability and security of the state, it was ipso facto good.

In the final result, *The Prince* is a work so candid and pragmatic that it has shocked, fascinated, and influenced its readers since its first appearance, for its approach is surprisingly new. Machiavelli addresses specific contemporary issues and problems, and he demonstrates how effectively a ruler can apply psychological pressure to accomplish his political aims. Indeed, throughout his little handbook, Machiavelli reveals that he is as clever a psychologist as a political analyst. By applying this combination of abilities, he offers insights into the nature of politics and political behavior that are both original and disturbing in their candor and truthfulness.

To appreciate how he came to understand political life so clearly, we must briefly review his role in the struggle for power in the Italy of his day. The son of a lawyer, Niccolò Machiavelli was born into a well-established Florentine family in the year that Lorenzo de' Medici, called "the Magnificent," became the political head of the city, leading it to one of the greatest periods in its history. Niccolò's own career in politics began in 1494 when the Medicis were driven out of Florence for their refusal to oppose the French invasion of Italy by Charles VIII. The new Florentine republic employed Machiavelli in diplomatic service, and for the next eighteen years he worked to consolidate Florentine power in Tuscany, to represent the interests of his government at the French court, and to report on relations with Germany and the Holy Roman Emperor, Maximilian I. In 1512, weakened by Spanish victories and the power of the papacy under Julius II, Florence allowed the Medicis to return, and they soon took control of the government. Implicated in a conspiracy against them, Machiavelli was briefly imprisoned and tortured; finally released, he retired to a small property he owned in the country. In 1513, during this period of enforced leisure, he began writing in the hope of gaining preferment, ultimately dedicating *The Prince* to Lorenzo II, the grandson of Lorenzo the Magnificent. By this time, Italy had suffered nearly twenty years of foreign oppression: the Spanish were at Naples, the Swiss in Lombardy, and the French were about to begin a new invasion. Machiavelli's hope was that his advice would enable a strong ruler to drive out foreign powers and unify the country; his title for the last chapter of *The Prince* is: "Exhortation to Free Italy from the Barbarians."

Machiavelli's book was not published in Italy until 1532, five years after his death; it appeared in a French translation in 1551 and in Latin in 1560. Within twenty years after its first printing, the work went through twenty-five editions, becoming so infamous that the Church placed it on the Index of Prohibited Books in 1559, and the Inquisition, with the approval of the Council of Trent, ordered the burning of all Machiavelli's writings. Although publication of *The Prince* was long banned in England, its notoriety was so great that copies in Italian and

French found their way across the Channel; Thomas Cromwell, Walter Raleigh, and Francis Bacon were well acquainted with it. And those who had not read it, knew something about it by reputation or through the distortions of a French Huguenot, Innocent Gentillet. Gentillet's *Contra-Machiavel* (1576), translated into English and published in London in 1602, accuses Machiavelli's writing of having destroyed "all virtues at once." Describing *The Prince* as a "deadly poison sent out of Italy," Gentillet's analysis reveals "how wicked, impious and detestable the doctrine of that most filthy Atheist is, who hath left out no kind of wickedness to build a tyranny, accomplished of all abhominable vices" (p. 374). This view, confirming the suspicions of the Elizabethans about things Italian, helped to shape the character type of the Machiavel, a disciple of Machiavelli who appears frequently in the literature of the period.

Unprincipled and power-hungry, the English Machiavel is a popular figure, a villain-hero who appears on stage often with his henchman. Indeed, the practice of using and discarding an agent or hit man—what Hotspur in *Henry IV* (1597) calls a "base second means"—becomes so common that it is another distinguishing mark of the Machiavel. Marlowe's Barabas and Ithamore in *The Jew of Malta* (1589) and Shakespeare's Richard III and Buckingham are examples, as are similar type characters in the tragedies and histories not only of Marlowe and Shakespeare but also of Kyd, Marston, Chapman, Webster, and Thomas Middleton and William Rowley. After a time, playwrights even ridicule the Machiavel—for instance, Jonson in *Volpone*, Chapman in *All Fools* (1598?), and Shakespeare in *The Merry Wives of Windsor.*

The excerpts that follow are from the first published English translation of *The Prince* by Edward Dacres in 1640.

Of Those Things in Respect Whereof Men and Especially Princes Are Praised or Dispraised

It now remains that we consider what the conditions of a prince ought to be, and his terms of government over his subjects and towards his friends. And because I know that many have written hereupon, I doubt lest I, venturing also to treat thereof, may be branded with presumption, especially seeing I am like enough to deliver an opinion different from others.[1] But my intent being to write for the advantage of him that understands me, I thought it fitter to follow the effectual truth of the matter than the imagination thereof. And many principalities and republics have been in imagination which neither have been seen nor known to be indeed, for there is such a distance between how men do live and how men ought to live that he who leaves that which is done for that which ought to be done learns sooner his ruin than his preservation. For that man who will profess honesty in all his actions must needs go to ruin among so many that are dishonest. Whereupon it is necessary for a prince, desiring to preserve himself, to be able to make use of that honesty and to lay it aside again as need shall require.[2]

Passing by, then, things that are only in imagination belonging to a prince, to discourse upon those that are really true, I say that all men, whensoever mention is made of them, and especially princes, because they are placed aloft in view of all, are taken notice of for some of these qualities which procure them either commendations or blame. And this is that some one is held liberal, some miserable[3]—miserable, I say, not covetous, for the covetous desire to have though it were by rapine, but a miserable man is he that too much forbears to make use of his own; some free givers, others extortioners; some cruel, others piteous; the one a league breaker, another faithful; the one effeminate and of small courage, the other fierce and courageous; the one courteous, the other proud; the one lascivious, the other chaste; the one of fair dealing, the other wily and crafty; the one hard, the other easy; the one grave, the other light; the one religious, the other incredulous, and suchlike.

I know that everyone will confess it were exceedingly praiseworthy for a prince to be adorned with all these above-named qualities that are good. But because this is not possible, nor do human conditions admit such perfection in virtues, it is necessary for him to be so discreet that he know how to avoid the infamy of those vices which would thrust him out of his state and, if it be possible, beware of those also which are not able to remove him thence. But where it cannot be, let them pass with less regard.[4]

1. Machiavelli is fully aware of the well-established classical tradition of writing manuals on government for princes. Moreover, he is preparing his reader for the fact that some of his advice is very different from, if not actually the opposite of, what classical works recommend.

2. Rather than being idealistic and emphasizing ethical values, Machiavelli gives pragmatic advice; his approach is based on the evidence of human behavior.

3. *miserable*: stingy.

4. Machiavelli is arguing that no one has only good qualities in his character; and that even if such a person existed, he could hardly retain power in an evil world by practicing only perfect virtue. On the other hand, a prince should be clever enough to avoid damaging his reputation so that he will not be overthrown because he is thought wicked or decadent. Those vices in his nature that will not cost him his position and that he cannot give up should not trouble him.

And yet, let him not stand much upon[5] it, though he incur the infamy of those vices without which he can very hardly save the state, for if all be thoroughly considered, some things we shall find which will have the color and very face of virtue, and following them, they will lead thee to thy destruction; whereas some others, that shall as much seem vice, if we take the course they lead us, shall discover unto us the way to our safety and well-being.[6]

Of Cruelty and Clemency and Whether It Is Better to Be Beloved or Feared

Descending afterwards unto the other fore-alleged qualities, I say that every prince should desire to be held pitiful and not cruel. Nevertheless ought he beware that he ill uses not this pity. Cesare Borgia was accounted cruel, yet had his cruelty redressed the disorders in Romania, settled it in union, and restored it to peace and fidelity—which, if it be well weighed, we shall see was an act of more pity than that of the people of Florence who to avoid the term of cruelty suffered Pistoia to fall to destruction.[7]

Wherefore a prince ought not to regard the infamy of cruelty for to hold his subjects united and faithful. For by giving a very few proofs of himself the other way, he shall be held more pitiful than they who through their too much pity suffer disorders to follow, from whence arise murders and rapines, for these are wont to hurt an entire universality, whereas the executions practiced by a prince hurt only some particular. . . .

From hence arises a dispute whether it is better to be beloved or feared.[8] I

5. *Stand upon:* give importance to.
6. Note that Machiavelli has no illusions about the basic goodness of human nature or about the rewards of virtue.
7. Pistoia suffered from factional riots (1500–1501) between two rival families because the Florentines failed to suppress the fighting by taking strong measures. In contrast, Cesare Borgia by strong and decisive action brought peace to the Romania, the area north of Florence on the Adriatic. Machiavelli is particularly interested in Cesare Borgia's method for consolidating power in the Romania. In chapter 7 he explains that Cesare named as his deputy Remiro d'Orco, a fiercely cruel and autocratic administrator, who soon brought the territory under control. When his harsh and unpopular methods were no longer necessary, Cesare arranged for Remiro's murder; the body of the former governor was cut into two and displayed one morning on the public square. In this way Cesare dissociated himself from Remiro's cruelty yet benefited from its effects. The populace was both pleased and horrified by Remiro's death and not unhappy to be now under Cesare's immediate protection and rule. In fact, we should note that of all political leaders, Cesare Borgia (1476–1507) receives the closest attention in *The Prince*, for he had many of the qualities Machiavelli most admired. In this instance, Machiavelli is describing how to use what Elizabethan dramatists called a "tool villain," the instrument or henchman of a Machiavel who enforces his will and is then eliminated.
8. This is a traditional subject in books of advice to rulers. Machiavelli disagrees with Cicero's recommendation in *De Officiis* 2.7.234 that it is better to be loved than feared.

answer, a man would wish he might be the one and the other; but because hardly can they subsist both together, it is much safer to be feared than be loved, being that one of the two must needs fail. For touching men, we may say this in general: they are unthankful, inconstant dissemblers; they avoid dangers and are covetous of gain. And whilst thou dost them good they are wholly thine—their blood, their fortunes, lives and children are at thy service, as is said before, when the danger is remote. But when it approaches, they revolt. And that prince who wholly relies upon their words, unfurnished of all other preparations, goes to wrack, for the friendships that are got with rewards and not by the magnificence and worth of the mind are dearly bought indeed, but they will neither keep long nor serve well in time of need. And men do less regard to offend one that is supported by love than by fear, for love is held by a certainty of obligation which because men are mischievous is broken upon any occasion of their own profit. But fear restrains with a dread of punishment which never forsakes a man.[9]

Yet ought a prince cause himself to be beloved in such a manner that if he gains not love he may avoid hatred, for it may well stand together that a man may be feared and not hated which shall never fail if he abstain from his subject's goods and their wives. And whensoever he should be forced to proceed against any of their lives, do it when it is to be done upon a just cause and apparent conviction. But above all things, forbear to lay his hands on other men's goods, for men forget sooner the death of their father than the loss of their patrimony. Moreover, the occasions of taking from men their goods do never fail and always he that begins to live by rapine finds occasion to lay hold upon other men's goods; but against men's lives they are seldomer found and sooner fail.

But when a prince is abroad in the field with his army and hath a multitude of soldiers under his government, then is it necessary that he stands not much upon it though he be termed cruel, for unless he be so, he shall never have his soldiers live in accord one with another nor ever well-disposed to any brave piece of service. . . .

I conclude, then, returning to the purpose of being feared and beloved. Insomuch as men love their own pleasure and to serve their own turn, and their fear depends upon the prince's pleasure, every wise prince ought to ground upon that which is of himself and not upon that which is of another. Only this, he ought to use his best wits to avoid hatred, as was said.

---

9. Machiavelli has none too high an opinion of human behavior and finds humanity psychologically prone to fixed responses and reactions.

In What Manner Princes Ought to Keep Their Words

How commendable in a prince it is to keep his word and live with integrity, not making use of cunning and subtlety, everyone knows well. Yet we see by experience in these our days that those princes have effected great matters who have made small reckoning of keeping their words and have known by their craft to turn and wind men about and in the end have overcome those who have grounded upon the truth.

You must then know there are two kinds of combating or fighting, the one by right of the laws the other merely by force. The first way is proper to men, the other is also common to beasts. But because the first many times suffices not, there is a necessity to make recourse to the second, wherefore it behooves a prince to know how to make good use of that part which belongs to a beast as well as that which is proper to a man. 10

This part hath been covertly showed to princes by ancient writers who say that Achilles and many others of those ancient princes were entrusted to Chiron the centaur to be brought up under his discipline. The moral of this, having for their teacher one that was half a beast and half a man, was nothing else but that it was needful for a prince to understand how to make his advantage of the one and the other nature because neither could subsist without the other.

A prince, then, being necessitated to know how to make use of that part belonging to a beast, ought to serve himself of the conditions of the fox and the lion, for the lion cannot keep himself from snares nor the fox defend himself against the wolves. He had need then be a fox that he may beware of the snares, and a lion that he may scare the wolves. 11 Those that stand wholly upon the lion understand not well themselves.

And therefore a wise prince cannot nor ought not keep his faith given when the observance thereof turns to disadvantage and the occasions that made him promise are past. For if men were all good, this rule would not be allowable, but being they are full of mischief and would not make it good to thee, neither art thou tied to keep it with them, nor shall a prince ever want lawful occasions to give color to this breach.

Very many modern examples hereof might be alleged wherein might be showed how many peaces concluded and how many promises made have been violated and broken by the infidelity of princes, and ordinary things have best succeeded with him that hath been nearest the fox in condition. But it is necessary to understand how to set a good color upon this disposition

10. Cicero, *De Officiis* 1.2.34.
11. Cicero, *De Officiis* 1.13.41; also Plutarch, *Lives, Lysander,* vii.

and to be able to feign and dissemble thoroughly. And men are so simple and yield so much to the present necessities that he who hath a mind to deceive shall always find another that will be deceived.

I will not conceal any one of the examples that have been of late. Alexander VI[12] never did anything else than deceive men and never meant otherwise, and always found whom to work upon. Yet never was there man would protest more effectually nor aver anything with more solemn oaths and observe them less than he. Nevertheless, his cozenages all thrived well with him, for he knew how to play this part cunningly.

Therefore is there no necessity for a prince to be endowed with all these above-written qualities, but it behooves well that he seem to be so. Or rather I will boldly say this, that having these qualities and always regulating himself by them, they are hurtful, but seeming to have them, they are advantageous. As to seem pitiful, faithful, mild, religious, and of integrity and indeed to be so, provided withal thou beest of such a composition that if need require thee to use the contrary, thou canst and knowst how to apply thy self thereto.

And it suffices to conceive this, that a prince and especially a new prince cannot observe all those things for which men are held good, he being often forced for the maintenance of his state to do contrary to his faith, charity, humanity, and religion. And therefore, it behooves him to have a mind so disposed as to turn and take the advantage of all winds and fortunes, and, as formerly I said, not forsake the good while he can, but to know how to make use of the evil upon necessity.

A prince, then, ought to have a special care that he never let fall any words but what are all seasoned with the five above-written qualities, and let him seem to him that sees and hears him, all pity, all faith, all integrity, all humanity, all religion. Nor is there anything more necessary for him to seem to have than this last quality,[13] for all men in general judge thereof rather by the sight than by the touch. For every man may come to the sight of him, few come to the touch and feeling of him. Every man may come to see what thou seemest, few come to perceive and understand what thou art. And those few dare not oppose the opinion of many who have the majesty of state to protect them. And in all men's actions, especially those of princes wherein there is no judgment to appeal unto, men forbear to give their censures till the events and ends of things.

Let a prince therefore take the surest courses he can to maintain his life

---

12. Rodrigo de Borja y Doms (1431?–1503), father of Cesare Borgia, was pope from 1492 to 1503.
13. Aristotle, *Politics*, 5.9.15.

and state. The means shall always be thought honorable and commended by everyone, for the vulgar is overtaken with the appearance and event of a thing. And for the most part of people, they are but the vulgar. The others, that are but few, take place where the vulgar have no subsistence. A prince there is in these days, whom I shall not do well to name, that preaches nothing else but peace and faith, but had he kept the one and the other, several times had they taken from him his state and reputation.[14]

How Great Power Fortune Hath in Human Affairs, and What Means There Is to Resist It

In this chapter, Machiavelli is arguing against those classical writers (such as Plutarch, Cicero, and Livy) and their followers (such as Petrarch, Boccaccio, and Dante) who believe that the power of fortune is irresistible. On the contrary, he finds that the prince can shape affairs as he wishes if fortune offers him the opportunity. According to Machiavelli, fortune gives a man of ability the occasion to prove himself: if he is lucky enough to have the chance, a leader with intelligence and drive (*virtù*) can achieve success.

Machiavelli's emphasis on the strength of an individual's will to accomplish what he desires adds a third force to the two usually claimed to affect the outcome of events, the pagan goddess Fortuna and the Judeo-Christian God. The older of these, the Roman goddess Fortuna, is often portrayed by Christian writers as operating independently of God, possibly as a consequence of the Fall or as a proof of Heaven's inscrutability. Enigmatic, malignant, and fickle, she rules over events without order, blindly turning her wheel and raising for a time both the innocent and the wicked. The popular medieval tradition of collecting the tales of those historical figures brought low by Fortuna, the "fall of illustrious men and women," was continued by the Elizabethans in *A Mirror for Magistrates* (1559). In this compendium, each of the characters, speaking from the grave, tells the story of his rise and fall "to show the slippery deceits of the wavering lady." And, of course, heaven itself can actively intervene, shaping events: the Old Testament presented a divinity who is "jealous, . . . showing mercy . . . and visiting iniquity." The New Testament God is even more immediate and watchful. And with the Reformation doctrine of predestination (see above, pages 44–48), heaven's involvement in human affairs is all-pervasive: accord-

14. Most scholars believe that here and in the first paragraph of this chapter Machiavelli is referring to Ferdinand V, King of Spain (1452–1516).

ing to Calvin, "God doth claim and will have us give unto Him an almightiness . . . busied in continual doing."

English Renaissance plays often refer to one or another of these views. In *Tamburlaine* (1587), for example, Marlowe's hero brags that he holds "the fates bound fast in iron chains, / And with my hand turn fortune's wheel about." In contrast, the antagonist of Marlowe's *Edward II* (1592) stoically acknowledges that fortune is independent of human will:

> *Base Fortune, now I see, that in thy wheel*
> *There is a point, to which when men aspire,*
> *They tumble headlong down: that point I touched,*
> *And, seeing there was no place to mount up*
>   *higher,*
> *Why should I grieve at my declining fall?*
>
> (V.vi.)

In some cases, dramatists actually combine all three of these elements—the goddess Fortuna, the intervention of Providence, and the individual will—for they contribute to the shaping of the action and to the dramatization of the tragic hero. For example, in *Romeo and Juliet* (1595) the lovers are fated for destruction by Fortuna. Shakespeare's Chorus describes them as "star-cross'd" and their love is "death-mark'd." Romeo even calls himself "fortune's fool" when in fury he stabs Juliet's cousin Tybalt. But Providence, too, has a role to play. The prince sums up the moral for the grieving families at the close of the action with the line: "heaven finds means to kill your joys with love." Yet the events are also determined, it seems, to a great extent by the will of the young lovers. Their innocence and passion, their haste and intensity, their commitment and absolute devotion largely explain what they do and what happens to them. In effect, the lives of tragic characters are nearly always shaped by incompatible forces: on the one hand, by powers over which they have no control, and on the other hand, by their own disposition that leads them to make certain choices. In *Antony and Cleopatra* (1607), Antony, angry with himself, acknowledges that his predicament is largely the result of his own weak nature. His fate is a direct consequence of his character:

> *When we in our viciousness grow hard—*
> *O misery on't!—the wise gods seel our eyes,*

> *In our own filth drop our clear judgments, make us*
> *Adore our errors, laugh at's while we strut*
> *To our confusion.*
>
> (III.xiii.)

Because Machiavelli insists on the importance of *virtù*—that individual will that can greatly shape the course of events—*The Prince* also strengthens an element essential to the development of tragedy in the Renaissance.

From *How Great Power Fortune Hath in Human Affairs, and What Means There Is to Resist It*

It is not unknown unto me how that many have held opinion and still hold it that the affairs of the world are so governed by fortune and by God that men by their wisdom cannot amend or alter them, or rather that there is no remedy for them. And hereupon they would think that it were of no avail to take much pains in anything but leave all to be governed by chance.[15]

This opinion hath gained the more credit in our days by reason of the great alteration of things which we have of late seen and do every day see beyond all human conjecture, upon which I sometimes thinking am in some part inclined to their opinion. Nevertheless, not to extinguish quite our own free will, I think it may be true that fortune is the mistress of one half of our actions, but yet that she lets us have rule of the other half or little less. And I liken her to a precipitous torrent, which when it rages overflows the plains, overthrows the trees and buildings, removes the earth from one side and lays it on another. Everyone flies before it; everyone yields to the fury thereof, as unable to withstand it; and yet, however it be thus, when the times are calmer, men are able to make provisions against these excesses with banks and fences so that afterwards when it swells again it shall all pass smoothly along within its channel, or else the violence thereof shall not prove so licentious and hurtful.[16] In like manner befalls it us with fortune, which there shows her power where virtue is not ordained to resist her, and thither turns she all her forces where she perceives that no provisions nor resistances are made to uphold her.[17]

I believe also that he proves the fortunate man whose manner of proceed-

15. The power of fortune is a standard subject in handbooks for rulers.
16. Horace, *Odes*, 3.29.36ff.
17. By *virtue*, Dacres is translating Machiavelli's word *virtù*—a personality trait that combines energy and determination with strength, courage, intelligence, and boldness.

ing meets with the quality of the times and so likewise he unfortunate from whose course of proceeding the times differ, for we see that men in the things that induce them to the end which everyone propounds to himself, as glory and riches, proceed therein diversely, some with respects, others more bold and rashly; one with violence and the other with cunning; the one with patience, the other with its contrary; and everyone by several ways may attain thereto.

We see also two very respective and wary men, the one come to his purpose and the other not. And in like manner two equally prosper taking divers courses, the one being wary, the other headstrong—which proceeds from nothing else but from the quality of the times which agree or not with their proceedings. From hence arises that which I said, that two working diversely produce the same effect and two equally working, the one attains his end, the other not.

Hereupon also depends the alteration of the good, for if to one that behaves himself with wariness and patience, times and affairs turn so favorably that the carriage of business prove well, he prospers. But if the times and affairs change, he is ruined, because he changes not his manner of proceeding, nor is there any man so wise that can frame himself hereunto as well because he cannot go out of the way from that whereunto nature inclines him, as also for that one having always prospered walking such a way, cannot be persuaded to leave it. And therefore the respective and wary man when it is fit time for him to use violence and force knows not how to put it in practice, whereupon he is ruined; but if he could change his disposition with the times and the affairs, he should not change his fortune. . . .

I conclude, then, fortune varying and men continuing still obstinate to their own ways prove happy, while these accord together; and as they disagree, prove unhappy. And I think it true that it is better to be heady[18] than wary because fortune is a mistress, and it is necessary to keep her in obedience, to ruffle and force her. And we see that she suffers herself rather to be mastered by those than by others that proceed coldly. And therefore, as a mistress, she is a friend to young men because they are less respective, more rough, and command her with more boldness.

18. *heady:* headstrong, bold, impetuous.

Resistance
and Nonresistance

Machiavelli had looked to the lay ruler, in the person of Lorenzo de'
Medici, to save Italy from foreign domination. Luther looked to the lay
ruler to bring about a regeneration of religion. This had traditionally
been the function of the Roman Catholic Church under its papal head,
but the Papacy seemed to have lost the capacity, if not the will, to carry
out this task, and the Church was floundering. Luther, when he made
his historic challenge to the pope, denied that the Church had any
powers of coercion. These, he said, belonged of right to the secular
rulers, and it was their responsibility to create within their states the
conditions in which true religion could flourish. Luther was not optimistic about the capacity of secular rulers to fulfill such a daunting
obligation, nor did he believe that they should be blindly obeyed, but he
accepted St. Paul's injunction that secular authority must not be resisted, because it was divinely ordained. If God chose to appoint a
wicked ruler, this was a punishment for the people's sins, and one they
should not seek to evade. While subjects had a right—indeed a duty—
to refuse to carry out an unjust or ungodly order, they should not under
any circumstances actively oppose their prince's will. If they did so they
would be going against God, who disposed everything in the world as
He thought fit.

Luther had little choice but to appeal to the lay princes, since without
their support his challenge to papal power might well have been
unsuccessful. In his patron, the Elector of Saxony, he found a ruler
after his own heart, but it could not be taken for granted that temporal
princes would always support the 'right' religion, however this was

defined. Indeed, during Luther's own lifetime the greatest ruler in Christendom, the Emperor Charles V, launched a counterattack upon the Protestants that threatened their very existence. This prompted them to look again at the doctrine of nonresistance, for surely they argued, God did not mean them to remain so passive that the true religion, which He had chosen to reveal to them, would be stifled at birth? Calvinists faced a similar dilemma, particularly since Calvin himself shared Luther's view about the sinfulness of active opposition to secular authority.

However, the pressure of events drove first the Lutherans and then the Calvinists into articulating a theory of resistance.

Philippe Duplessis-Mornay:
Vindiciae Contra Tyrannos

Belief in the sanctity of resistance provided a justification for the French Calvinists, the Huguenots, when they chose to fight the royal government in defense of their faith. The Wars of Religion, which broke out in 1562, plunged France into a quarter of a century of bitter and bloody conflict. Among those who fought on the Huguenot side was Philippe Duplessis-Mornay, who had been brought up as a Protestant by his mother and sent abroad to be educated at the Calvinist center of Heidelberg. In 1571 he wrote a couple of tracts supporting the struggle of the people of the Netherlands against the heavy-handed rule of their nominal sovereign, Philip II of Spain, the embodiment of Catholic absolutism. He returned to Paris just in time for the massacre of the Huguenots on St. Bartholomew's Day, 1572, from which he was lucky to escape with his life, and then engaged in a vigorous pamphlet war as well as actual fighting on the battlefield. His most famous work—even though he published it under an assumed name and the authorship was long disputed—is the *Vindiciae Contra Tyrannos*, which appeared in 1579.

In the *Vindiciae* Duplessis-Mornay unequivocally asserts the right of subjects to overthrow their rulers. Like Hooker, he derived the origin of political societies from a covenant between the prince and the people, but he added to this a simultaneous covenant between both these parties and God. The newly created community was therefore, from its very beginning and by the nature of its constitution, a godly community, and its members were God's people, whose primary obligation was to Him and not to their ruler, who was merely God's deputy. If the ruler exceeded the limits of his authority by acting against God's will, his subjects were bound to resist him. However, Duplessis-Mornay, unlike some of the more radical Huguenots, did not accord this right of resistance to the subjects as individuals. He distrusted "the people," thinking of them as little better than a mob, and insisted that only the magistrates—drawn from the upper sections of society—had the authority, indeed the obligation, to decide when and how to lead resistance to an unjust ruler.

Although the Huguenots were fighting against their Catholic king, they were not opposed to monarchy as such. Duplessis-Mornay had a vested interest in it, since he was the close adviser of Henry of Navarre, the Protestant claimant to the throne, who was eventually acknowledged as Henry IV. Yet although Duplessis-Mornay never denied the godly origin of monarchical rule, it is clear from the following extracts that he saw "the people"—or rather those who spoke in their name—as the voice of God. This raised a difficulty, in that although kings might originally have been chosen by popular acclaim, in practice they now held their thrones through hereditary succession. Duplessis-Mornay overcame this difficulty by pointing to the ceremony of coronation as a symbolic acceptance of the new king by his subjects. It had been the custom in many monarchies, including England, to date the beginning of a king's rule from his coronation rather than his accession, and although this was no longer the case, the coronation service retained an element of election: in 1604, for instance, prior to the crowning of James I, the new king was formally presented to "the people," who were asked, "Will you take this worthy Prince James, right heir of the realm, and have him to your King, and become subjects to him and submit yourselves to his commandments?," to which they responded by shouting, "Yea. Yea. God save the King."

However, these elective elements were little more than vestigial survivals, and in practice hereditary succession was an established custom throughout Christendom. Hooker, who had the *Vindiciae* very much in mind when he was composing his *Laws of Ecclesiastical Polity*, rejected any suggestion that the kingly office was elective, since this would have opened the way to "unquiet spirits" to assert a claim to the throne, thereby plunging England back into the anarchy of the Wars of the Roses, from which she had been rescued only by the advent of the Tudor dynasty. This period was still fresh in the minds of English men and women, who valued "good order" and dreaded any relapse into chaos. From this point of view Shakespeare's histories were not so much about the past as the present—political tracts couched in historical terms but with an immediate relevance to the major issues of their own day.

Although Hooker rejected Duplessis-Mornay's claim that all monarchies were essentially elective, the two men were at one in their insistence that the kingly office was a trust, and that rulers were instituted in order to promote the welfare of their subjects. They also shared the belief that the best-governed societies were those that were directed by law rather than individual caprice. When Sir Philip Sidney, in his *Arcadia* (c. 1580), described the reordering of a kingdom in which the people properly overthrew a tyrant, he made the new monarch a prince of the royal blood who was willing to agree to "such conditions and cautions of the conditions, as might assure the people (with as much assurance as worldly matters bear) that not only that governor, of whom indeed they looked for all good, but the nature of the government should be no way apt to decline to tyranny" (2.8.). In short, Sidney, a close friend and admirer of Duplessis-Mornay, supported the position that rulers, like subjects, must be bound by the law. Kings who ignored their subjects' interests, and rode roughshod over their rights, were not true kings but tyrants, and as Duplessis-Mornay powerfully argued, tyrants could and should be resisted and overthrown. This was the essential message of the *Vindiciae Contra Tyrannos*.

The First Question: Whether Subjects Are Bound and Ought to Obey Princes, if They Command That Which is Against the Law of God?

This question may seem at the first view to be altogether superfluous and unprofitable, for that it seems to make a doubt of an axiom always held infallible amongst Christians, confirmed by many testimonies in Holy Scripture, divers examples of the histories of all ages, and by the death of all the holy martyrs. For it may well be demanded wherefore Christians have endured so many afflictions, but that they were always persuaded that God must be obeyed simply and absolutely, and kings with this exception, that they command not that which is repugnant to the law of God. Otherways wherefore should the apostles have answered that God must rather be obeyed then men? And also seeing that the only will of God is always just, and that of men may be, and is, oftentimes unjust, who can doubt but that we must always obey God's commandments without any exception, and men's ever with limitation?

But for so much as there are many princes in these days calling themselves Christians which arrogantly assume an unlimited power over which God himself hath no command, and that they have no want of flatterers which adore them as gods upon earth . . . I fear me that whosoever shall nearly and thoroughly consider these things will confess this question to be not only most profitable, but also, the times considered, most necessary. . . . The princes exceed their bounds, not contenting themselves with that authority which the almighty and all good God hath given them, but seek to usurp that sovereignty which He hath reserved to Himself over all men, being not content to command the bodies and goods of their subjects at their pleasure, but assume license to themselves to enforce the consciences, which appertains chiefly to Jesus Christ. Holding the earth not great enough for their ambition, they will climb and conquer heaven itself. The people, on the other side . . . instead of resisting them, if they have means and occasion, suffer them to usurp the place of God, making no conscience to give that to Caesar which belongs properly and only to God. . . .

It then belongs to princes to know how far they may extend their authority, and to subjects in what they may obey them, lest the one encroaching on that jurisdiction which no way belongs to them, and the others obeying him which commandeth further than he ought, they be both chastised when they shall give an account thereof before another judge. Now the end and scope of the question propounded, whereof the Holy Scripture shall principally give the resolution, is that which followeth. The question is, if subjects be bound to obey kings in case they command that which is against the law of God: that is to say, to which of the two (God or king) must we rather obey?

First, the Holy Scripture doth teach that God reigns by His own proper authority, and kings by derivation; God from Himself, kings from God; that God hath a jurisdiction proper, kings are His delegates. It follows then that the jurisdiction of God hath no limits, that of kings is bounded; that the power of God is infinite, that of kings confined; that the kingdom of God extends itself to all places, that of kings is restrained within the confines of certain countries. In like manner God hath created of nothing both heaven and earth, wherefore by good right He is lord and true proprietor . . . and all men, of what degree or quality soever they be, are His servants, farmers, officers, and vassals, and owe account and acknowledgment to Him, according to that which He hath committed to their dispensation. The higher their place is, the greater their account must be, and according to the ranks whereunto God hath raised them must they make their reckoning before His divine majesty. . . .

God does not at any time divest Himself of His power. He holds a scepter in one hand to repress and quell the audacious boldness of those princes who mutiny against Him, and in the other a balance to control those who administer not justice with equity as they ought. Than these, there cannot be expressed more certain marks of sovereign command. . . . Therefore all kings are the vassals of the King of Kings, invested into their office by the sword, which is the cognizance of their royal authority, to the end that with the sword they maintain the law of God, defend the good, and punish the evil. . . .

Now if we consider what is the duty of vassals, we shall find that what may be said of them agrees properly to kings. . . . The vassal receives laws and conditions from his sovereign. God commands the king to observe his laws and to have them always before his eyes, promising that he and his successors shall possess long the kingdom if they be obedient, and, on the contrary, that their reign shall be of small continuance if they prove rebellious to their sovereign king. . . . The vassal loses his fee [fief] if he commit a felony, and by law forfeits all his privileges. In the like case the king loses his right, and many times his realm also, if he despise God, if he complot with His enemies, and if he commit felony against that royal majesty. This will appear more clearly by the consideration of the covenant which is contracted between God and the king, for God does that honor to His servants to call them His confederates. Now we read of two sorts of covenants at the inaugurating of kings: the first between God, the king, and the people, that the people might be the people of God; the second between the king and the people, that the people shall obey faithfully and the king command justly. . . . If a prince usurps the right of God, and puts himself forward, after the manner of the giants, to scale the heavens, he is no less guilty of high treason to his sovereign, and commits felony in the same manner as if one of his vassals should seize on the rights of his crown, and puts himself into evident danger to be despoiled of his estates; and that so much the more justly, there being no proportion between God and an earthly king, between the Almighty and a mortal man, whereas yet between the lord and the vassal there is some relation of proportion. . . .

Now for that we see that God invests kings into their kingdoms almost in the same manner that vassals are invested into their fees by their sovereign, we must needs conclude that kings are the vassals of God and deserve to be deprived of the benefit they receive from their lord if they commit felony, in the same fashion as rebellious vassals are of their estates. These premises being allowed, this question may be easily resolved; for if God hold the place of sovereign lord, and the king as vassal, who dare deny but that we must rather obey the sovereign than the vassal? If God commands one thing and the king commands the contrary, what is that proud man that would term him a rebel who refuses to obey the king, when else he must disobey God? But, on the contrary, he should rather be condemned and held for truly rebellious who omits to obey God, or who will obey the king when he forbids him to yield obedience to God.

The Second Question: Whether It Be Lawful to Resist a Prince Who Doth Infringe the Law of God or Ruin His Church? By Whom, How, and How Far Is It Lawful?

The question is, if it be lawful to resist a prince violating the law of God, or ruinating the church, or hindering the restoring of it? If we hold ourselves to the tenure of the Holy Scripture it will resolve us. For if in this case it had been lawful to the Jewish people (the which may be easily gathered from the books of the Old Testament), yea, if it had been enjoined them, I believe it will not be denied that the same must be allowed to the whole people of any Christian kingdom or country whatsoever. . . .

But I see well, here will be an objection made. What will you say? That a whole people, that beast of many heads, must they run in a mutinous disorder to order the business of the commonwealth? What address or direction is there in an unruly and unbridled multitude? What counsel or wisdom to manage the affairs of state?

When we speak of all the people we understand by that only those who hold their authority from the people: to wit, the magistrates, who are inferior to the king, and whom the people have substituted or established, as it were, consorts in the empire and with a kind of tribunitial authority to restrain the encroachments of sovereignty and to represent the whole body of the people. We understand also the assembly of the estates, which is nothing else but an epitome or brief collection of the kingdom, to whom all public affairs have special and absolute reference. . . . To be short, as it is lawful for a whole people to resist and oppose tyranny, so likewise the principal persons of the kingdom may, as heads and for the good of the whole body, confederate and associate themselves together. And as in a public state that which is done by the greatest part is esteemed and taken as the act of all, so in like manner must it be said to be done which the better part of the most principal have acted—briefly, that all the people had their hand in it.

It remains now that we speak of particulars who are private persons. First, particulars or private persons are not bound to take up arms against the prince who would compel them to become idolaters. The covenant between

God and all the people who promise to be the people of God does not in any sort bind them to that. For as that which belongs to the whole universal body is in no sort proper to particulars, so in like manner that which the body owes and is bound to perform cannot by any sensible reason be required of particular persons. Neither does their duty anything oblige them to it, for everyone is bound to serve God in that proper vocation to which he is called. Now private persons, they have no power, they have no public command, nor any calling to unsheathe the sword of authority. And therefore, as God has not put the sword into the hands of private men, so does He not require in any sort that they should strike with it. It is said to them "Put up thy sword into thy scabbard."[1] On the contrary, the apostles say of magistrates "They carry not the sword in vain."[2] If particular men draw it forth, they make themselves delinquents. If magistrates be slow and negligent to use it when just occasion is offered, they are likewise justly blameable of negligence in performing their duties, and equally guilty with the former. . . . For as all the subjects of a good and faithful prince, of what degree soever they be, are bound to obey him, but some of them, notwithstanding, have their particular duty . . . in like manner, all men are bound to serve God, but some are placed in a higher rank, have received greater authority, in so much as they are accountable for the offenses of others if they attend not the charges of the commonalty carefully.

The Third Question: Whether It Be Lawful to Resist a Prince Who Doth Oppress or Ruin a Public State, and How Far Such Resistance May Be Extended? By Whom, How, and by What Right or Law It Is Permitted.

We have showed before that it is God that does appoint kings, who chooses them, who gives the kingdom to them. Now we say that the people establish kings, put the scepter into their hands, and with their suffrages approve the election. God would have it done in this manner, to the end that the kings should acknowledge that, after God, they hold their power and sovereignty from the people, and that it might the rather induce them to apply and address the utmost of their care and thoughts for the profit of the people, without being puffed with any vain imagination that they were formed of any matter more excellent than other men. . . . Let them remember and know that they are of the same mould and condition as others; raised from the earth by the voice and acclamations, now as it were upon the shoulders of

1. John 18:11.
2. Romans 13:4.

the people, unto their thrones, that they might afterwards bear on their own shoulders the greatest burdens of the commonwealth. . . .

Briefly, for so much as none were ever born with crowns on their heads and scepters in their hands, and that no man can be a king by himself, nor reign without people—whereas, on the contrary, the people may subsist of themselves, and were long before they had any kings—it must of necessity follow that kings were at the first constituted by the people. And although the sons and dependents of such kings, inheriting their fathers' virtues, may in a sort seem to have rendered their kingdoms hereditary to their offsprings, and that in some kingdoms and countries the right of free election seems in a sort buried, yet notwithstanding, in all well-ordered kingdoms this custom is yet remaining. The sons do not succeed the fathers before the people have first, as it were, anew established them by their new approbation. Neither were they acknowledged in quality as inheriting it from the dead, but approved and accounted kings then only when they were invested with the kingdom by receiving the scepter and diadem from the hands of those who represent the majesty of the people. One may see most evident marks of this in Christian kingdoms which are at this day esteemed hereditary. For the French king, he of Spain and England, and others, are commonly sacred [crowned] and, as it were, put into possession of their authority by the peers, lords of the kingdom, and officers of the crown, who represent the body of the people, no more nor less than the emperors of Germany are chosen by the electors, and the kings of Poland by the vaivodes[3] and palatines[4] of the kingdom, where the right of election is still in force. In like manner also, the cities give no royal reception nor entries unto the king but after their inauguration, and anciently they used not to count the times of their reign but from the day of their coronation, the which was strictly observed in France.

If it be objected that kings were enthronised and received their authority from the people who lived five hundred years ago, and not by those now living, I answer that the commonwealth never dies, although kings be taken out of this life one after another. For as the continual running of the water gives the river a perpetual being, so the alternative revolution of birth and death renders the people immortal. And further, as we have at this day the same Seine and Tiber as was 1,000 years ago, in like manner also is there the same people of Germany, France and Italy; neither can the lapse of time, nor changing of individuals, alter in any sort the right of those people.

The only duty of kings and emperors is to provide for the people's good. The kingly dignity, to speak properly, is not a title of honor but a weighty and

3. *Vaivodes:* local rulers or officials in Southeastern Europe, especially Hungary and Poland.
4. *Palatines:* those holding power over provinces or dependencies of an empire or realm.

burdensome office. It is not a discharge or vacation from affairs to run a licentious course of liberty, but a charge and vocation to all industrious employments for the service of the commonwealth—the which has some glimpse of honor with it, because in those first and golden ages no man would have tasted of such continuous troubles if they had not been sweetened with some relish of honor. Insomuch as there was nothing more true than that which was commonly said in those times: "If every man knew with what turmoils and troubles the royal wreath was wrapt withal, no man would vouchsafe to take it up, although it lay at his feet."

When therefore that these words of *mine* and *thine* entered into the world, and that differences fell amongst fellow citizens touching the propriety of goods, and wars amongst neighboring people about the right of their confines, the people bethought themselves to have recourse to someone who both could and should take order that the poor were not oppressed by the rich, nor the patriots wronged by strangers. . . . See then wherefore kings were created in the first ages: to wit, to administer justice at home, and to be leaders in the wars abroad. . . . Seeing then that kings are ordained by God and established by the people to procure and provide for the good of those who are committed unto them, and that this good or profit be principally expressed in two things—to wit, in the administration of justice to their subjects and in the managing of armies for the repulsing their enemies—certainly we must infer and conclude from this that the prince who applied himself to nothing but his peculiar profits and pleasures, or to those ends which most readily conduce thereunto; who contemns and perverts all laws; who uses his subjects more cruelly than the barbarous enemy would do: he may truly and really be called a tyrant; and those who in this manner govern their kingdoms, be they of never so large an extent, are more properly unjust pillagers and freebooters than lawful governors.

Must the kings be subject to the law? Or does the law depend upon the king? . . . There is nothing which exempts the king from the obedience which he owes to the law . . . neither should they think their authority the less because they are confined to laws. For seeing the law is a divine gift coming from above, which human societies are happily governed by and addressed to their best and blessedest end, those kings are as ridiculous and worthy of contempt to repute it a dishonor to conform themselves to law . . . Who can doubt but that it is a thing more profitable and convenient to obey the law than the king, who is but one man? The law is the soul of a good king, it gives him motion, sense, and life. The king is the organ and, as it were, the body by which the law displays her forces, exercises her functions, and expresses her conceptions. Now it is a thing much more reasonable to obey the soul than the body. The law is the wisdom of diverse sages, recollected in few words; but many see more clear and further than one alone. It is much better to follow the law than any one man's opinion, be he never so acute. The law is reason and wisdom itself, free from all perturbation, not subject to be moved with choler, ambition, hate, or acceptances of persons. Entreaties nor threats cannot make it to bow nor bend. On the contrary, a man, though endued with reason, suffers himself to be led and transported with anger, desire of revenge, and other passions which perplex him, in such sort that he loses his understanding, because being composed of reason and disordered affections he cannot so contain himself, but sometimes his passions become his master. . . .

Neither the emperor, the king of France, nor the kings of Spain, England, Poland, and Hungary, and all other lawful princes . . . are not admitted to the government of their estates before they have promised . . . that they will render to everyone right according to the laws of the country; yea, so strictly that they cannot alter or innovate anything contrary to the privileges of the countries without the consent of the towns and provinces. If they do it, they are no less guilty of rebellion against the laws than the people are in their kind if they refuse obedience when kings command according to law. Briefly, lawful princes receive the laws from the people as well as the crown, in lieu of honour, and the scepter, in lieu of power; which they are bound to keep and maintain. And therein reposes their chiefest glory. . . .

We must remember that all princes are born men, and therefore reason and passion are as hardly to be separated in them as the soul is from the body whilst the man lives. We must not then expect princes absolute in perfection, but rather repute ourselves happy if those who govern us be indifferently good. And therefore although the prince observe not exact mediocrity [moderation] . . . , if sometimes passions overrule his reason, if some careless omission make him neglect the public utility, or if he do not always carefully execute justice with equality, or repulse not with ready valor an invading enemy, he must not therefore be presently declared a tyrant. . . . But if a prince purposely ruin the commonwealth, if he presumptuously pervert and resist legal proceedings of lawful rights, if he make no reckoning of faith, covenants, justice nor piety, if he prosecute his subjects as enemies—briefly, if he express all or the chiefest of those wicked practices we have formerly spoken of—then we may certainly declare him a tyrant, who is as much an enemy both to God and men. . . .

It becomes wise men to try all ways before they come to blows, to use all other remedies before they suffer the sword to decide the controversy. If, then, those who represent the body of the people foresee any innovation or machination against the state, or that it be already embarked into a course of perdition, their duty is first to admonish the prince and not to attend that the disease, by accession of time and accidents, becomes unrecoverable. . . . Therefore small beginnings are to be carefully observed, and by those whom it concerns diligently prevented. If the prince therefore persists in his violent courses, and contemns frequent admonitions, addressing his designs only to that end that he may oppress at his pleasure and effect his own desires without fear or restraint, he then doubtless makes himself liable to that detested crime of tyranny, and whatsoever either the law or lawful authority permits against a tyrant may be lawfully practiced against him. . . . And if the tyranny have gotten such sure footing as there is no other means but force to remove him, then it is lawful for them to call the people to arms, and to enroll and raise forces, and to employ the utmost of their power, and use against him all advantages and stratagems of war, as against the enemy of the commonwealth and the disturber of the public peace.

Jean Bodin:
The Six Bookes of a Commonweale

The passions that led to the Wars of Religion and convulsed France for a quarter of a century provoked some of the most influential political writing of the whole Renaissance period. Philippe Duplessis-Mornay saw the root of the trouble in the overweening ambitions of princes and therefore argued that their power should be limited. Jean Bodin went in exactly the opposite direction. He came to believe that the misfortunes of France had been caused by weak government, not strong, and that the restoration of order could only be accomplished by elevating the authority of the crown and denying to the subject any right of resistance.

Bodin, who was born in 1529/30, began life as a monk and received a traditional education in scholastic philosophy, based on Aristotle and Aquinas. He subsequently abandoned both the cloister and scholasticism, but the rigorous formal training left its mark on him, as will be seen. He embarked on a career as a lawyer at a time when the New Learning was undermining the reverence hitherto accorded to the *Lex Civile*, the law of the Roman Empire as it had been handed down to posterity in the *Digest* compiled by the order of the Emperor Justinian in the early sixth century. The study of Roman law had been revived in Italy in the eleventh century, from where it spread to most of Europe. It won admiration and respect for its coherence and apparent universality, especially when set against the mosaic of regional laws and customary observances that characterized the European states. This high valuation carried over into the Renaissance, for many of the early humanists were themselves civil lawyers.

A change of attitude came about, however, as a consequence of the humanists' success in bringing to light classical works that had been lost sight of in the Middle Ages. So much was discovered that it became necessary to develop techniques for distinguishing between good and bad copies and establishing authentic texts. Erasmus and the northern humanists applied these techniques to the Bible and early fathers, thereby fueling the demand for reform of the Church; but in a parallel development French humanists in the sixteenth century brought the *Digest* under critical scrutiny and, as they did so, became aware that it was itself a compilation of earlier texts, and nothing like so unified and coherent as had hitherto been assumed. Moreover, by putting Roman law back into its historical context, they lessened its universality; they showed that it had been designed for a particular community at a particular time, and had only a limited relevance to the very different world of their own day. Admittedly, Roman law told one a great deal about the Romans and their society, but by the same token so would other systems of law about the societies that had given birth to them. Indeed, a comparative study of laws might reveal common denominators from which it would be possible to construct not simply a philosophy of jurisprudence but even perhaps a theory of politics that really would be universally applicable.

Bodin took a leading part in the investigations into the origins of French laws, and in 1566 published his conclusions in *The Method for the Easy Comprehension of History*. His studies had reinforced his conviction that historically speaking the French monarchy could claim only limited and not absolute authority. However, by this time the Wars of Religion were already devastating France, and as they became increasingly bitter, so the prospects of bringing them to an end receded. The intransigence of both Catholics and Protestants provoked the emergence of a center group, the *Politiques*, who argued that the only way in which to restore peace was by uniting around the monarchy. The nominal head of the *Politiques* was the Duke d'Alençon, brother of King Henry III, and in 1571 Bodin entered the Duke's household. Five years later he published *The Six Bookes of a Commonweale*, in which he provided a detailed historical and philosophical defense of absolutism. To many Frenchmen who longed for peace but despaired of finding it, Bodin's arguments seemed like the voice of sanity. Over the course of the next twenty years ten editions of *The Six Bookes* appeared, as well as an expanded version in Latin, the *De Republica*. Bodin's fame rapidly spread to England, and Spenser's friend Gabriel Harvey reported from

Cambridge that "you cannot step into a scholar's study but (ten to one) you shall litely find open . . . Bodin *De Republica*."[1] The English, not surprisingly, were passionately concerned about events in France, and even the peace-loving and parsimonious Elizabeth sent an army to support Henry of Navarre. Marlowe wrote a drama about the St. Bartholomew's Day massacre, and George Chapman's plays about Bussy d'Ambois and the Duke of Biron took contemporary French politics as their theme.

Bodin's *Six Bookes* were consciously modeled on Aristotle's *Politics*, and he intended, by surveying the constitutions of existing states as well as the lessons of history, to construct a modern theory of politics. Machiavelli had set out on a similar course, but Bodin believed that his range of evidence was too confined and his conclusions therefore suspect. Although Bodin asked the same sort of questions as Machiavelli, he arrived at more conventionally moral answers, partly because he was concerned to shore up traditional values at a time when they seemed to be disintegrating.

Bodin's major contribution to political thought was his definition of sovereignty as an "absolute and perpetual power" vested in the ruler. This power, according to Bodin, derived not from the people but from God, and it was to God alone, and not to the people, that the ruler was accountable. It followed from this premise that law—unlike covenants that the ruler freely entered into—was the expression of the sovereign's will and bound him only as long as he saw fit. Since the people were subordinate to the sovereign, they could not possibly have the right to oppose his will. "What subject can give sentence on his king?" asks the Bishop of Carlisle in Shakespeare's *Richard II* (IV.i.), echoing Bodin's belief that the subject's duty, when confronted with absolute power, consists in absolute obedience. Richard himself reminds the lords who have rebelled against him that "no hand of blood and bone / Can gripe the sacred handle of our sceptre." Their challenge, he insists, is doomed to fail, for "my master, God omnipotent, / Is mustering in his clouds on our behalf / Armies of pestilence, and they shall strike / Your children yet unborn, and unbegot, / That lift your vassal hands against my head, / And threat the glory of my precious crown," (III.iii.).

In his approach to sovereignty Bodin shows a "Machiavellian" realism. Yet although he had earlier rejected scholasticism, he retained its

1. Quoted by J. H. M. Salmon in *The French Religious Wars in English Political Thought* (Oxford, 1959), p. 24.

basic imprint. Like Aquinas, and like Hooker, he believed that the universe was a work of reason governed by natural law, to which all human beings, including rulers, were subject. Moreover, since political societies had been created in order to preserve property, a sovereign had no justification for infringing his subjects' property rights. The same point is made by Shakespeare in *Richard II*, when the king's uncle warns the young autocrat not to confiscate his cousin's estate: "If you do wrongfully seize Herford's rights / . . . You lose a thousand well-disposed hearts, / And prick my tender patience to those thoughts / Which honor and allegiance cannot think" (II.i). The sovereign, in short, had a moral obligation to observe the fundamental laws and to rule in the best interests of his people. What if he failed to rule justly? Bodin's answer was that such matters must be left to God. Human kings were merely the vassals of the King of Kings, and He would ultimately call them to account for their actions. If subjects attempted to do so, they were usurping God's prerogative.

To a twentieth-century reader such a conclusion may seem tame and inadequate. But in the second half of the sixteenth century it made a great deal of sense. In his earlier "constitutional" phase Bodin had assumed, along with Aristotle, that the best regulated states were those that had a mix of the three primary elements—monarchy, aristocracy, and democracy. The experience of the Wars of Religion had persuaded him otherwise. Absolute monarchy now seemed to him to be the only true form of government, especially since it reflected the sovereignty of God over the whole universe. Any rule was better than none at all, and given that God appointed rulers, it seemed a reasonable assumption that He would endow them with the appropriate qualities. There was an element of divinity about monarchy, for kings were God's surrogates, but their exalted status demanded an equally exalted sense of responsibility, for in the last resort they were not so much kings as viceroys, the embodiments of a power that was greater than themselves and to which they were therefore subject. Again, Shakespeare offers perhaps the most direct statement of this position in *Richard II*. The king may well have been responsible for the death of his uncle, Thomas of Woodstock, but Thomas's brother refuses to take vengeance:

> God's is the quarrel—for God's substitute,
> His deputy anointed in His sight,
> Hath caused his death; the which if wrongfully,

Let heaven revenge, for I may never lift
An angry arm against His minister.

(I.ii.)

But such arguments are never clear-cut or simple, as Shakespeare knew only too well. In this instance, heaven may, in fact, be avenging the king's wrongdoings, for Bolingbroke, the usurper of the throne, intimates that he is acting with divine sanction. When reminded that "the heavens are o'er our heads," he responds by claiming: "I oppose not myself / Against their will" (III.iii.).

What a Citizen is

A citizen . . . is no other in proper terms than a free subject holding of the sovereignty of another man. For before there was either city or citizen, or any form of a commonweal amongst men, every master of a family was a master in his own house, having power of life and death over his wife and children. But after that force, violence, ambition, covetousness, and desire of revenge had armed one against another, the issues of wars and combats giving victory unto the one side, made the other to become unto them slaves. And amongst them that overcame, he that was chosen chief and captain, under whose conduct and leading they had obtained the victory, kept them also in his power and command, as his faithful and obedient subjects, and the other as his slaves. Then that full and entire liberty by nature given to every man, to live as himself best pleased, was altogether taken from the vanquished, and in the vanquishers themselves in some measure also diminished, in regard of the conqueror. For that now it concerned every man in private to yield his obedience unto his chief sovereign; and he that would not abate anything of his liberty, to live under the laws and commandment of another, lost all. So the word of *lord* and *servant*, of *prince* and *subject*, before unknown unto the world, were first brought into use. Yea, reason, and the very light of nature, leadeth us to believe very force and violence to have given course and beginning unto commonweals.

Of Sovereignty

Majesty or sovereignty is the most high, absolute, and perpetual power over the citizens and subjects in a commonweal. . . . So here it behoveth first to define what majesty or sovereignty is, which neither lawyer nor political philosopher hath yet defined, although it be the principal and most necessary point for the understanding of the nature of a commonweal. And forasmuch as we have before defined a commonweal to be the right government of many families, and of things common amongst them, with a most high and perpetual power, it resteth to be declared what is to be understood by the names of a most high and perpetual power.

We have said that this power ought to be perpetual, for that it may be that that absolute power over the subjects may be given to one or many, for a short or certain time; which expired, they are no more than subjects themselves. So that whilst they are in their puissant authority, they cannot call themselves sovereign princes, seeing that they are but men put in trust, and keepers of this sovereign power, until it shall please the people or the prince that gave it them to recall it, who always remained seized thereof. For as they which lend or pawn unto another man their goods remain still the lords and owners thereof, so it is also with them who give unto others power and authority to judge and command, be it for a certain time limited or so great and long time as shall please them—they themselves nevertheless continuing still seized of the power and jurisdiction, which the other exercise but by way of loan or borrowing. . . .

But let us grant an absolute power, without appeal or controlment, to be granted by the people to one or many, to manage their estate and entire government. Shall we therefore say him or them to have the state of sovereignty, whenas he only is to be called absolute sovereign who next unto God acknowledgeth none greater than himself? Wherefore I say no sovereignty to be in them, but in the people, of whom they have a borrowed power, or power for a certain time; which once expired, they are bound to yield up their authority. Neither is the people to be thought to have deprived itself of the power thereof, although it have given an absolute power to one or more for a certain time: and much more if the power (be it given) be revocable at the pleasure of the people, without any limitation of time. For both the one and the other hold nothing of themselves, but are to give account of their doings unto the prince or the people of whom they had the power to command. Whereas the prince or people themselves, in whom the sovereignty resteth, are to give account unto none but to the immortal God alone. . . .

Now let us prosecute the other part of our propounded definition, and show what these words *absolute power* signify. For we said that unto majesty, or sovereignty, belongeth an absolute power not subject to any law. For the people or the lords of a commonweal may purely and simply give the sovereign and perpetual power to anyone, to dispose of the goods and lives and of all the state at his pleasure, and so afterward to leave it to whom he list; like as the proprietor or owner may purely and simply give his own goods, without any other cause to be expressed than of his own mere bounty—which is indeed the true donation, which no more receiveth condition, being once accomplished and perfected. As for the other donations, which carry with them charge and conditions, [they] are not indeed true donations. So also the chief power, given unto a prince with charge and condition, is not properly sovereignty, nor power absolute—except that such charge or condition annexed unto the sovereignty at the creation of a prince be directly comprehended within the laws of God and nature. . . .

If we shall say that he only hath absolute power which is subject unto no law, there should then be no sovereign prince in the world, seeing that all princes of the earth are subject unto the laws of God, of nature, and of nations. . . . But it behoveth him that is a sovereign not to be in any sort subject to the command of another. . . . [His] office it is to give laws unto his subjects, to abrogate laws unprofitable, and in their stead to establish other; which he cannot do that is himself subject unto laws, or to others which have command over him. And that is it for which the law saith that the prince is acquitted from the power of the laws. And this word, the law, in the Latin importeth the commandment of him which hath the sovereignty. . . . If then the sovereign prince be exempted from the laws of his predecessors, much less should he be bound unto the laws and ordinances he maketh himself. For a man may well receive a law from another man, but impossible it is in nature for to give a law unto himself, no more than it is to command a man's self in a matter depending of his own will. . . . And as the pope can never bind his own hands (as the canonists say), so neither can a sovereign prince bind his own hands, albeit that he would. We see also in the end of all edicts and laws these words, *Quia sic nobis placuit*, "Because it hath so pleased us"; to give us to understand that the laws of a sovereign prince, although they be grounded upon good and lively reasons, depend nevertheless upon nothing but his mere and frank goodwill.

But as for the laws of God and nature, all princes and people of the world are unto them subject. Neither is it in their power to impugn them, if [they] will not be guilty of high treason to the divine majesty, making war against God, under the greatness of whom all monarchs of the world ought to bear the yoke and to bow their heads in all fear and reverence. Wherefore, in that we said the sovereign power in a commonweal to be free from all laws, [that] concerneth nothing the laws of God and nature. For amongst the popes, he that of all others best knew the laws of majesty or sovereignty, and had almost brought under him the power of all the Christian emperors and princes,[2] said him to be indeed a sovereign that was able to derogate from the ordinary right (which is, as I understand it, from the laws of his country) but not from the laws of God or nature.

But further question may be: whether a prince be a subject to the laws of his country, that he hath sworn to keep, or not? Wherein we must distinguish. If the prince swear unto himself that he will keep his law, he is no more bound to his law than by the oath made unto himself. For the subjects themselves are not any way bound by oath, which they make in their mutual conventions, if the covenants be such as from which they may by law shrink, although they be both honest and reasonable. But if a sovereign prince promise by oath to keep the laws which he or his predecessors have made, he is bound to keep them . . . not for that the prince is bound to his laws, or by his predecessors, but to the just conventions and promises that he hath made, be it by oath or without any oath at all, as should a private man be. And for the same causes that a private man may be relieved from his unjust and unreasonable promise—as for that it was too grievous, or for that he was by deceit or fraud circumvented, or induced thereinto by error or force of just fear, or by some great hurt—even for the same causes the prince may be restored in that which toucheth the diminishing of his majesty, if he be a sovereign prince. And so our maxim resteth, that the prince is not subject to his laws, nor to the laws of his predecessors; but well to his own just and reasonable conventions, and in the observation whereof the subjects in general or particular have interest. . . .

So was there no need of money, or of oath, to bind the sovereign prince, if it concerned his subjects (to whom he had promised) to have the law kept. For the word of a prince ought to be as an oracle, which loseth his dignity if his subjects have so evil an opinion of him as not to believe him except he swear; or else to be so covetous, as not to regard his promise except therefore he receive money. And yet nevertheless the maxim of right still standeth in force: that the sovereign prince may derogate unto the laws that he hath promised and sworn to keep, if the equity thereof ceases; and that of himself, without consent of his subjects. . . . But if there be no probable cause of abrogating the law he hath promised to keep, he shall do against the duty of a good prince if he shall go about to abrogate such a law. And yet, for all that, is he not bound unto the covenants and oaths of his predecessors further than standeth with his profit, except he be their heir. . . .

We must not, then, confound the laws and contracts of sovereign princes. For that the law dependeth of the will and pleasure of him that hath the

2. The reference is to Pope Innocent IV (1243–54).

sovereignty, who may bind all his subjects but cannot bind himself. But the contract betwixt the prince and his subjects is mutual, which reciprocally bindeth both parties, so that the one party may not start therefrom to the prejudice or without the consent of the other. In which case the prince hath nothing above the subject, but that the equity of the law, which he hath sworn to keep, ceasing, he is no more bound to the keeping thereof by his oath or promise, as we have before said: which the subjects cannot do among themselves, if they be not by the prince relieved. The sovereign princes also, well advised, will never take oath to keep the laws of their predecessors, for otherwise they are not sovereigns. . . .

But touching the laws which concern the state of the realm and the establishing thereof: forasmuch as they are annexed and united to the crown, the prince cannot derogate from them—such as is the Law Salic[3]—and albeit that he do so, the successor may always disannul that which hath been done unto the prejudice of the laws royal, upon which the sovereign majesty is stayed and grounded. . . . But as for general and particular laws and customs which concern not the establishing of the state of the realm, but the right of men in private, they have not used to have been with us otherwise changed but after general assembly of the three estates of France[4] well and truly made. . . . Not for that it is necessary for the king to rest on their advice, or that he may not do the contrary to that they demand, if natural reason and justice so require. And in that the greatness and majesty of a true sovereign prince is to be known, when the estates of all the people assembled together in all humility present their requests and supplications to their prince, without having any power in any thing to command or determine, or to give voice; but that that which it pleaseth the king to like or dislike of, to command or forbid, is holden for law, for an edict and ordinance.

Wherein they which have written of the duty of magistrates, and other suchlike books, have deceived themselves in maintaining that the power of the people is greater than the prince—a thing which oft times causeth the true subjects to revolt from the obedience which they owe unto their sovereign prince, and ministereth matter of great troubles in common-weals. . . . For otherwise, if the king should be subject unto the assemblies and decrees of the people, he should neither be king nor sovereign, and the commonwealth neither realm nor monarchy, but a mere aristocracy of many

3. The Salic Law, originally a code of law of the Salian Franks, was held by some of its interpreters to bar women from succession to the French throne. The question is discussed at length by the archbishop of Canterbury in Shakespeare's *Henry V* (I.ii).

4. The three estates that together made up the Estates-General of France were the spiritual peers, the temporal peers, and the commonalty or "Third Estate."

lords in power equal, where the greater part commandeth the less in general. . . .

And albeit that in the parliaments of England, which have commonly been holden every third year, there the states seem to have a very great liberty (as the northern people almost all breathe thereafter), yet so it is that in effect they proceed not but by way of supplications and requests unto the king. . . . Now also the estates of England are never otherwise assembled (no more than they are in this realm of France, or Spain) than by parliament writs and express commandment proceeding from the king. Which showeth very well that the estates have no power of themselves to determine, command, or decree anything; seeing that they cannot so much as assemble themselves; neither, being assembled, depart, without express commandment from the king. . . . But here might some object and say that the estates of England suffer not any extraordinary charges and subsidies to be laid upon them, if it be not first agreed upon and consented unto in the high court of parliament. . . . Whereunto mine answer is, that other kings have in this point no more power than the kings of England; for that it is not in the power of any prince in the world at his pleasure to raise taxes upon the people, no more than to take another man's goods from him. . . .

From which we are not to except either the pope or the emperor, as some pernicious flatterers do, saying that those two—viz the pope and the emperor—may of right, without cause, take unto themselves the goods of their subjects. Which opinion the canonists themselves, the interpreters of the pope's law, detest, as contrary to the law of God. . . . Now certainly it is a greater offense to infect princes with this doctrine than it is to rob and steal. For poverty commonly causeth thieves to seek after other men's goods; but they that maintain such opinions show the lion his claws and arm the prince, so instructed, to pretend unto his outrages this godly show of law and justice; who . . . proving to be a tyrant, maketh no question most shamefully to confound and break all the laws both of God and man. And afterward, enflamed with corrupt desires and affections, which altogether weaken the more noble parts of the mind, he quickly breaketh out from covetousness to unjust confiscations, from lust to adultery, from wrath to murder.

Of the True Marks of Sovereignty

Seeing that nothing upon earth is greater or higher, next unto God, than the majesty of kings and sovereign princes, for that they are in a sort created His lieutenants for the welfare of other men, it is meet diligently to consider of their majesty and power, as also who and of what sort they be; that so we may in all obedience respect and reverence their majesty, and not to think or speak of them otherwise than of the lieutenants of the most mighty and immortal God: for that he which speaketh evil of his prince, unto whom he oweth all duty, doth injury unto the majesty of God Himself, whose lively image he is upon earth. . . .

Wherefore let this be the first and chief mark of a sovereign prince: to be of power to give laws to all his subjects in general, and to every one of them in particular. Yet is not that enough, but that we must join thereunto [that he does so] without consent of any other greater, equal, or lesser than himself. For if a prince be bound not to make any law without consent of a greater than himself, he is then a very subject. If not without his equal, he then hath a companion. If not without the consent of his inferiors, whether it be of his subjects, of the senate, or of the people, he is then no sovereign. . . . Under this same sovereignty of power for the giving and abrogating of the law are comprised all the other rights and marks of sovereignty. So that to speak properly, a man may say that there is but this only mark of sovereign power, considering that all other the rights thereof are contained in this: viz to have power to give laws unto all and every one of the subjects, and to receive none from them.

Whether It Be Lawful to Lay Violent Hand upon a Tyrant

If the prince be an absolute sovereign . . . it is not lawful for any one of the subjects in particular, or all of them in general, to attempt anything, either by way of fact [i.e., deed] or of justice against the honor, life, or dignity of the sovereign, albeit that he had committed all the wickedness, impiety, and cruelty that could be spoken. For as to proceed against him by way of justice, the subject hath no such jurisdiction over his sovereign prince, of whom dependeth all power and authority to command. . . . Now if it be not lawful for the subject by way of justice to proceed against his prince . . . how should it then be lawful to proceed against him by way of fact or force? For question is not here of what men are able to do by strength and force, but what they ought of right to do: as not whether the subjects have power and strength, but whether they have lawful power to condemn their sovereign prince. Now the subject is not only guilty of treason in the highest degree who hath slain his sovereign prince, but even he also which hath attempted the same; who hath given counsel or consent thereunto; yea, if he have concealed the same, or but so much as thought it. . . .

I cannot use a better example than of the duty of a son towards his father. The law of God saith that he which speaketh evil of his father or mother shall be put to death. Now if the father shall be a thief, a murderer, a traitor to his country . . . or what so you will else, I confess that all the punishments that can be devised are not sufficient to punish him. Yet I say that it is not for the son to put his hand thereunto. . . . Wherefore the prince, whom you may justly call the father of the country, ought to be unto every man dearer and more reverend than any father, as one ordained and sent unto us by God. I say, therefore, that the subject is never to be suffered to attempt anything against his sovereign prince, how naughty and cruel soever he be. Lawful it is, not to obey him in things contrary unto the laws of God and nature; to fly and hide ourselves from him; but yet to suffer stripes, yea, and death also, rather than to attempt anything against his life or honor.

A Comparison of the Three Lawful Commonweals
—that is, a Popular Estate, an Aristocratical, and a Royal; and that a Royal Monarchy is the Best

The chief point of a commonweal, which is the right of sovereignty, cannot be, nor subsist (to speak properly) but in a monarchy. For none can be sovereign in a commonweal but one alone. If they be two, or three, or more, no one is sovereign, for that no one of them can give or take a flaw from his companion. And although we imagine a body of many lords, or of a whole people, to hold the sovereignty, yet hath it no true ground nor support if there be not a head with absolute and sovereign power to unite them together. . . . We see the difficulties which are, and always have been, in popular states and seigneuries, whereas they hold contrary parts, and for divers magistrates. Some demand peace; others war. Some will have this law; others that. Some will have one commander; others another. . . . Moreover, in a popular and aristocratical estate, always the greater number will be believed, although the wiser and the most virtuous be fewest in number; so as most commonly the sounder and the better part is forced to yield unto the greater, at the appetite of an impudent tribune or a brazen-faced orator. But a sovereign monarch may join with the sounder and better part, and make choice of wise men and well practices in matters of state; whereas necessity doth force them in other commonweals to admit wise men and fools and altogether to offices and counsel. It is also impossible for a popular state or an aristocracy to command with sovereign power, or to do any act which cannot be done but by one person only—as to conduct an army and suchlike things; but they must create magistrates and commissaries to that end, who have neither the sovereign power, authority, nor majesty of a monarch. . . .

And therefore, whereas we said before that in a well-ordered state the sovereign power must remain in one only, without communicating any part thereof unto the state (for in that case it should be a popular government, and no monarchy), and that all wise politicians, philosophers, divines, and historiographers have highly commended a monarchy above all other commonweals; it is not to please the prince that they hold this opinion, but for the safety and happiness of the subjects. And contrariwise, whenas they shall limit and restrain the sovereign power of a monarch, to subject him to the general estates, or to the council, the sovereignty hath no firm foundation, but they frame a popular confusion, or a miserable anarchy, which is the plague of all states and commonweals. The which must be duly considered; not giving credit to their goodly discourses which persuade subjects that it is necessary to subject monarchs and to prescribe their prince a law; for that it is not only the ruin of the monarch, but also of the subjects.

James I

James VI of Scotland, who in 1603 became James I of England, was Plato's ideal of a ruler, namely a philosopher king. He had been a monarch almost since his birth, for his mother, Mary, Queen of Scots, fled into exile in England while he was still a baby, and when he was crowned King at Stirling he was a mere one year old. Not long after his fourth birthday the distinguished philosopher George Buchanan was appointed as his tutor, and although James—who was highly intelligent and a lover of scholarship—subsequently took pride in having had such a mentor, his feelings toward Buchanan were far from friendly. This was not merely a question of age—although Buchanan was over sixty at the time, with a temper made harsh by repeated attacks of gout. Buchanan had spent the greater part of his life in France—including a spell of teaching at Bordeaux, where his pupils included the young Montaigne—and had imbibed a good deal of the radicalism that later surfaced among the French Protestants. Like Duplessis-Mornay he believed that rulers derived their power from the people and held it conditionally. In fact, he went ever further than the author of the *Vindiciae Contra Tyrannos* by asserting that the right of resistance belonged to every individual and that kings were little more than public officials, liable to dismissal if they misbehaved. Using just such arguments, Buchanan justified the deposition of Mary, Queen of Scots, in 1568.

Buchanan's radical and abrasive theories were anathema to James; they savored too much of Calvinist republicanism. No sooner did the King come of age than he persuaded the Scottish Parliament to order the suppression of the *De Jure Regni*, in which Buchanan had expounded his beliefs. But James was not content with negative actions.

Confident in his own ability, he set about developing a philosophical defense of kingship and making his views known to the world. In 1599 he produced the *Basilicon Doron*, nominally addressed to his son and heir, Prince Henry. This was in the "advice-to-princes" genre, which first appeared in fourteenth-century Italy and was later taken up and enthusiastically expanded by the Renaissance humanists. James's advice to the young Henry is couched in conventional terms, but his insistence on the duty of kings to rule in a godly manner is evidence that humanist propaganda was having just the effect that was intended and hoped for.

The *Basilicon Doron* was not James's first work of political philosophy, for it had been preceded by *The Trew Law of Free Monarchies*, printed in 1598 and aptly subtitled a study of "the reciprock and mutual duty betwixt a free King and his subjects." Whether or not James had actually read Bodin, there is no doubt that he shared Bodin's assumptions; the *Trew Law* fits very neatly into the overall pattern laid down in *The Six Bookes of a Commonweale*. James, like Bodin, derives the royal authority from God, and insists that it is as natural as that exercised by a father over his family. Kings are above the law, in the sense that they cannot be compelled to obey it, but a good king will choose to rule in accordance with law, particularly since he takes an oath to do so at his coronation. Since all kings, bad as well as good, are appointed by God, there can be no question of resisting their authority. It is permissible to fly from a wicked ruler or to pray that he may amend his life, but there is no justification for a subject to raise his hand against the Lord's anointed. In the words of Shakespeare's Richard II: "The breath of worldly men cannot depose / The deputy elected by the Lord" (*Richard II*, III.ii).

As this quotation indicates, the nature of monarchical authority was a theme that had already made its appearance in Elizabethan literature, but the accession of James I prompted Shakespeare to place it in a specifically Scottish context. *Macbeth* was written for James and deals with questions of kingship, rebellion, and retribution. James himself received direct and fulsome praise in what may be Shakespeare's last work, *Henry VIII* (1613). In a prophetic speech delivered at the baptism of the infant Elizabeth, the archbishop predicts that, after Elizabeth's death, her heir:

> *Shall star-like rise, as great in fame as she was,*
> *And so stand fix'd. Peace, plenty, love, truth, terror,*
> *That were the servants to this chosen infant,*
> *Shall then be his, and like a vine grow to him;*

Wherever the bright sun of heaven shall shine,
His honour and the greatness of his name
Shall be, and make new nations. He shall flourish,
And like a mountain cedar, reach his branches
To all the plains about him.

(V.v.)

The glory, wisdom, and peace-loving nature of James I are also celebrated in the splendid court masques of Ben Jonson and Inigo Jones. Their themes are suggested in such titles as *The Golden Age Restored* (1615) and *The Fortunate Isles, and their Union* (1625).

Basilicon Doron
or His Majesty's Instructions to His Dearest Son, Henry the Prince

First of all things, l⸜⸜ ⸜o know and love that God whom-to ye have a double obligation; first, for that He made you a man; and next, for that He made you a little God to sit on His throne and rule over other men. Remember that as in dignity He hath erected you above others, so ought ye in thankfulness towards Him go as far beyond all others. . . . Think not therefore that the highness of your dignity diminisheth your faults (much less giveth you license to sin); but, by the contrary, your fault shall be aggravated according to the height of your dignity, any sin that ye commit not being a single sin, procuring but the fall of one, but being an exemplary sin, and therefore drawing with it the whole multitude to be guilty of the same. Remember then that this glistering worldly glory of kings is given them by God to teach them to press so to glister and shine before their people in all works of sanctification and righteousness that their persons, as bright lamps of godliness and virtue, may, going in and out before their people, give light to all their steps. Remember also that by the right knowledge and fear of God (which is the beginning of wisdom, as Solomon saith)[1] ye shall know all the things necessary for the discharge of your duty both as a Christian and as a king; seeing in Him, as in a mirror, the course of all earthly things, whereof He is the spring and only mover.

1. Proverbs 9:10.

The Trew Law of Free Monarchies
or the Reciprock and Mutual Duty Betwixt a Free King and
His Natural Subjects

In the coronation of our own kings, as well as of every Christian monarch, they give their oath, first to maintain the religion presently professed within their country, according to their laws whereby it is established, and to punish all those that should press to alter or disturb the profession thereof. And next, to maintain all the lowable [i.e., allowable, permissible] and good laws made by their predecessors, to see them put in execution, and the breakers and violators thereof to be punished, according to the tenor of the same. And lastly, to maintain the whole country, and every state herein, in all their ancient privileges and liberties, as well against all foreign enemies as among themselves. And, shortly, to procure the weal and flourishing of his people, not only in maintaining and putting to execution the old lowable laws of the country and by establishing of new (as necessity and evil manners will require), but by all other means possible to foresee and prevent all dangers that are likely to fall upon them, and to maintain concord, wealth, and civility among them, as a loving father and careful watchman, caring for them more than for himself, knowing himself to be ordained for them, and they not for him; and therefore accountable to that great God who placed him as His lieutenant over them, upon the peril of his soul to procure the weal of both souls and bodies, as far as in him lieth, of all them that are committed to his charge. And this oath in the coronation is the clearest civil and fundamental law whereby the king's office is properly defined.

By the law of nature the king becomes a natural father to all his lieges at his coronation. And as the father, of his fatherly duty, is bound to care for the nourishing, education, and virtuous government of his children, even so is the king bound to care for all his subjects. . . . And shortly, as the father's chief joy ought to be in procuring his children's welfare, rejoicing at their weal, sorrowing and pitying at their evil; to hazard for their safety, travail for their rest, wake for their sleep; and, in a word, to think that his earthly felicity and life standeth and liveth more in them nor in himself; so ought a good prince think of his people.

As to the other branch of this mutual and reciprock band is the duty and allegiance that the lieges owe to their king; the ground whereof I take out of the words of Samuel, dited by God's spirit, when God had given him commandment to hear the people's voice in choosing and anointing them a king. . . .[2] It is plain and evident that this speech of Samuel to the people

2. I Samuel 8:5–22.

was to prepare their hearts beforehand to the due obedience of that king which God was to give unto them; and therefore opened up unto them what might be the intolerable qualities that might fall in some of their kings, thereby preparing them to patience, not to resist to God's ordinance . . . since He that hath the only power to make him hath the only power to unmake him, and ye only to obey. . . .

To end, then, the ground of my proposition taken out of the Scripture, let two special and notable examples, one under the law, another under the evangel, conclude this part, of my allegiance. Under the law, Jeremy threateneth the people of God with utter destruction for rebellion to Nebuchadnezzar, the king of Babel;[3] who, although he was an idolatrous persecutor, a foreign king, a tyrant and usurper of their liberties, yet, in respect they had once received and acknowledged him for their king, he not only commandeth them to obey him, but even to pray for his prosperity—adjoining the reason to it: because in his prosperity stood their peace.

And under the evangel, that king whom Paul bids the Romans obey and serve for conscience' sake[4] was Nero, that bloody tyrant, an infamy to his age and a monster to the world, being also an idolatrous persecutor, as the king of Babel was. If, then, idolatry and defection from God, tyranny over their people, and persecution of the saints for their profession' sake, hindered not the spirit of God to command His people, under all highest pain, to give them all due and hearty obedience for conscience' sake, giving to Caesar that which was Caesar's, and to God that which was God's, as Christ saith . . .[5] what shameless presumption is it to any Christian people nowadays to claim to that unlawful liberty which God refused to His own peculiar and chosen people?

Shortly, then, to take up in two or three sentences, grounded upon all these arguments out of the law of God, the duty and allegiance of the people to their lawful king: their obedience, I say, ought to be to him as to God's lieutenant in earth, obeying his commands in all thing (except directly against God) as the commands of God's minister, acknowledging him a judge set by God over them, having power to judge them but to be judged only by God, whom-to only he must give account of his judgment; fearing him as their judge, loving him as their father, praying for him as their protector; for his continuance if he be good; for his amendment if he be wicked; following and obeying his lawful commands; eschewing and flying his fury in his unlawful, without resistance, but by sobs and tears to God, according to that

3. Jeremiah 27:8.
4. Romans 13.
5. Matthew 22:21.

sentence used in the primitive Church in the time of the persecution: *Preces et lachrymae sunt arma ecclesiae.*[6]

The kings . . . in Scotland were before any estates or ranks of men within the same, before any parliaments were holden or laws made; and by them was the land distributed (which at the first was whole theirs), states erected and decerned [i.e., determined, delimited], and forms of government devised and established. And so it follows, of necessity, that the kings were the authors and makers of the laws, and not the laws of the kings. . . . And according to these fundamental laws already alleged, we daily see that in the Parliament (which is nothing else but the head court of the king and his vassals) the laws are but craved by his subjects and only made by him at their rogation and with their advice. For albeit the king makes daily statutes and ordinances, enjoining such pains thereto as he thinks meet, without any advice of Parliament or estates; yet it lies in the power of no Parliament to make any kind of law or statute without his scepter be to it, for giving it the force of a law. . . .

The same ground of the king's right over all the land and subjects thereof remaineth alike in all other free monarchies, as well as in this. For when the bastard of Normandy came into England and made himself king,[7] was it not by force and with a mighty army? Where he gave the law and took none; changed the laws; inverted the order of government; set down the strangers his followers in many of the old possessors' rooms—as at this day well appeareth: a great part of the gentlemen in England being come of the Norman blood, and their old laws, which to this day they are ruled by, are written in his language, and not in theirs. And yet his successors have with great happiness enjoyed the crown to this day. . . .

As ye see it manifest that the king is overlord of the whole land, so is he master over every person that inhabiteth the same, having power over the life and death of every one of them. For although a just prince will not take the life of any of his subjects without a clear law, yet the same laws whereby he taketh them are made by himself or his predecessors. And so the power flows always from himself. As by daily experience we see, good and just princes will from time to time make new laws and statutes, adjoining the penalties to the breakers thereof, which before the law was made had been no crime to the subject to have committed.

Not that I deny the old definition of a king and a law, which makes the king to be a speaking law, and the law a dumb king. For certainly a king that

6. "Prayers and tears are the weapons of the Church."
7. William, Duke of Normandy, became William I of England after the battle of Hastings in 1066.

governs not by his law can neither be accountable to God for his administration, nor have a happy and established reign. For albeit it be true that I have at length proved, that the king is above the law, as both the author and giver of strength thereto, yet a good king will not only delight to rule his subjects by the law, but even will conform himself in his own actions thereunto, always keeping that ground that the health of the commonwealth be his chief law. . . . Although I have said a good king will frame all his actions to be according to the law, yet he is not bound thereto but of his goodwill and for good example giving to his subjects.

It is casten up by divers that employ their pens upon apologies for rebellions and treasons, that every man is born to carry such a natural zeal and duty to his commonwealth, as to his mother, that seeing it so rent and deadly wounded as whiles it will be by wicked and tyrannous kings, good citizens will be forced, for the natural zeal and duty they owe to their own native country, to put their hand to work for freeing their commonwealth from such a pest.

Whereunto I give two answers. First, it is a sure axiom in theology, that evil should not be done that good may come of it. The wickedness, therefore, of a king can never make them that are ordained to be judged by him, to become his judges. And if it be not lawful to a private man to revenge his private injury upon his private adversary (since God hath only given the sword to the magistrate), how much less is it lawful to the people, or any part of them (who all are but private men; the authority being always with the magistrate, as I have already proved), to take upon them the use of the sword, whom-to it belongs not, against the public magistrate, whom-to only it belongeth.

Next, in place of relieving the commonwealth out of distress (which is their only excuse and color) they shall heap double distress and desolation upon it, and so their rebellion shall procure the contrary effects that they pretend it for. For a king cannot be imagined to be so unruly and tyrannous but the commonwealth will be kept in better order, notwithstanding thereof, by him than it can be by his way-taking. For first, all sudden mutations are perilous in commonwealths, hope being thereby given to all bare men to set up themselves and fly with other men's feathers, the reins being loosed, to all the insolencies that disordered people can commit, by hope of impunity because of the looseness of all things. . . .

The second objection they ground upon the curse that hangs over the commonwealth where a wicked king reigneth. And, say they, there cannot be a more acceptable deed in the sight of God, nor more dutiful to their commonweal, than to free the country of such a curse, and vindicate to them their liberty, which is natural to all creatures to crave.

Whereunto, for answer, I grant indeed that a wicked king is sent by God for a curse to his people and a plague for their sins. But that it is lawful for them to shake off that curse at their own hand which God hath laid on them, that I deny, and may do so justly. . . . Patience, earnest prayers to God, and amendment of their lives, are the only lawful means to move God to relieve them of that heavy curse. As for vindicating to themselves their own liberty, what lawful power have they to revoke to themselves again those privileges which, by their own consent before, were so fully put out of their hands? For if a prince cannot justly bring back again to himself the privileges once bestowed by him or his predecessors upon any state or rank of his subjects; much less may the subjects reave [i.e., rob] out of the prince's hand that superiority which he and his predecessors have so long brooked over them. . . .

Not that by all this former discourse of mine, and apology for kings, I mean that whatsoever errors and intolerable abominations a sovereign prince commit, he ought to escape all punishment; as if thereby the world were only ordained for kings, and they, without controlment, to turn it upside down at their pleasure. But, by the contrary, by remitting them to God (who is their only ordinary judge) I remit them to the sorest and sharpest schoolmaster that can be devised for them. For the further a king is preferred by God above all other ranks of men, and the higher that his seat is above theirs, the greater is his obligation to his maker. And therefore, in case he forget himself (his unthankfulness being in the same measure of height) the sadder and sharper will his correction be; and according to the greatness of the height he is in, the weight of his fall will recompense the same. . . . Neither is it ever heard that any king forgets himself towards God, or in his vocation, but God with the greatness of the plague revengeth the greatness of his ingratitude.

Neither think I by the force and argument of this my discourse so to persuade the people that none will hereafter be raised up and rebel against wicked princes. But remitting to the justice and providence of God to stir up such scourges as pleaseth Him for punishment of wicked kings (who made the very vermin and filthy dust of the earth to bridle the insolency of proud Pharaoh), my only purpose and intention in this treatise is to persuade, as far as lieth in me, by these sure and infallible grounds, all such good Christian readers . . . to keep their hearts and hands free from such monstrous and unnatural rebellions, whensoever the wickedness of a prince shall procure the same at God's hands. That when it shall please God to cast such scourges of princes and instruments of his fury in the fire, ye may stand up with clean hands and unspotted consciences, having proved yourselves in all your actions true Christians towards God and dutiful subjects towards your king; having remitted the judgment and punishment of all his wrongs to Him whom-to only of right it appertaineth.

The Coronation Oath
of James I, 1603

ARCHBISHOP: SIR, will you grant and keep and by your oath confirm to the people of England the laws and customs to them granted by the kings of England your lawful and religious predecessors? And namely the laws, customs and franchises granted to the clergy and to the people by the glorious king, St. Edward, your predecessor [according and conformable to the laws of God and true profession of the gospel established in this kingdom, and agreeing to the prerogatives of the kings thereof, and to the ancient customs of this realm]?[1]

KING: I grant and promise to keep them.

ARCHBISHOP: Will you keep peace and godly agreement entirely, according to your power, both to God, the holy church, the clergy and the people?

KING: I will keep it.

ARCHBISHOP: Will you, to your power, cause law, justice and discretion in mercy and truth to be executed in all your judgments?

KING: I will.

ARCHBISHOP: Sir, will you grant to hold and keep the laws and rightful customs which the commonalty of your kingdom have, and to defend and uphold them to the honor of God, so much as in you lie?

KING: I grant and promise so to do.

---

1. The section within square brackets appears in three of the six surviving manuscript accounts of James's coronation ceremony, but not in the other three. Assuming that these words were added, it seems probable that they were directed against the claims of the Papacy rather than the liberties of James's newly acquired subjects.

Common Law
and the
English Constitution

❧

E ven though Renaissance influences were increasingly powerful in Shakespeare's England, they did not totally sweep away older traditions. The prevailing assumptions about the limited nature of English monarchy and the existence of constitutional conventions guaranteeing the rights of the subject derived in large part from the common law, which was itself an inheritance from the Middle Ages. Common lawyers were taught their craft through the study of precedents, which meant that for them the past was ever-present, and they regarded the writings of great medieval English jurists such as Henry de Bracton and Sir John Fortescue not simply as authoritative and worthy of reverence but also as immediately relevant to their own day.

Sir John Fortescue:
De Laudibus Legum Angliae

Sir John Fortescue was Chief Justice of England in the mid–fifteenth century. Caught up in the Wars of the Roses, he adhered to the Lancastrians and accompanied Queen Margaret and her son, Prince Edward, into exile in Burgundy. When they returned to England with an army in 1471, Fortescue again went with them, but the brief restoration to power of Margaret's husband, Henry VI, ended with the Lancastrian defeat at Tewkesbury. Prince Edward was killed in battle, and both Margaret and Fortescue were captured. With the Lancastrian cause in total eclipse, Fortescue made his peace with the new Yorkist sovereign, Edward IV, and entered his service.

Fortescue's best-known work, the *De Laudibus Legum Angliae,* was probably composed during his exile in 1468–70, and it circulated widely in manuscript until it was eventually printed in 1537. It takes the form of a dialogue between Fortescue, the "Chancellor," and Prince Edward, Henry VI's son and prospective heir, in which Fortescue instructs his future sovereign on the nature of his responsibilities and discusses the origins of political communities. These were of two main sorts, according to Fortescue. The first consisted of absolute monarchies, in which the ruler's will was law: as witness Goneril, in *King Lear,* who claimed, after defeating her father and sister, "The laws are mine. . . . Who can arraign me?" (V.iii). The second was made up of constitutional monarchies, such as England, which originated from agreements freely entered into and were therefore governed not by the arbitrary will of the ruler but by those laws to which the subjects had given their assent.

The great importance of the common law in securing the rights of the subject was not lost on Tudor writers. The very first "tragedy" in that popular compilation of stories about the fall of illustrious men and women known as *The Mirror for Magistrates* is that of Robert Tresilian, Chief Justice of England under Richard II. Tresilian and "other his fellows" were highly regarded for their understanding of the law—"in the common law our skill was so profound"—but they allowed themselves to become the King's creatures and rendered judgments that were "always to his profit where any word might sound." As a consequence, "the subject was not sure / Of life, land, nor goods, but at the Prince's will." When the people rose in revolt, Tresilian was accused of "misconstruing the laws and expounding them to serve the Prince's affections," and for this heinous offense he was "damned to the gallows."

Tudor writers were also aware of another threat to law, that came not from the ruler but from overmighty subjects who rejected the constraints it imposed upon their freedom of action. Shakespeare, for instance, when he dealt with the Wars of the Roses, began with the bickering of the Earls of Somerset and Suffolk, who acknowledged no limits upon their ambition. In Suffolk's words "I have been a truant in the law / And never yet could frame my will to it, / And therefore frame the law unto my will." (*King Henry VI, Part One*, II.iv.)

Although Fortescue had been involved in the Wars of the Roses, his principal concern in *De Laudibus Legum Angliae* was with the danger of tyranny. To buttress his arguments in favor of constitutional monarchy he makes extensive references to the Bible and to English history. He also displays a knowledge of Aristotle and other authorities, but his acquaintance with these was almost certainly at second hand, through one or more of the collections of philosophical maxims that were so popular in his own day. Renaissance humanists prided themselves on bypassing such unreliable compilations and returning to the originals, but Fortescue may serve as a reminder that classical learning was not unknown to the Middle Ages, and that the influence of Aristotle, albeit at several removes, was exerting a powerful sway even before the humanists appeared on the scene.

From *De Laudibus Legum Angliae*

CHANCELLOR: The next thing, my Prince, at which you seem to hesitate, shall with the same ease be removed and answered: that is, whether you ought to apply yourself to the study of the laws of England or to that of the civil laws, [1] for that the opinion is with them everywhere, in preference to all other human laws.

Let not this difficulty, sir, give you any concern. A King of England cannot, at his pleasure, make any alterations in the laws of the land, for the nature of his government is not only regal but political. Had it been merely regal, he would have a power to make what innovations and alterations he pleased in the laws of the kingdom, impose tallages [i.e., taxes] and other hardships upon the people, whether they would or no, without their consent—which sort of government the civil laws point out when they declare *Quod principi placuit legis habet vigorem.* [2] But it is much otherwise with a king whose government is political, because he can neither make any alteration or change in the laws of the realm without the consent of the subject, nor burthen them against their wills with strange impositions; so that a people governed by such laws as are made by their own consent and approbation enjoy their properties securely and without the hazard of being deprived of them, either by the king or any other.

The same things may be effected under an absolute prince, provided he do not degenerate into the tyrant. Of such a prince, Aristotle, in the third of his *Politics,* says, "It is better for a city to be governed by a good man than by good laws." [3] But because it does not always happen that the person presiding over a people is so qualified, St. Thomas, in the book which he wrote to the King of Cyprus *(De Regimine Principum)* [4] wishes that a kingdom could be so instituted as that the king might not be at liberty to tyrannize over his people; which only comes to pass in the present case—that is, when the sovereign power is restrained by political laws. Rejoice therefore, my good Prince, that such is the law of that kingdom to which you are to inherit, because it will afford both to yourself and subjects the greatest security and satisfaction.

PRINCE: How comes it to pass, my Chancellor, that one king may govern his subjects in such an absolute manner, and a power in the same extent is unlawful for another king? Seeing kings are equal in dignity, I am surprised that they are not likewise equal in the extent and exercise of their power.

CHANCELLOR: I have sir . . . sufficiently made appear that the king who governs by political rules has no less power than him who governs his subjects at his mere will and pleasure. Yet that the authority which each has

1. The *Lex Civile* or "civil law" of classical Rome was known to late medieval and Renaissance Europe through the survival of the *Institutes* and *Digest* commissioned by the Emperor Justinian in the sixth century A.D.

2. The prince's will has the force of law.

3. Aristotle *Politics* iii.

4. One of the two works that bear the title *De Regimine Principum* was written by St. Thomas Aquinas. It was subsequently extended by his pupil, Ptolemy of Lucca, whose views were significantly different from Aquinas's.

over their subjects is vastly different, I never disputed it. The reason of which I shall, in the best manner I can, endeavor to explain.

Formerly, men who excelled in power, being ambitious of honor and renown, subdued the nations which were round about them by force of arms. They obliged them to a state of servitude, absolutely to obey their commands, which they established into laws as the rules of their government. By long continuance and suffering whereof, the people, though under such subjection, finding themselves protected by their governors from the violence and insults of others, submitted quietly to them, thinking it better to be under the protection of some government than to be continually exposed to the ravages of everyone who should take it into their heads to oppress them. From this original and reason, some kingdoms date their commencement; and the persons invested with the power during such their government, *a regendo* (from ruling), assumed and usurped to themselves the name of *Rex* (ruler or king), and their power obtained the name of "regal". . . . And thus, if I mistake not, most excellent Prince, you have had a true account how those kingdoms first began where the government is merely "regal." I shall now endeavor to trace the original of those kingdoms where the form of government is "political," that so, the first rise and beginning of both being known, you may more easily discern the reason of that wide difference which occasioned your question.

Saint Augustine, in his book *De Civitate Dei*, has it "that a people is a body of men joined together in society by a consent of right, by an union of interests, and for promoting the common good."[5] Not that a people so met together in society can properly be called a body, as long as they continue without a head; for as in the body natural, the head being cut off, we no longer call it a body, but a trunk, so a community without a head to govern it cannot in propriety of speech be called a body politic. Wherefore the philosopher, in the first of his *Politics*, says "Whensoever a multitude is formed into one body or society, one part must govern, and the rest be governed."[6] Wherefore it is absolutely necessary, where a company of men combine and form themselves into a body politic, that some one should preside as the governing principal, who goes usually under the name of "King." In this order, as out of an embryo, is formed a human body, with one head to govern and control it; so, from a confused multitude, is formed a regular kingdom, which is a sort of mystical body, with one person, as the head, to guide and govern.

And as in the natural body (according to the philosopher) the heart is the first thing which lives, having in it the blood which it transmits to all the

5. St. Augustine *De Civitate Dei*, book 19, 24.
6. Aristotle *Politics* i.

other members, thereby imparting life and growth and vigor; so in the body politic the first thing which lives and moves is the intention of the people, having in it the blood—that is, the prudential care and provision for the public good—which it transmits and communicates to the head, as the principal part, and to all the rest of the members of the said body politic, whereby it subsists and is invigorated.

The law, under which the people is incorporated, may be compared to the nerves or sinews of the body natural. For as by these the whole frame is fitly joined together and compacted, so is the law that ligament (to go back to the truest derivation of the word *lex* from *ligando*) by which the body politic and all its several members are bound together and united in one entire body. And as the bones and all the other members of the body preserve their functions and discharge their several offices by the nerves, so do the members of the community by the law. And as the head of the body natural cannot change its nerves or sinews, cannot deny to the several parts their proper energy, their due proportion and aliment of blood, neither can a king who is the head of the body politic change the laws thereof, nor take from the people what is theirs by right, against their consents.

Thus you have, sir, the formal institution of every political kingdom from whence you may guess at the power which a king may exercise with respect to the laws and the subject. For he is appointed to protect his subjects in their lives, properties, and laws. For this very end and purpose he has the delegation of power from the people; and he has no just claim to any other power but this. Wherefore, to give a brief answer to that question of yours concerning the different powers which kings claim over their subjects: I am firmly of opinion that it arises solely from the different natures of their original institution.

The Governance of England

The Governance of England, almost certainly Fortescue's last work, was probably composed after he entered Edward IV's service in 1471: indeed, it may have been intended as a book of advice to the new sovereign. Fortescue was a conservative, in the sense that he believed the English system of limited monarchy, which was the product of a long history, should not be changed. He was aware from his travels in France that the French kings were consolidating their power by undermining the customary rights and privileges as well as the representative institutions which that country, in common with England, had hitherto enjoyed. He wanted to demonstrate to Edward IV that in his case no such fundamental alteration was necessary. In fact, it would be harmful, since it would almost certainly impoverish and enfeeble the English people and turn Edward into a mere king of beggars.

Fortescue showed originality in linking the social and economic health of a country with its type of government. But the major impact of his book came through his distinction between a *dominium regale,* in which the king was supreme, and a *dominium politicum et regale,* in which the royal power was constrained by law. There was nothing particularly novel about these concepts. Royal authority was a fact of contemporary life, but so also were feudal law and conventions that checked and balanced it. What Fortescue did was to give lucid and persuasive expression to a view of the English constitution that not only his contemporaries but also later generations found immensely appealing and persuasive. It provided one of the principal buttresses for the assertive patriotism that informs so much English writing during the Renaissance period.

From *The Governance of England*

There be two kinds of kingdoms, of the which that one is a lordship called in Latin *dominium regale,* and that other is called *dominium politicum et regale.* And they diversen in that the first king may rule his people by such laws as he maketh himself. And therefore he may set upon them *tailles*[7] and other impositions, such as he will himself, without their assent. The second king may not rule his people by other laws than such as they assenten unto. And therefore he may set upon them none impositions without their own assent.

And howsobeit that the French king reigneth upon his people *dominio regale,* yet Saint Louis,[8] sometime king there, nor any of his progenitors set never *tailles* or other imposition upon the people of that land without the assent of the three estates,[9] which when they be assembled be like to the court of the Parliament in England. And this order kept many of his successors into late days, [when] that Englandmen made such war in France that the three estates durst not come together. And then, for that cause and for great necessity which the French king had of good for the defense of that land, he took upon him to set *tailles* and other impositions upon the commons without the assent of the three estates; but yet he would not set any such charges, nor hath set, upon the nobles, for fear of rebellion.

7. *Tailles* were direct taxes levied by the king of France on his subjects.
8. Louis IX (St. Louis) was King of France from 1226 to 1270. He was canonized in 1297.
9. i.e., the spiritual peers, the temporal peers, and the representatives of the commonalty, the third estate.

And because the commons there, though they have grudged, have not rebelled or be hardy to rebel, the French kings have yearly sithence set such charges upon them, and so augmented the same charges, as the same commons be so improverished and destroyed that they are scarcely able to live. They drink water, they eat apples, with bread right brown made of rye. They eat no flesh but if it be right seldom a little lard, or of the entrails and heads of beasts slain for the nobles and merchants of the land. They wear no wool, but if it be a poor coat under their uttermost garment, made of great canvas and called a frock. Their hose be of like canvas and pass not their knee, wherefore they be gartered and their thighs bare. Their wives and children go barefoot; they may in no other wise live. For some of them that were wont to pay to his lord for his tenement, which he hireth by the year, a crown, payeth now to the king, over that crown, five crowns. Wherethrough they be obliged by necessity so to work, labor and grub in the ground for their sustenance that their nature is wasted and the kind of them brought to naught. They go crooked and be feeble, not able to fight nor to defend the realm; nor they have weapon, nor money to buy them weapon withal. But verily they live in the most extreme poverty and misery, and yet dwell they in one the most fertile realm of the world . . . Lo, this is the fruit of his [the French king's] *jus regale*.

But, blessed be God, this land [of England] is ruled under a better law, and therefore the people thereof be not in such penury nor hereby hurt in their persons, but they be wealthy and have all things necessary to the sustenance of nature. Wherefore they be mighty, and able to resist the adversaries of his realm, and to beat other realms that do or would do them wrong. Lo, this is the fruit of *jus politicum et regale* under which we live. . . . It is the king's honor, and also his office, to make his realm rich; and it is dishonor when he hath but a poor realm, of which men will say that he reigneth but upon beggars. Yet it were much greater dishonor if he found his realm rich and then made it poor. And it were also greatly against his conscience, that ought to defend them and their goods, if he took from them their goods without lawful cause; from the infamy whereof, God defend our king and give him grace to agument his realm in riches, wealth, and prosperity, to his perpetual laud and worship.

Sir Edward Coke:
Reports

Under Elizabeth and James I, Sir Edward Coke became the outspoken champion of Fortescue's view of England as a community of free men and women secured in their rights by a common law that embodied the accumulated wisdom of countless generations of their forebears. Born in 1552, Coke received his legal training at the Inns of Court, which he described as "the most famous university for profession of law only, or of any one human science, that is in the world." He quickly made a name for himself through his prodigious capacity for hard work and his excellent memory, which enabled him to marshal precedents from five hundred years of English history and use them to resolve the problems of his own day. Queen Elizabeth made him first her Solicitor General and subsequently her Attorney General, and in 1601 he entertained her at his great house at Stoke Poges in Buckinghamshire. Under James I, Coke rose to the top of the legal profession as Chief Justice of the Court of King's Bench, but his claim that the judges should act as independent arbiters between the King and his people led to a stormy relationship with his new sovereign. James believed that the judges should be, in Bacon's phrase, "lions under the throne," upholding the royal authority instead of constantly calling it into question, which he accused Coke of doing. In the end, James lost patience and took the almost-unprecedented step of dismissing his Chief Justice from office.

Coke was over sixty by this time and James doubtless assumed that he would retire from public life. But the stubborn and cantankerous lawyer had no such intention. Coke had been a member of Parliament in Elizabeth's reign and served as Speaker of the House of Commons in

1592–93. Following his abrupt departure from the judicial bench, he again secured election to the Lower House and almost immediately became one of its unofficial spokesmen, foremost in criticizing aspects of royal policy or the conduct of royal officials that he believed to be against the public interest. At a time when European monarchies were moving in an absolutist direction, Coke followed the example of Fortescue—whom he frequently quoted—by stressing the need for England to adhere to its traditional constitution. His moment of triumph came in 1628 when he masterminded the parliamentary campaign that effectively compelled Charles I to accept the Petition of Right—a latter-day Magna Carta, which brought the royal prerogative under formal restraint.

If Coke had done nothing more, he would be remembered as a formidable judge and a great parliamentarian. But his passion for the law, and his recognition of the need to make it more coherent, led him to publish a series of *Reports* that recorded the legal arguments used in important cases and listed the relevant precedents. The first volume of the *Reports* was published in 1600, and ten more appeared before his death in 1634. In the preface to Book 1, from which an extract is given below, Coke uses language that recalls not only Fortescue but also Shakespeare to praise Queen Elizabeth for her commitment to the rule of law, which enabled her subjects to enjoy peace and security while the inhabitants of less fortunate lands were enduring the violence of arbitrary power. The second extract sums up Coke's belief that laws were the quintessence of human wisdom, while the third records his conviction, which he derived from Fortescue, that the origins of the common law were as old as England itself.

"Bless God for Queen Elizabeth"

There is no jewel in the world comparable to learning; no learning so excellent both for Prince and subject as knowledge of laws; and no knowledge of any laws (I speak of human) so necessary for all estates and for all causes concerning goods, lands, or life as the common laws of England. If the beauty of other countries be faded and wasted with bloody wars, thank God for the admirable peace wherein this realm hath long flourished under the due administration of these laws. If thou readest of the tyranny of other nations, wherein powerful Will and Pleasure stands for Law and Reason, and where, upon conceit of mislike, men are suddenly poisoned or otherwise murdered and never called to answer, praise God for the justice of thy gracious sovereign, who (to the world's admiration) governeth her people by God's goodness in peace and prosperity by these laws, and punisheth not the greatest offender—no, though his offense be *Crimen Laesae Majestatis*, Treason against her Sacred Person—but by the just and equal proceedings of Law.

If in other kingdoms the Laws only seem to govern, but the judges had rather misconstrue Law, and do injustice, than displease the king's humor . . . bless God for Queen Elizabeth, whose continual charge to her justice, agreeable with her ancient laws, is that for no commitment under the great or privy seal, writs or letters,[1] common right be disturbed or delayed. And if any such commitment (upon untrue surmises) should come, that the justices of her laws should not therefore cease to do right in any point. And this agreeth with the ancient law of England, declared by the Great Charter and spoken in the person of the king: *Nulli vendemus, nulli negabimus aut differemus justitiam, vel Rectum.*[2]

"The Wisdom of Those That Were before Us"

We are but of yesterday (and therefore had need of the wisdom of those that were before us) and our days upon the earth are but as a shadow in respect of the old ancient days and times past, wherein the laws have been by the wisdom of the most excellent men, in many successions of ages, by long and continual experience (the trial of right and truth) fined and refined, which no one man (being of so short a time), albeit he had in his head the wisdom of all the men in the world, in any one age could ever have effected or attained unto. And therefore . . . no man ought to take upon him to be wiser than the laws. Secondly, in respect of our forefathers . . . they shall teach thee and tell thee and shall utter the words of their heart without all equivocation or mental reservation. They (I say) that cannot be daunted with fear of any power above them, nor be dazzled with the applause of the popular about them, nor fretted with any discontentment (the matter of opposition and contradiction) within them; but shall speak the words of their heart without all affection or infection whatsoever.

1. Writs and letters authenticated by the great seal or the privy seal were used by the government to enforce its commands.
2. This is clause 40 of Magna Carta: "To no-one will we sell, to no-one will we deny or delay, justice or right."

"These Ancient and Excellent Laws of England"

It doth appear most plain by successive authority in history what I have positively affirmed out of record, that the grounds of our common laws at this day were beyond the memory or register of any beginning, and the same which the Norman Conqueror then found within this realm of England. The laws that William the Conqueror swore to observe were *bonae et approbatae antiquae regni leges*, that is, the laws of this kingdom were in the beginning of the Conqueror's reign good, approved, and ancient. . . .

The certain and continual practice of the common laws of England soon after the Conquest, even in the time of King Henry I, the Conqueror's son (which almost was within the smoke of that fiery conquest) and continued ever since, do plainly demonstrate that these laws were before the days of William the Conqueror. For it had not been possible to have brought the laws to such a perfection as they were in the reign of King Henry II succeeding, if the same had been so suddenly brought in or instituted by the Conqueror. Of which laws, this I will say: that there is no human law within the circuit of the whole world, by infinite degrees, so apt and profitable for the honorable, peaceful, and prosperous government of this kingdom as these ancient and excellent laws of England be.

Social Graces—
Conduct and
Language

~❦~

Baldassare Castiglione's *The Book of the Courtier* established an
ideal for the Elizabethan gentleman who hoped to gain the grace
and favor of his queen. It described the social, athletic, and martial
abilities necessary for one who sought advancement in a sophisticated
and competitive society: in the words of its English translator, the book
is "a storehouse of most necessary implements for the conversation, use,
and training up of man's life with courtly demeanors." Ease, charm,
appreciation of feminine beauty, and a seeming negligence that deliberately hides the courtier's skills are essential elements of his fictional self-
image, his public persona. In this way, playing the modest amateur, he
can delight his audience when he unexpectedly displays the talents of a
professional.

Thomas Wilson in his *Arte of Rhetorique* also recommends much
that can be found in Castiglione—the need for humor, the importance
of insinuation and suggestion, the ways that role-playing or artifically
conceived self-presentations can affect one's audience. And his manual
may have encouraged Puttenham in the *The Arte of English Poesie*, for
Wilson offers a model and argues for principles that Puttenham later
makes his own. From Castiglione, Puttenham probably derived the
premise that a true poet can only be fashioned from a true courtier, that
action and behavior are reflected in speech and writing: "the good

maker or poet who is in decent speech and good terms to describe all things . . . ought to know the comeliness of an action as well as of a word." And all three men are in agreement that civilization and culture are reflected by the beauty and pleasure of life, that art is best when, as Puttenham phrases it, the "artificial [is] well dissembled," and that a courtier's "feats of . . . language and utterance . . . [owe as much to] nature to be suggested and uttered as by art to be polished and re-formed."

Finally, all three writers direct their efforts toward the same end: to fashion a courtier whose service to his prince will advance both himself and the state. And it is toward a career as counselor, diplomat, or statesman that all his training and education are ultimately directed.

Baldassare Castiglione, *The Courtier*

Through the witty conversations of an elegant and sophisticated gathering, *The Book of the Courtier* gradually builds up a picture of the perfect Renaissance aristocrat. But rather than presenting the sort of philosophic ideal that a classical writer might establish through a dialogue on ethics and moral behavior, Castiglione's speakers are concerned with social deportment. For them, good and bad are matters of grace and style. Manners, charm, poise, and such virtues as knowing dancing and languages have taken preeminence as the most desirable aspects of conduct. The pleasures of such a life, the high-spiritedness of this society, and particularly the importance of love, which provides the spiritual and emotional link between man and woman and between humanity and God, are all amply demonstrated. Castiglione's presentation is so winning, persuasive, and enjoyable that his model, the court at Urbino, became the model for the rest of Europe and England. And, indeed, the court at Urbino was for Castiglione himself as close to perfection as human society could ever attain.

Born near the city of Mantua, Baldassare Castiglione (1478–1529), was a relative of the Gonzagas, the ruling family there. Educated at Milan, where he studied Greek and Latin, he briefly entered the diplomatic service of the duke of Milan. In 1500, when the duke was taken to France as a prisoner, Castiglione returned to Mantua. Four years later, he attached himself to the court of Guidobaldo di Montefeltro, the duke of Urbino, who had married Elisabetta Gonzaga and who had inherited from his famous father a court, a library, and a government admired throughout Italy. Under the wise and cultured administration of Guidobaldo and his successor, his nephew Francesco Maria della Rovere, Castiglione passed his happiest years at Urbino—in fact, the conversations that make up *The Courtier* were imagined as taking place there in March 1507 when some attendants of Pope Julius II remained behind after a papal visit. Castiglione lived an active life pursuing his career as courtier, diplomat, and soldier. In 1524, charged with negotiating the differences between pope and emperor, he became papal representative for Clement VII to the Spanish court of the Emperor Charles V. But three years later, Rome was sacked by Charles's forces, the pope was taken prisoner, and Castiglione, duped by the intrigues and deceit of the Spanish court, was even accused of complicity. Francesco Maria della Rovere had been driven from Urbino during the period when Castiglione was writing *The Courtier*, and now, in 1527, the year before the book was to be published, Castiglione himself was accused of treason. Overwhelmed by shame and sorrow, he retired to Toledo, where he died.

In a letter to a friend Castiglione claimed that he wrote the book "in a few days," but in fact he worked at it from 1508 to 1516, even consulting with Pietro Bembo, the major speaker in Book 4. In keeping with the manners he recommends, Castiglione is understating his effort, making his achievement seem simple and easy; like his ideal courtier, he practices the art that conceals art. Castiglione also modestly reduces his own role in the book to that of reporter, for he does not present himself as a participant in the conversations that he relates.

These conversations, spread out over four evenings, are the heart of *The Courtier*. They are imagined as taking place during the regular evening activities at the ducal court among the various men and women one might find there:

> The manner of the gentlemen in the house was immediately after supper to assemble together where the Duchess was. Where among other recreations, music and dancing, which they used continually, sometime they propounded feat questions,[1] otherwhile they invented certain witty sports and pastimes, at the devise sometime of one, sometime of another. . . . At other times there arose other disputations of divers matters, or else jestings with prompt inventions. Many times they fell into purposes, (as we nowadays term them) where in this kind of talk and debating of matters, there was wondrous great pleasure on all sides because (as I have said) the house was replenished with most noble wits.

1. *feat questions:* intriguing issues for discussion and debate.

In this setting of great sophistication, culture, and refinement, the members of the court attempt "to shape in words a good courtier, specifying all such conditions and particular qualities as of necessity must be in him that deserveth this name." This theme is taken up in four books: in Book 1, they attempt to define the courtier's proper education, manners, and talents; in Book 2, they describe his training and conduct on the battlefield and at court "so that every possible thing may be easy to him, and all men wonder at him, and he at no man"; in Book 3 they turn their attention to women, describing "a gentlewoman of the palace so fashioned in all perfections as these lords have fashioned the perfect courtier"; and in Book 4, on the last night of their conversation, Pietro Bembo delivers his great defense of love, explaining its importance in the universe and its positive effects on humanity.

From these topics we can judge that Castiglione is not interested in moral problems or political dilemmas; ethics as a subject of philosophic concern receives scarcely any consideration. Attention instead is focused on the courtier's social values, on his personal achievements, and on the necessity of his acquiring a style of behavior that is courteous and graceful.

Castiglione's masterpiece, called "the golden book" by the Italians, was an instant success: more than one hundred editions were published by the end of the century, by which time it had been translated into Latin, French, Spanish, and English. Adopted by young men who hoped to win a place at court, it was the most respected of all manners-books. Sir Philip Sidney (1554–1586), who was for the Elizabethans the pattern of a perfect courtier, kept a copy of Castiglione in his pocket. His conduct reflected its influence. Sidney modestly denied any importance to his *Apology for Poetry* (c. 1579), claimed his famous sonnet sequence—indebted to Bembo's praise of love—was created only as an idle amusement, and supposedly wrote the *Arcadia* simply to please his sister. When he rode into battle at Zutphen, where he was mortally wounded because he negligently wore no leg-armor, Sidney was acting with the *sprezzatura*, the nonchalance and bravado, which mark him as a disciple of Castiglione.

For a number of reasons *The Courtier* made a powerful impression in England. It used humanist concepts derived from the writing of such classical authorities as Plato, Aristotle, Cicero, and Plutarch to define the role of the courtier and the education necessary for a diplomat. As a handbook for proper conduct on both social and political occasions, commenting on everything from dress to the display of skills in music and dancing, it made its recommendations not in a heavy-handed, didactic manner but indirectly through the witty banter of the participants. Moreover, the behavior and sophistication of these court members at Urbino demonstrated polite society at its finest: here was a model for civilized men and women everywhere. An English version even flourished in the last twenty years of the sixteenth century. Sir Philip Sidney's sister Mary, Countess of Pembroke, acted as patroness of a group of courtiers, poets, and clergymen, admirers of her late brother, who met informally at her home at Wilton. Praised as superior to Castiglione's original, the Countess's "kind of little court" was concerned not only with politics and personalities but also with religious issues: "Who hath read of the Duchess of Urbino may say the Italians wrote well. But who knows the Countess of Pembroke, I think hath cause to write better," noted Nicolas Breton, a popular writer of lyrics and religious allegories and a favorite at Wilton.

But it is the last section of Castiglione's book that may have had the most profound and lasting impact on its audience, for here the reader discovers how Platonic love could be translated from a philosophic concept to a literary one. Bembo's analysis, indebted to Plato's *Symposium* and colored by the writings of such fifteenth-century Florentine neoplatonists as Marsilio Ficino and Pico della Mirandola, traces the course by which one moves from human to divine love and in the process provided subject matter for playwrights and poets of the English Renaissance. The witty conversations, games, and dances of the members of the court in *Love's Labour's Lost* and in *Much Ado About Nothing* (1598) are indebted to the actions of their predecessors at Urbino. In *Twelfth Night* (1600), Viola, thinking of her own feelings for her employer, describes to her rival how a true lover suffers and acts. The intensity of her emotions and the conventionalized elements of her description—the willow cabin, the songs of condemned love, the persistence with which she would press her suit—give her words a lyrical persuasiveness that owes a heavy debt to Bembo's argument, as does her total dedication even to the point of self-sacrifice: "And I most jocund, apt, and willing, / To do you rest, a thousand deaths would die." (V.i.) And the lyric poems and sonnet sequences of Sidney, Spenser, and Michael Drayton that take as their subject matter the conflicting drives of soul and body, or of physical passion and sexual sublimation, or of ideal love were all influenced to some degree by Castiglione.

Even in the chronicle history plays we come to judge characters by Castiglione's precepts: Shakespeare's Hotspur in *Henry IV, Part One*, energetic, outspoken, high-principled, and brave, demonstrates serious failings for a courtier when he argues with a royal messenger, contradicts the king, loses patience with his elders, shows no taste for music, and fights when outnumbered. He is far too rough-and-ready, too unsubtle, too naive.

Finally, Castiglione's prose was itself highly regarded. In his collected observations on life and literature called *Timber, or Discoveries*, Ben Jonson praised *The Courtier* for the vigorousness, the "life and quickness" of its writing. By including "pithy sayings, similitudes, and conceits" as well as "allusions [to] some known history or other commonplace," Castiglione gives his style its "strength and sinews."

The English translator of *Il Cortegiano*, Thomas Hoby (1530–1566), served as a diplomat in the Protestant courts of Edward VI and Elizabeth. In fact, at his death he was the Queen's ambassador to France. During the reign of the Catholic Mary Tudor, Hoby fled England, and, while living in Italy, in the years from 1554 to 1556, completed his version of Castiglione's book. Published first in 1561, *The Courtier* was reprinted in 1577, 1588, and 1603.

What a Perfect Courtier Ought to Be

Then answered the Count[2]: . . . "I will have this our courtier therefore to be a gentleman born and of a good house. For it is a great deal less dispraise for him that is not born a gentleman to fail in the acts of virtue than for a gentleman. If he swerve from the steps his of ancestors, he staineth the name of his family. . . . The noble of birth count it a shame not to arrive at the least at the bounds of their predecessors set forth unto them. . . . Some there are born indued with such graces that they seem not to have been born but rather fashioned with the very hand of some god, and abound in all goodness both of body and mind. . . . And to give you an example, mark me the Lord Hippolytus d'Este, Cardinal of Ferrara;[3] he hath had so happy a birth, that his person, his countenance, his words, and all his gestures are so fashioned and compact with this grace that among the most ancient prelates, for all he is but young, he doth represent so grave an authority that a man would ween he were more meet to teach than needful to learn.

"Likewise in company with men and women of all degrees, in sporting, in laughing, and in jesting, he hath in him certain sweetness, and so comely

2. Count Lodovico da Canossa, thirty-one, a relative of the author who later became papal ambassador to England and France and Bishop of Bayeux.
3. Made a cardinal at fourteen by Pope Alexander VI, Ippolito (1479–1520) was the third son of Duke Ercole of Ferrara, a patron of Ludovico Ariosto, and a friend of Leonardo da Vinci.

demeanors, that who so speaketh with him, or yet beholdeth him, must needs bear him an affection forever. . . .

"The courtier, therefore, besides nobleness of birth, I will have him to be fortunate in this behalf, and by nature to have not only a wit and a comely shape of person and countenance, but also a certain grace and, as they say, a hue[4] that shall make him at the first sight acceptable and loving unto who so beholdeth him. . . . And to avoid envy and to keep company pleasantly with every man, let him do whatsoever other men do, so he decline not at any time from commendable deeds, but governeth himself with that good judgment that will not suffer him to enter into any folly. But let him laugh, dally, jest, and dance yet in such wise that he may always declare himself to be witty and discreet and everything that he doth or speaketh, let him do it with a grace."

Then answered the Lord Cesar:[5] . . . "If I do well bear in mind, me think, Count Lewis, you have this night oftentimes repeated that the courtier ought to accompany all his doings, gestures, demeanors, finally all his motions with a grace. And this, me think, ye put for a sauce to everything, without the which his other properties and good conditions were little worth. . . . I would fain know with what art, with what learning, and by what mean they shall compass this grace as well in the exercises of the body, wherein ye think it so necessary a matter, as in all other things that they do or speak."

. . . "Bound I am not," quoth the Count, "to teach you to have good grace nor anything else, saving only to show you what a perfect courtier ought to be. . . . But I, imagining with myself oftentimes how this grace cometh, leaving apart such as have it from above,[6] find one rule that is most general which in this part, me thinketh, taketh place in all things belonging to a man in word or deed above all other. And that is to eschew as much as a man may, and, as a sharp and dangerous rock, too much curiousness,[7] and, to speak a new word, to use in everything a certain disgracing to cover art withal, and seem whatsoever he doth and saith, to do it without pain and, as it were, not minding it. . . .[8] Therefore, that may be said to be a very art that appeareth not to be art, neither ought a man to put more diligence in any thing than in covering it,[9] for in case it be open, it loseth credit clean and maketh a man little set by."

4. *hue:* air.
5. Lord Cesar Gonzaga, about thirty-two, a relative of the duchess and of Castiglione, to whom he was also a close friend.
6. "such as have it from above": from birth.
7. *curiousness:* affectation.
8. Sir Philip Sidney modestly described his prose romance *The Arcadia* as "a trifle, and that but triflingly handled."
9. "covering it": hiding or concealing the effort.

The Lord Julian[10] answered, "There is no doubt but so excellent and perfect a courtier hath need to understand . . . not only to speak but also to write well."

"Nay, everyone shall understand him," answered the Count, "for fineness hindereth not the easiness of understanding. Neither will I have him to speak always in gravity, but of pleasant matters, of merry conceits, of honest devices, and of jests according to the time. . . . And when he shall then commune of a matter that is dark and hard, I will have him, both in words and sentences well pointed, to express his judgment, and to make every doubt clear and plain after a certain diligent sort without tediousness.

"Likewise, when he shall see time,[11] to have the understanding to speak with dignity and vehemency and to raise those affections which our minds have in them, and to inflame or stir them according to the matter, sometime with a simplicity of such meekness of mind that a man would ween nature herself spake to make them tender and, as it were, drunken with sweetness; and with such conveyance of easiness that who so heareth him may conceive a good opinion of himself and think that he also with very little ado might attain to that perfection, but when he cometh to the proof, shall find himself far wide."

The Lord Octavian[12] said: "I think . . . that the courtier, if he be of the perfection that Count Lewis and Sir Frederick have described him, may indeed be a good thing and worthy praise, but for all that not simply, nor of himself but for respect of that whereto he may be applied.

"For doubtless if the courtier with his nobleness of birth, comely behavior, pleasantness, and practice in so many exercises should bring forth no other fruit but to be such a one for himself, I would not think to come by this perfect trade of courtiership that a man should of reason bestow so much study and pains about it, as who so will compass it must do. But I would say rather that many of the qualities appointed him—as dancing, singing, and sporting—were lightness and vanity, and in a man of estimation rather to be dispraised than commended. . . .

"The end therefore of a perfect courtier, whereof hitherto nothing hath been spoken, I believe is to purchase him, by the means of the qualities which these lords have given him, in such wise the goodwill and favor of the prince he is in service withal, that he may break his mind to him and always inform him frankly of the truth of every matter meet for him to understand,

10. Giuliano de Medici, twenty-nine, son of Lorenzo the Magnificent. A close friend of Castiglione's, he was residing at the Court of Urbino during the period that his family was in exile from Florence (1494–1512).

11. *when he shall see time*: on appropriate occasions.

12. Lord Octavian Fregoso and his younger brother Sir Frederick were half-nephews of the Duke. Octavian was elected doge of Genoa in 1513 and later appointed governor of the city by Francis I.

without fear or peril to displease him. And when he knoweth his[13] mind is bent to commit anything unseemly for him, to be bold to stand with[14] him in it, and to take courage after an honest sort at the favor which he hath gotten him through his good qualities, to dissuade him from every ill purpose and to set him in the way of virtue. . . .

"And, therefore, in mine opinion, as music, sports, pastimes, and other pleasant fashions are, as a man would say, the flower of courtliness, even so is the training and helping forward of the prince to goodness, and the fearing him from evil, the fruit of it."

"A Little Discourse to Declare What Love Is"

In Book 4 the discussion focuses on the subject of love. The chief skeptic, Master Morello, thinks that love is only a dream, but Pietro Bembo (1470–1547) delivers a rhapsodic account of the lover that turns him into both a philosopher and a saint. Bembo derives his analysis of love from the poetry of his countrymen Dante (1265–1321) and Petrarch (1304–74) as well as from the writings of the Neoplatonist philosopher Marsilio Ficino (1433–99). In their interpretation, love is freed from a physical attraction and turned into an intellectual one. The process involves two elements of the human soul. The sensitive soul is aroused by physical beauty; its desire is to possess the beautiful object. This impulse may supplement but does not limit man's reactions. The higher part of his nature, his rational soul, is attracted by abstract beauty; it experiences an intellectual longing to unite with the beauty of another soul. Accepting the notion that all worldly beauty is a reflection of heavenly or spiritual beauty, Bembo argues that the beloved's perfection and remoteness, qualities that were once admired by medieval poets of courtly love, can ultimately lead one to contemplate disembodied beauty (or virtue) in its purest form. Once the soul has escaped its incorporation in a fallen body, "without any veil or cloud, she seeth the main sea of the pure heavenly beauty and receiveth it into her, and enjoyeth the sovereign happiness that cannot be comprehended of the senses."

Love is often compared to a stairway linking the sensual and earthly to the spiritual and heavenly. This metaphor, which originated in Plato's *Symposium* and was popularized through Ficino's writing on Platonic love and through Bembo's speech, had great staying power in English Renaissance literature: Sidney's youthful heroes, Pyrocles and Mus-

13. *his:* the prince's.
14. *stand with:* oppose.

idorus, discuss this notion in Book 1 of *Arcadia;* Lyly dramatizes the various levels of love in his play *Endymion;* and Jonson's Lovel, "a complete gentleman, a soldier, and a scholar," restates the whole argument in *The New Inn* (1629).

According to this conception, love is experienced by the rational soul as a desire to gain perfection, to join with higher forms, to unite with God. The beloved enables the poet to glimpse the soul under its fleshly covering; her beauty sets him on an upward path. Moreover, since the intellectual faculties have no physical embodiment, they are available to the soul after death. Intellectual love, then, can transcend mortality—its object is the eternal. Sensual love may change, but the love of the rational soul is fixed, permanent.

In his *Four Hymns,* Spenser incorporates many of these ideas, tracing the connections between love and beauty on earth and in heaven. In the two earthly hymns, love is distinguished from lust and inner from outer beauty. In the heavenly hymns, Christ is contrasted with Cupid, and Sapience, "the sovereigne darling of the Deity," with Venus. At the conclusion of the "Hymn to Heavenly Beauty," the speaker can:

> *Look at last up to that Soveraine Light.*
> *From whose pure beams al perfect Beauty springs,*
> *That kindleth love in every godly spright,*
> *Even the love of God, which loathing brings*
> *Of this vile world and these gay seeming things;*
> *With whose sweet pleasures being so possest,*
> *Thy straying thoughts henceforth forever rest.*

Many of the ideas in Bembo's speech also find expression in the lyric love poetry of the English Renaissance. Shakespeare adopts elements of this convention in Sonnet 69 when, addressing his beloved, he speaks of "the beauty of thy mind" and in Sonnet 116, when he claims that "the marriage of true minds" is unalterable, enduring "even to the edge of doom." Sidney can treat Platonic love ironically. In Sonnet 71 he points out that intellectual admiration for Stella does not ease his physical longing for her. He praises Stella as "perfection's heir / Thyself dost strive all minds that way to move," and he acknowledges that "thy beauty draws the heart to love, / As fast thy virtue bends that love to good." But in his closing line he admits, "Desire still cries, 'Give me some food!'" English writers of lyric poetry, often as interested in psychological truth as in literary convention, made rich and varied use of the tradition handed on to them by their Italian predecessors.

Then spake the Duchess:[15] "I am glad, Master Peter,[16] that you have not been much troubled in our reasonings this night, for now we may be the bolder to give you in charge to speak and to teach the courtier this so happy a love, which bringeth with it neither slander nor any inconveniency; for perhaps it shall be one of the necessariest and profitablest qualities that hitherto hath been given him. Therefore, speak of good fellowship, as much as you know therein.

Master Peter laughed and said: "I would be loath, madam, where I say that it is lawful for old men to love, it should be an occasion for the ladies to think me old. Therefore, hardly give ye this enterprise to another."

The Duchess answered: "You ought not to refuse to be counted old in knowledge, though ye be young in years. Therefore, say on, and excuse yourself no more."

. . . Then Master Peter after a while's silence, somewhat settling himself as though he should entreat upon a weighty matter, said thus: "My lords, to show that old men may love not only without slander but otherwhile more happily than young men, I must be enforced to make a little discourse to declare what love is, and wherein consisteth the happiness that lovers may have. Therefore I beseech you give the hearing with heedfulness, for I hope to make you understand that it were not unfitting for any man here to be a lover, in case he were fifteen or twenty years elder than M. Morello."[17]

And here, after they had laughed awhile, M. Peter proceeded. "I say, therefore, that according as it is defined of the wise men of old time, love is nothing else but a certain coveting to enjoy beauty; and, for so much as coveting longeth for nothing but for things known, it is requisite that knowledge go evermore before coveting, which of his own nature willeth the good, but of himself is blind and knoweth it not. Therefore hath nature so ordained that to every virtue of knowledge there is annexed a virtue of longing. And because in our soul there be three manner ways to know, namely, by sense, reason, and understanding: of sense there ariseth appetite or longing, which is common to us with brute beasts; of reason ariseth election or choice, which is proper to man; of understanding, by the which man may be partner with angels, ariseth will.

"Even as, therefore, the sense knoweth not but sensible matters, and that which may be felt, so the appetite or coveting only deserveth the same; and

15. Lady Elisabetta Gonzaga, thirty-six. She married Guidobaldo in 1489. He became an invalid before he was twenty, and since his poor health forced him to retire early, the Duchess acted as hostess for guests at the court.

16. Pietro Bembo, thirty-seven, a Venetian man of letters who lived at the court from 1506–12. He served as papal secretary to Leo X and became a cardinal in 1539.

17. Sigismondo Morello, the one older member of the group; Castiglione elsewhere refers to him as a musician.

even as the understanding is bent but to behold things that may be understood, so is that will only fed with spiritual goods.

"Man of nature endowed with reason, placed, as it were, in the middle between these two extremities, may through his choice inclining to sense or reaching to understanding, come nigh to the coveting, sometime of the one, sometime of the other part.

"In these sorts, therefore, may beauty be coveted, the general name wherefore may be applied to all things, either natural or artificial, that are framed in good proportion and due temper, as their nature beareth.

"But speaking of the beauty that we mean—which is only it that appeareth in bodies, and especially in the face of man, and moveth this fervent coveting which we call love—we will term it an influence of the heavenly bountifulness, the which, for all it stretcheth over all things that be created (like the light of the sun), yet when it findeth out a face well proportioned, and framed with a certain lively agreement of several colors, and set forth with lights and shadows, and with an orderly distance and limits of lines, thereinto it distilleth itself and appeareth most well favored and decketh out and lighteneth the subject where it shineth with a marvelous grace and glistering (like the sunbeams that strike against beautiful plate of fine gold wrought and set with precious jewels). So that it draweth unto it men's eyes with pleasure, and piercing through them imprinteth himself in the soul, and with an unwonted sweetness all to-stirreth her and delighteth, and setting her on fire maketh her to covet him.

"When the soul then is taken with coveting to enjoy this beauty as a good thing, in case she suffer herself to be guided with the judgment of sense, she falleth into most deep errors, and judgeth the body in which beauty is discerned to be the principal cause thereof: whereupon to enjoy it she reckoneth it necessary to join as inwardly as she can with that body, which is false.

"And therefore, who so thinketh in possessing the body to enjoy beauty, he is far deceived, and is moved to it, not with true knowledge by the choice of reason, but with false opinion by the longing of sense.[18] Whereupon the pleasure that followeth it is also false and of necessity full of errors. . . .

"These kind of lovers therefore love most unlucky, for either they never come by their covetings, which is a great unluckiness; or else, if they do come by them, they come by their hurt and end their miseries with other greater miseries. For both in the beginning and middle of this love, there is never other thing felt but afflictions, torments, griefs, pining, travail, so that to be wan, vexed with continual tears and sighs, to live with a discontented

18. *sense:* sensual desire.

mind, to be always dumb, or to lament, to covet death, in conclusion most unlucky are the properties which, they say, belong to lovers.[19]

"The cause therefore of this wretchedness in men's minds is principally sense, which in youthful age beareth most sway because the lustiness of the flesh and blood in that season addeth unto him even so much force as it withdraweth from reason. . . .

"Setting case therefore this to be so, which is most true, I say that the contrary chanceth to them of a more ripe age. For in case they, when the soul is not now so much weighed down with the bodily burden, and when the natural burning assuageth and draweth to a warmth,[20] if they be inflamed with beauty, and to it bend their coveting, guided by reasonable choice, they be not deceived, and possess beauty perfectly, and therefore through the possessing of it, always goodness ensueth to them because beauty is good, and consequently the true love of it is most good and holy and evermore bringeth forth good fruits in the souls of them that with the bridle of reason restrain the ill disposition of sense, the which old men can much sooner do than young.

"It is not therefore out of reason to say that old men may also love without slander and more happily than young men, taking notwithstanding this name old, not for the age at the pit's brink, nor when the canals of the body be so feeble that the soul cannot through them work her feats, but when knowledge in us is in his right strength.

"And I will not also hide from you: namely, that I suppose where sensual love in every age is naught, yet in young men it deserveth excuse, and perhaps in some case lawful,[21] for although it putteth them in afflictions, dangers, travails, and the unfortunateness that is said, yet are there many that to win them the goodwill of their ladies practice virtuous things, which for all they be not bent to a good end, yet are they good of themselves.

"And so of that much bitterness they pick out a little sweetness, and through the adversities which they sustain, in the end they acknowledge their error.

"As I judge therefore those young men that bridle appetites and love with reason to be godly, so do I hold excused such as yield to sensual love, whereunto they be so inclined through the weakness and frailty of man, so[22] they show therein meekness, courtesy, and prowess, and the other worthy conditions that these lords have spoken of. And when these youthful years be gone and past, leave it off clean, keeping aloof from this sensual coveting as

19. Bembo is describing the symptoms of love melancholy.
20. Cf *Hamlet* (III.iv.) where the prince tells his mother that at her age "the heyday in the blood is tame, it's humble / And waits upon the judgment."
21. *lawful*: is lawful.
22. *so*: so long as.

from the lowest step of the stairs by the which a man may ascend to true love.

"But in the case after they draw in years once, they reserve still in their cold heart the fire of appetites, and bring stout reason in subjection to feeble sense, it cannot be said how much they are to be blamed, for like men without sense they deserve with an everlasting shame to be put in the number of unreasonable living creatures, because the thoughts and ways of sensual love be far unfitting for ripe age."

. . . "Do you believe, Master Morello," quoth then Count Lewis, "that beauty is always so good a thing as Master Peter Bembo speaketh of?"

"Not I, in good sooth," answered Master Morello. "But I remember rather that I have seen many beautiful women of a most ill inclination, cruel and spiteful, and it seemeth that, in a manner, it happeneth always so, for beauty maketh them proud, and pride cruel."

Master Peter Bembo laughed and said, . . . "I say that beauty cometh of God and is like a circle, the goodness whereof is the center. And therefore, as there can be no circle without a center, no more can beauty be without goodness.

"Wherefore doth very seldom an ill soul dwell in a beautiful body. And therefore is the outward beauty a true sign of the inward goodness, and in bodies this comeliness is imprinted more and less, as it were, for a mark of the soul whereby she is outwardly known. . . .[23]

"The foul, therefore, for the most part be also evil, and the beautiful good. Therefore it may be said that beauty is a face pleasant, merry, comely, and to be desired for goodness; and foulness a face dark, uglesome, unpleasant, and to be shunned for ill. And in case you will consider all things, ye shall find that whatsoever is good and profitable hath also evermore the comeliness of beauty. . . .

"Therefore, beauty is the true monument and spoil[24] of the victory of the soul when she with heavenly influence beareth rule over martial and gross nature, and with her light overcometh the darkness of the body. . . .

"Because the influence of that beauty when it is present giveth a wondrous delight to the lover, and, setting his heart on fire, quickeneth and melteth certain virtues in a trance and congealed in the soul, . . . the soul taketh a delight, and with a certain wonder is aghast. And yet enjoyeth she it, and, as it were, astonished together with the pleasure, feeleth the fear and reverence that men accustomably have toward holy matters, and thinketh herself to be

23. According to Plato, virtue or inner beauty was reflected by outer or physical beauty. See, for example, the discussion in *Hamlet* (III.i.104ff) or the many references in *Richard III* to the correspondence between Richard's appearance and his true nature. The idea is often repeated in the poetry and drama of the period.
24. *spoil:* prize, reward.

in paradise. The lover, therefore, that considereth only the beauty in the body loseth this treasure and happiness. . . .

"And besides, through the virtue of imagination, he shall fashion with himself that beauty much more fair than it is in deed. But among these commodities, the lover shall find another yet far greater, in case he will take this love for a stair, as it were, to climb up to another far higher than it. The which he shall bring to pass, if he will go and consider with himself what a strait bond it is to be always in the trouble to behold the beauty of one body alone. And, therefore, to come out of this so narrow a room, he shall gather in his thought by little and little so many ornaments that meddling all beauty together he shall make a universal conceit, and bring the multitude of them to the unity of one alone, that is generally spread over all the nature of men. And thus shall he behold no more the particular beauty of one woman, but a universal, that decketh out all bodies. Whereupon being made dim with this greater light, he shall not pass upon[25] the lesser, and, burning in a more excellent flame, he shall little esteem it that he set great store by at the first. . . .

"When our courtier, therefore, shall be come to this point, although he may be called a good and happy lover, in respect of them that be drowned in the misery of sensual love, yet will I not have him to set his heart at rest, but boldly proceed farther, following the highway after his guide, that leadeth him to the point of true happiness. And thus, instead of going out of his wit with thought, as he must do that will consider the bodily beauty, he may come into his wit to behold the beauty that is seen with the eyes of the mind, which then begin to be sharp and thoroughly-seeing when the eyes of the body lose the flower of their sightliness. . . .

"Therefore, the soul, . . . waxed blind about earthly matters, is made most quick[26] of sight about heavenly. And otherwhile when the stirring virtues[27] of the body are withdrawn alone through earnest beholding, either fast bound through sleep, when she is not hindred by them, she feeleth a certain privy smell[28] of the right angel-like beauty, and, ravished with the shining of that light, beginneth to be inflamed, and so greedily followeth after, that in a manner she waxeth drunken and beside herself, for coveting to couple herself with it, having found, to her weening,[29] the footsteps of God in the beholding of whom, as in her happy end, she seeketh to settle herself. . . . Whereupon, not thoroughly satisfied with this benefit, love

25. *pass upon:* care for.
26. *quick:* eager.
27. *virtues:* powers.
28. *a certain privy smell*—a certain distant perfume.
29. *weening:* opinion.

giveth unto the soul a greater happiness. For like as through the particular beauty of one body he guideth her to the universal beauty of all bodies, even so in the least degree of perfection through particular understanding he guideth her to the universal understanding.

"Thus the soul kindled in the most holy fire of true heavenly love fleeth to couple herself with the nature of angels,[30] and not only clean forsaketh sense, but hath no more need of the discourse of reason, for, being changed into an angel, she understandeth all things that may be understood.[31] And without any veil or cloud she seeth the main sea of the pure heavenly beauty, receiveth it into her, and enjoyeth the sovereign happiness that cannot be comprehended of the senses. . . .

"Let us, therefore, bend all our force and thoughts of soul to this most holy light, that showeth us the way which leadeth to heaven; and after it, putting off the affections we were clad [in] at our coming down, let us climb up the stairs which at the lowermost step have the shadow of sensual beauty, to the high mansion place where the heavenly, amiable, and right beauty dwelleth, which lieth hidden in the innermost secrets of God, lest unhallowed eyes should come to the sight of it. And there shall we find a most happy end for our desires. . . .

"What mortal tongue is there then, O most holy love, that can sufficiently praise thy worthiness? . . . Thou with agreement bringest the elements in one, stirrest nature to bring forth, and that which ariseth and is borne for the succession of the life.[32] Thou bringest severed matters into one; to the unperfect givest perfection; to the unlike likeness; to enmity amity; to the earth fruits; to the sea calmness; to the heaven lively light. . . . Accept our souls that be offered unto thee for a sacrifice. Burn them in the lively flame that wasteth all gross filthiness, that after they be clean sundered from the body they may be coupled with an everlasting and most sweet bond to the heavenly beauty. And we, severed from ourselves, may be changed like right lovers into the beloved, and, after we be drawn from the earth, admitted to the feast of the angels."[33]

. . . When Bembo had hitherto spoken with such vehemency that a man would have thought him, as it were, ravished and beside himself, he stood

30. *holy fire* describes the nature of angels according to St. Augustine, for they were created from light on the very first day of Genesis.

31. As intellectual presences, angels apprehend, using an intuitive reason that enables them to understand. This faculty is superior to man's comprehension or discursive reason that works by means of language and logic.

32. Love moves nature to produce all that is born or grown for life. See Spenser's presentation of this notion in the description of the Garden of Adonis, *The Faerie Queen* (III.vi.).

33. Revelation 19:7–9.

still without once moving, holding his eyes toward heaven as astonished, when the Lady Emilia,[34] which together with the rest gave most diligent ear to this talk, took him by the plait of his garment and plucking him a little, said, "Take heed, Master Peter, that these thoughts make not your soul also to forsake the body."

"Madam," answered Master Peter, "it should not be the first miracle that love hath wrought in me."

34. Emilia Pia, thirty-eight, widow of Antonio di Montefeltro, the natural half-brother of Duke Guidobaldo. She was a faithful and inseparable companion of the Duchess.

Thomas Wilson
The Arte of Rhetorique

A manual that can show us how to select, organize, and present, in speeches or writing, a message that is persuasive for its coherence and logic as well as for its style is invaluable—as every student of freshman composition knows. And that substantial task is what Thomas Wilson undertook in *The Arte of Rhetorique*, the first and most influential book in English to analyze this material in a comprehensive manner.

Thomas Wilson (1523?–1581) was born in Lincolnshire, the son of a prosperous yeoman farmer. Educated at Eton and King's College, Cambridge, Wilson began to turn his new learning into works that could advance his reputation. In 1551, he published *The Rule of Reason*, the first manual on logic in English, and in 1553, *The Arte of Rhetorique*. With the establishment of a Catholic monarchy under Mary Tudor, Wilson became a political refugee, settling in Padua where he took up the study of law. While in Italy—for reasons not entirely clear—he agreed to deliver letters from the English Cardinal, William Peto, to Pope Paul IV. These activities were reported back to London by Queen Mary's ambassador in Rome with the result that Wilson was ordered to return to England. When he refused, the English ambassador, possibly at the Queen's command, arranged for the Inquisition to arrest Wilson on a charge of heresy. He was imprisoned, interrogated, and tortured. Fortunately for him, the public unrest against the Inquisition that broke out with the death of Paul IV in 1559 enabled Wilson to escape and go into hiding. He resumed the study of law at Ferrara, took his degree there, and returned to a Protestant England in 1560.

Through his law practice Wilson became acquainted with members of Elizabeth's Privy Council. With their help and through the patronage of Protestant clergymen, he secured substantial financial benefits. Entering Parliament in 1561, Wilson also managed to attract attention through his rhetorical skills so that he was called upon for diplomatic service, becoming Elizabeth's ambassador to the Low Countries and ultimately Secretary of State.

Written early in Wilson's career, *The Arte of Rhetorique* was the first manual in English to treat this subject thoroughly. Based on the influential Latin texts of Quintilian, Cicero, and the pseudo-Ciceronian *To Herennius*, it is a fine example of Renaissance humanism, for it combines belief in the moral value of classical learning with faith in the spiritual value of Christianity. Moreover, its tribute to eloquence and appreciation of the arts of persuasion and insinuation were topics also discussed by Castiglione as necessary for the courtier. Finally, the book's plain language, its direct, pragmatic approach, and its firm Protestant sympathies assured its popularity: eight editions were printed between 1553 and 1585. Wilson takes up each of the five traditional categories of his subject: selecting a topic *(inventio)*; organizing its presentation to achieve the desired effect on the audience *(dispositio)*; choosing means to express the subject in memorable words *(elocutio)*; learning it *(memoria)*; and delivering it *(pronuntiatio)*. In addition, Wilson analyzes the three kinds of orations—demonstrative, deliberative, and judicial—and describes some eighty figures and tropes—that is, devices for enhancing what is said. And in all of this, he manages to use examples that appeal to English values.

Wilson's book had a profound effect on writers as well as politicians. After all, eloquence and persuasiveness, as Castiglione had shown, were as important to playwrights as to diplomats, for conflicts are often brought to a climax or resolved through the skillful use of language. Shakespeare repeatedly proves his inventiveness at writing such crucial speeches: in *Love's Labour's Lost*, Berowne delivers a joyous paean to love that convinces his colleagues to break their earlier vows and join him; in *Romeo and Juliet*, Friar Laurence proves his innocence by detailing in the best reportorial fashion the who, what, when, where, and why of his behavior; in *Julius Caesar*, Antony, practicing what Wilson calls "Insinuation," wins over the mob, turning them against the conspirators; and in *Coriolanus* (1608), Menenius calms the fury of the people by telling an amusing anecdote.

The Power of Eloquence

Man, in whom is poured the breath of life, was made at his first being an everliving creature, unto the likeness of God, endued with reason and appointed lord over all other things living.[1] But after the fall of our first father, sin so crept in that our knowledge was much darkened, and, by corruption of this our flesh, man's reason and intendment[2] were both overwhelmed. At what time, God, being sore grieved with the folly of one man, pitied of his mere goodness the whole state and posterity of mankind. And therefore, whereas through the wicked suggestion of our ghostly[3] enemy the joyful fruition of God's glory was altogether lost, it pleased our heavenly father to repair mankind of his free mercy, and to grant an everliving inheritance onto all such as would by constant faith seek earnestly thereafter. Long it was ere that man knew himself, being destitute of God's grace, so that all things waxed savage, the earth untilled, society neglected, God's will not known, man against man, one against another, and all against order. Some lived by spoil, some like brute beasts grazed upon the ground, some went naked, some roamed like woodwoses,[4] none did anything by reason, but most did what they could by manhood.[5] None almost considered the everliving God, but all lived most commonly after their own lust. By death they thought that all things ended; by life they looked for none other living. None remembered the true observation of wedlock; none tendered[6] the education of their children; laws were not regarded; true dealing was not once used. For virtue, vice bore the place; for right and equity, might used authority. And therefore, whereas man through reason might have used order, man through folly fell into error. And thus, for lack of skill and for want of grace, evil so prevailed that the devil was most esteemed, and God either almost unknown among them all or else nothing feared among so many. Therefore, even now when man was thus past all hope of amendment, God, still tendering his own workmanship, stirred up his faithful and elect[7] to persuade with reason all men to society. And gave his appointed ministers knowledge both to see the natures of men and also granted them the gift of utterance, that they might with ease win folk at their will and frame them by reason to all good order.[8]

And, therefore, whereas men lived brutishly in open fields, having neither house to shroud them in, nor attire to clothe their backs, nor yet any regard

1. In this, the preface to his book, Wilson has revised the opening of Cicero's *On Invention* so that its claims for the civilizing power of eloquence are here given a Christian context.
2. *intendment:* intelligence, understanding.
3. *ghostly:* spiritual.
4. *woodwoses:* wild men.
5. *manhood:* strength.
6. *tendered:* looked after, cared for.
7. *elect*—an allusion to the Protestant belief that certain human beings are chosen for salvation by God. See above, pages 44–48.
8. According to Wilson, the power of persuasive speech rests only in the hands of "appointed individuals"—that is, ethically approved, moral individuals.

to seek their best avail,[9] these appointed of God called them together by utterance of speech and persuaded with them what was good, what was bad, and what was gainful for mankind. And altogether at first the rude could hardly learn, and either for strangeness of the thing would not gladly receive the offer or else for lack of knowledge could not perceive the goodness. Yet being somewhat drawn and delighted with the pleasantness of reason and the sweetness of utterance, after a certain space they became, through nurture and good advisement, of wild, sober; of cruel, gentle; of fools, wise; and of beasts, men. Such force hath the tongue, and such is the power of eloquence and reason, that most men are forced even to yield in that which most standeth against their will. And therefore the poets do feign that Hercules, being a man of great wisdom, had all men linked together by the ears in a chain to draw them and lead them even as he lusted.[10] For his wit was so great, his tongue so eloquent and his experience such that no one man was able to withstand his reason, but everyone was rather driven to do that which he would and to will that which he did, agreeing to his advice both in word and work, in all that ever they were able.

Neither can I see that men could have been brought by any other means to live together in fellowship of life, to maintain cities, to deal truly, and willingly to obey one another, if men at the first had not by art and eloquence persuaded that which they full oft found out by reason. For what man, I pray you, being better able to maintain himself by valiant courage than by living in base subjection, would not rather look to rule like a lord than to live like an underling, if by reason he were not persuaded that it behooveth every man to live in his own vocation and not to seek any higher room than whereunto he was at the first appointed? Who would dig and delve from morn till evening? Who would travail and toil with the sweat of his brows? Yea, who would for his king's pleasure adventure and hazard his life, if wit had not so won men that they thought nothing more needful in this world, nor anything whereunto they were more bound, than here to live in their duty and to train their whole life according to their calling. Therefore, whereas men are in many things weak by nature and subject to much infirmity, I think in this one point they pass all other creatures living, that they have the gift of speech and reason.

And among all others, I think him most worthy fame and amongst men to be taken for half a god that therein doth chiefly and above all other excel men wherein men do excel beasts. For he that is among the reasonable of all

9. *avail:* good.

10. According to Lucian, the Celts depicted Hercules as having the power to draw men after him through his spoken words—as though he held men caught by their ears with golden chains linked to his tongue. Erasmus also refers to this episode in his *Dialogues of Lucian.*

most reasonable, and among the witty of all most witty, and among the eloquent of all most eloquent, him think I among all men not only to be taken for a singular man but rather to be counted for half a god. For, in seeking the excellency hereof, the sooner he draweth to perfection, the nigher he cometh to God, who is the chief wisdom, and therefore called God because he is most wise, or rather wisdom itself.

Now then, seeing that God giveth his heavenly grace unto all such as call unto him with stretched hands and humble heart, never wanting to those that want not to themselves, I purpose by his grace and special assistance to set forth precepts of eloquence, and to show what observation the wise have used in handling of their matters, that the unlearned, by seeing the practice of others, may have some knowledge themselves, and learn by their neighbor's device what is necessary for themselves in their own case.

Insinuation

Now resteth for me to speak of the other part of entrance into an oration which is called a close or privy getting of favor when the cause is dangerous and cannot easily be heard without displeasure.[11]

A privy beginning or creeping in, otherwise called insinuation, must then and not else be used when the judge is grieved with us and our cause hated of the hearers.

The cause [it]self oftentimes is not liked for three diverse causes: if either the matter [it]self be unhonest, and not meet to be uttered before an audience; or else if the judge himself by a former tale be persuaded to take part against us; or last, if at that time we are forced to speak when the judge is wearied with hearing of [an]other. For the judge himself being wearied by hearing will be much more grieved if any thing be spoken either overmuch or else against his liking. Yea, who seeth not that a wearied man will soon mislike a right good matter? If the matter be so heinous that it cannot be heard without offense—as if I should take a man's part who were generally hated—wisdom were to let him go and take some other whom all men liked; or if the cause were thought not honest, to take some other instead thereof which were better liked, till they were better prepared to hear the other, so that evermore nothing should be spoken at the first but that which might please the judge, and not be acknowen[12] once to think of that which yet we mind most of all to persuade. Therefore, when the hearers are somewhat calmed, we may enter by little and little into the matter and say that those

11. This definition and analysis is derived from *To Herennius*.
12. *Acknowen*: acknowledged. In this phrase, "not to be suspected."

things which our adversary doth mislike in the person accused we also do mislike the same.[13]

And when the hearers are thus won, we may say that all which was said nothing toucheth us and that we mind to speak nothing at all against our adversaries, neither this way nor that way. Neither were it wisdom openly to speak against them which are generally well esteemed and taken for honest men. And yet, it were not amiss for the furtherance of our own causes closely to speak our fantasy, and so straight to alter their hearts. Yes, and to tell the judges the like in a like matter that such and such judgment hath been given, and therefore, at this time considering the same case and the same necessity, like judgment is looked for. But if the adversary have so told his tale that the judge is wholly bent to give sentence with him, and that it is well-known unto what reasons the judge most leaned and was persuaded, we may first promise to weaken that which the adversary hath made most strong for himself and confute that part which the hearers did most esteem and best of all like. Or else, we may take advantage of some part of our adversary's tale and talk of that first which he spake last, or else begin so as though we doubted what were best first to speak or to what part it were most reason first of all to answer, wondering and taking God to witness at the strangeness of his report and confirmation of his cause. For when the standersby perceive that the answerer, whom the adversaries thought in their mind was wholly abashed, feareth so little the objections of his adversary and is ready to answer *Ad omnia quare*[14] with a bold countenance, they will think that they themselves rather gave rash credit and were overlight in believing the first tale than that he which now answereth in his own cause speaketh without ground or presumeth upon a stomach [disposition] to speak for himself without just consideration.

But if the time be so spent and the tale so long in telling that all men be almost wearied to hear anymore, then we must make promise at the first to be very short and to lap up our matter in few words.

Mirth making good at the beginning.

And if time may so serve, it were good when men be wearied to make them somewhat merry and to begin with some pleasant tale or take an occasion to jest wittily upon something then presently done.

Strange things some time needful to be told at the first.

Or if the time will not serve for pleasant tales, it were good to tell some strange thing, some terrible wonder that they all may quake at the only

13. Wilson has a good understanding of the need to be sensitive to his listeners, and he pays careful attention to their psychological reactions. In *Julius Caesar*, Antony, who was in a position similar to the one described here, clearly knew how effective Wilson's recommendations could be.
14. *Ad omnia quare*: "wherefore to all things."

hearing of the same. For like as when a man's stomach is full and can brook no more meat, he may stir his appetite either by some tart sauce or else quicken it somewhat by some sweet dish, even so when the audience is wearied with weighty affairs some strange wonders may call up their spirits or else some merry tale may cheer their heavy looks.

And assuredly it is no small cunning to move the hearts of men either to mirth or sadness, for he that hath such skill shall not lightly fail of his purpose whatsoever matter he taketh in hand.

Entrances apt to the purpose.

Thus have I taught what an entrance is, and how it should be used. Notwithstanding, I think it not amiss often to rehearse this one point, that evermore the beginning be not overmuch labored nor curiously made, but rather apt to the purpose, seeming upon present occasion evermore to take place, and so to be devised as though we speak altogether without any great study, framing rather our tale to good reason, than our tongue to vain painting of the matter.

Plainness, What It Is

Although many humanists recognized the expressive and communicative powers of the classical languages, they realized that the wholesale adoption into English of foreign words, especially from the Latin, would not simply enrich but overwhelm native speech with "inkhorn terms." Sir John Cheke, for example, believed English "should be written clean and pure, unmixed and unmangled with borrowing of other tongues." And Richard Mulcaster, the translator of Fortescue's *De Laudibus Legum Angliae* [see above, pages 142–46] and the first headmaster of the Merchant Taylors' School, offered arguably the most forceful Tudor expression of faith and pride in his native language. In his book on elementary education and rhetoric (1582), Mulcaster wrote: "I love Rome, but London better, I favor Italy but England more, I honor the Latin, but I worship the English. . . . I do not think that any language, be it whatsoever, is better able to utter all arguments either with more pith or greater plainness than our English tongue is."

But not all lovers of English placed so high a value on its purity. Sir Philip Sidney in *The Defense of Poetry* considered that his native speech was a "mingled language" improved by adding "the best" of Greek and Latin: "for the uttering sweetly and properly the conceits of the mind, which is the end of speech, that hath [English] equally with any other tongue in the world." And George Pettie (1581), pointing out that Latin made itself "flowing and flourishing" with vocabulary derived from the Greek, complained that if all the Latin recently added to English were called inkhorn terms, then "I know not how we should speak anything without blackening our mouths."

Sharing this love of his native tongue and this interest in words, Shakespeare dramatizes how ludicrous are such men as the classical pedant Holofernes in *Love's Labour's Lost*, who insists on pronouncing his English according to a falsely derived Latin etymology, or the court fop Osric in *Hamlet*, whose speech is highly artificial and affected. In the theater, the sharpest attack on an excessive importer of exotic vocabulary occurs in Ben Jonson's play *Poetaster* (1601). Crispinus, a stand-in for the playwright and satirist John Marston, is given an emetic and forced to vomit up such indigestible mouthfuls as "turgidous," "ventositous," "furibund," and "oblatrant." (Actually, time has given some of the joke back to Marston, for not all of Crispinus's jawbreakers remained so alien: "retrograde," "reciprocal," and "strenuous" have managed to make their way into common parlance.) Wilson, in a sensible and amusing passage, deals with this problem of using too many newly coined words.

From *Plainness, What It Is*[15]

Among all other lessons, this should first be learned, that we never affect any strange inkhorn terms, but so speak as is commonly received, neither seeking to be overfine, nor yet living overcareless, using our speech as most men do, and ordering our wits as the fewest have done. Some seek so far for outlandish English that they forget altogether their mother's language. And I dare swear this, if some of their mothers were alive, they were not able to tell what they say; and yet these fine English clerks will say they speak in their mother tongue, if a man should charge them for counterfeiting the King's English. Some far-journeyed gentlemen at their return home, like as they love to go in foreign apparel, so they will powder their talk with overseas language. He that cometh lately out of France will talk French-English and never blush at the matter. Another chops in with Angleso-Italiano. . . . The unlearned and foolish phantastical that smells but of learning (such fellows as have seen learned men in their days) will so Latin their tongues, that the simple cannot but wonder at their talk, and think surely they speak by some Revelation. I know them that think rhetoric to stand wholly upon dark

15. From Book III, *Of Apt Choosing and Framing Words and Sentences Together, Called Elocution* [The discussion of elocution is divided into four parts—plainness, aptness, composition, and exornation—following the example of Cicero's *De Oratore*].

words, and he that can catch an inkhorn term by the tail, him they accompt to be a fine Englishman and a good rhetorician. And the rather to set out this folly, I will add here such a letter as William Sommer himself[16] could not make a better for that purpose. Some will think, and swear it too, that there was never any such thing written; well, I will not force any man to believe it, but I will say thus much, and abide by it too, the like have been made heretofore and praised above the moon.

An Inkhorn Letter:

"Pondering, expending, and revoluting with myself your ingent affability and ingenious capacity for mundane affairs, I cannot but celebrate and extol your magnifical dexterity above all other. For how could you have adopted such illustrate perogative and dominical superiority if the fecundity of your ingenie had not been so fertile and wonderful pregnant. Now, therefore, being accerfited to such splendent renown and dignity splendidious, I doubt not but you will adivate such poor adnichilate orphans as whilom were condisciples with you, and of antique familiarity in Lincolnshire. Among whom I being a scholastical panion, obtestate your sublimity to extol mine infirmity. There is a sacerdotal dignity in my native country continguate to me where I now contemplate which your worshipful benignity could soon impetrate for me, if it would like you to extend your schedules and collaude me in them to the right honorable Lord Chancellor, or rather Archigrammacion of England. You know my literature, you know the pastoral promotion, I obtestate your clemency to invigilate thus much for me according to my confidence and as you know my condign merits for such a compendious living. But now I relinquish to fatigate your intelligence with any more frivolous verbosity, and therefore he that rules the climates be evermore your buttress, your fortress, and your bulwark. Amen."

. . . What wise man reading this letter will not take him for a very calf that made it in good earnest and thought by his inkpot terms to get a good parsonage? Doth wit rest in strange words, or else standeth it in wholesome matter and apt declaring of a man's mind? Do we not speak because we would have other to understand us, or is not the tongue given for this end that one might know what another meaneth? And what unlearned man can tell what half this letter signifieth? Therefore, either we must make a difference of English and say some is learned English and other some is rude English, or the one is court talk, the other is country speech, or else we must of necessity banish all such affected rhetoric and use altogether one manner of language.

16. William Sommer: jester to Henry VIII from 1525 until the king's death.

George Puttenham: *The Arte of English Poesie*

Although published in 1589 and including examples from much recent verse, *The Arte of English Poesie* is in large measure a product of the midcentury, for it shares the pioneering spirit of earlier humanist writers such as Thomas Elyot and Thomas Wilson. In fact, Wilson's *Arte of Rhetorique* (1553) may have served as a model, establishing a pattern by which the author of *The Arte of English Poesie* could accomplish for poets what Wilson had done for prose writers.

But unlike Elyot and Wilson, the author of *The Arte of English Poesie* affected courtly modesty by not signing his name to his work. From the references in the book to his personal experiences, diplomatic service, and literary creations, however, his contemporaries could have easily identified him, even if that knowledge is more difficult for us to acquire today. The most probable author is George Puttenham (c. 1529–90), who was educated at Christ's College, Cambridge, and the Middle Temple. A nephew of Sir Thomas Elyot and the husband of the aristocratic and twice-widowed Lady Elizabeth Windsor, Puttenham was related by both blood and marriage to prominent and wealthy families. He succeeded to some degree in making himself useful to the court, for toward the end of his life Puttenham was warmly commended by Queen Elizabeth for his faithful service and made one of her gentlemen pensioners.

Castiglione's manual for court advancement had clearly taught Puttenham much, for his writing advocates the playfulness and artfulness recommended by the Italian. But it is to his own abilities that we must credit Puttenham's success. The liveliness of his mind, the wittiness of his illustrations, and the deep conviction of his belief are what make

Puttenham's *The Arte of English Poesie* pleasurable reading. This is no small achievement, for Puttenham was treating a subject that can easily prove tedious, and he was writing before the finest works of Renaissance poetry had been published. Yet his analysis of the ways to embellish poetry through sound and syntax remains sensible and often delightful; his defense of the range, power, and potential of English poetry is stirring (and, indeed, proved prophetic); and, most important, his insistence on the need to balance art and nature helped establish a principle constantly repeated in Renaissance aesthetics: Puttenham's belief that "art is neither an aider nor a surmounter, but only a bare imitator of nature's works" is an attitude that Hamlet restates when he reminds the players not to overstep "the modesty of nature" but to "suit the action to the word, the word to the action."

Puttenham divided his material into three sections. Book 1, "Of Poets and Poesie," presents a defense of poetry as a civilizing art and identifies the various poetic genres as responses to human experience. Puttenham shares with the finest writers of the period an awareness of the range of human emotions, a sensitivity to the expressive power of language, and a delight in finding the language that expresses the progress of a passion. For example, he explains why love poetry must be capable of great variety:

> And because love is of all other human affections the most puissant and passionate, and most general to all sorts and ages of men and women, so as whether it be of the young or old, or wise or holy, or high estate or low, none ever could truly brag of any exemption in that case: it requireth a form of poesy variable, inconstant, affected, curious, and most witty of any others, whereof the joys were to be uttered in one sort, the sorrows in another, and by the many forms of poesy the many moods and pangs of lovers thoroughly to be discovered: the poor souls sometimes praying, beseeching; sometime honoring, advancing, praising; another while railing, reviling, and cursing; then sorrowing, weeping, lamenting. In the end laughing, rejoicing and solacing the beloved again with a thousand delicate devices, odes, songs, elegies, ballads, sonnets, and other ditties, moving one way and another to great compassion.

In Book 2, "Of Proportion Poetical," Puttenham reveals his enthusiasm for clear, strong rhyme, the "poet's chief music." Departing from those who would try and impose classical poetic meters on English, he understood the stress nature of English verse, what he calls its "natural emphasis." His enthusiasm for rhyme, however, prevented him from grasping the importance of blank verse, which had not yet demonstrated its potential; in fact, he never mentions it.

Finally, Book 3 of *The Arte of English Poesie* takes up tropes (or turns) and figures (or schemes). In his usage, tropes alter the meaning of a word from the literal to the imaginative—they include such devices as metaphor, allegory, synecdoche, and metonymy. Figures, in contrast, are particularly concerned with syntax, the placement of words in patterns—they include such devices as repetition, especially at the same point in a series of clauses or sentences; parallel constructions; periphrasis; ellipsis; and apostrophe. Puttenham replaces the usual classification system for tropes and figures into one of his own devising that allows him to analyze the sensory appeals of poetry. For instance, he explains that the Greek figure *Micterismus*, which he translates as "the fleering frumpe" [the jeering grimace], occurs "when we give a mock with a scornfull countenance as in some smiling sort looking aside, or by drawing the lip awry, or shrinking up the nose. . . . As he that said to one whose words he believed not, 'No doubt of that, sir.'" To Puttenham the Greek figure *Asterismus* may be termed "the civil jest because it is mirth full of civility," spoken "by manner of pleasantry, or merry scoff, that is, by a kind of mock, whereof the sense is far set, and without any gall or offense." His explanations are lively and practical, for he points out how these devices, properly employed, are the means that raise poetry above mere statement; they are the techniques by which it can "inveigle and appassionate the mind."

Puttenham's book was influential in a number of ways. First of all, it established solid principles for the artful deployment of rhetorical devices. Puttenham's work could stand as a measure of reasonableness against the later, more exuberant practices of pamphleteers and controversialists, such as Martin Marprelate and Thomas Nashe, with their colorful examples and neologisms, as well as of disciples of Euphues, with their excessive linguistic ingenuity. It defended English poetry, rather optimistically (and somewhat prematurely) arguing that it could be as great as the poetry of any language, ancient or modern. And above all, it argued that poetic greatness is measured by the results accomplished when a writer has perfectly matched means and ends, substance and style. Puttenham believed that decorum, which could be defined as the perfect blending of art and nature, was the ultimate criterion for art: "nature herself suggesteth the figure in this or that form, but art aideth the judgment of his [the poet's] use and application." For him the roles of art and nature are complementary. He resolves the art-nature dualism that is a recurring concern of Elizabethan writers by stating that the poet uses art correctly when he uses it "even as nature herself "—or, to borrow the words of Shakespeare's Polixenes in *The Winter's Tale* (1610)—when "the art itself is nature."

In *The Faerie Queene* (1590) Spenser takes up the art-nature opposition by contrasting the Bower of Bliss (II.xii), where art wrongly attempts to rival nature, with the Garden of Adonis (III.vi), where love and beauty are continually renewed by a fecund and creative nature, "not by art."

Shakespeare's development as a playwright can be traced through his application of Puttenham's principle of decorum, of matching language to character and action on the stage. In his earlier plays Shakespeare's rhetorical and poetic devices are often employed in ways that call attention to themselves simply to demonstrate the writer's skill: audiences, after all, had learned in grammar school the names and uses of the most popular tropes and schemes, and Shakespeare obliged them by enriching his work with these figures.

In his later works, however, Shakespeare uses the forms of rhetoric as a means of revealing character and clarifying action. *Troilus and Cressida*, a play written at about the midpoint of his career, offers a striking example of how speakers are characterized by their language. Agamemnon's prolixity is a mark of his failure to communicate—a failure that, in turn, leads to insubordination and procrastination among the Greeks under his command. Ulysses' balanced and complicated syntax, overly detailed and unnecessarily thorough, reflects not only a subtle and discriminating intelligence but also an inability to leave anything unspecified. Ajax's bombast befits a man stuffed with his own self-importance—how appropriate that he, quite literally, blows his own trumpet. And Thersites's foul name-calling, the vocabulary of a "deformed and scurrilous Greek," reduces the principals to fools, curs, whores, knaves, drabs, and cuckolds. These four figures of rhetoric— Agamemnon's *pleonasmus* or what Puttenham calls "too full speech," Ulysses' *periergeia* or "overlabour," Ajax's *bomphiologia* or "pompous speech," and Thersites' use of *tapinosis*, or "the abaser"—reflect the minds of the speakers and express their thoughts and feelings.

We can become even more appreciative of the works of Shakespeare's maturity when we realize how his characters use the figures of rhetoric with great flexibility and ease. The resources of language are put into the service of expressing remarkably complex mental attitudes and emotional states. In *King Lear* when Goneril and Regan together confront their father and insist that he accept their terms, the old man, who has already delivered terrible curses on his daughters, claims he will retaliate:

> *I will have such revenges on you both*
> *That all the world shall—I will do such things,*
> *What they are, yet I know not, but they shall be*
> *The terrors of the earth.*

(II.iv.281–84)

Shakespeare here uses *aposiopesis* "or the figure of silence"; that is, "when we begin to speak a thing, and break off in the middle way as if . . . by way of threatening." Unlike the Elizabethans, we are hardly aware of the figure, much less know its name; yet for us, as for Shakespeare's first audiences, the rhetorical construction is perfectly chosen to express the emotional intensity of the moment and the mental state of the character. Shakespeare's later plays do not use fewer schemes and tropes than his earlier ones; rather the figures are used with greater decorum, for they are more carefully adapted and more integrated into the dialogue. To paraphrase Puttenham's words, our poet is to be commended, for his art is well dissembled.

Other playwrights were also adept at using the schemes and tropes described by Puttenham. In his dying soliloquy, Marlowe's Faustus expresses his anguish and despair through apostrophe and antithesis; in *Sejanus* (1603) Jonson's devious emperor manages to condemn his former assistant by using what Puttenham calls "*amphibologia* or the ambiguous—when we speak or write doubtfully and that the sense may be taken two ways." Once we have become aware of the rhetorical figures that make Elizabethan verse such a powerfully expressive medium, we shall find them everywhere in Renaissance English drama. As Jonson explained, dramatists must relate language to character: "Language most shows a man. . . . No glass renders a man's form or likeness so true as his speech."[1] And like Puttenham and Shakespeare, Jonson argued that in ideal works of art the writer's means and ends—the rhetorical figures he uses to depict a certain type of character—are in complete accord: "Without Art, Nature can ne'er be perfect; and without Nature, art can claim no being."[2]

1. *Discoveries*, 2031–35.
2. *Discoveries*, 2503–4.

Of Figures and Figurative Speeches

As figures be the instruments of ornament in every language, so be they also
in a sort abuses or rather trespasses in speech, because they pass the ordinary
limits of common utterance, and be occupied of purpose to deceive the ear
and also the mind, drawing it from plainness and simplicity to a certain
doubleness, whereby our talk is the more guileful and abusing, for what else
is your *metaphor* but an inversion of sense by transport; your *allegory* by a
duplicity of meaning or dissimulation under covert and dark intendments:
one while speaking obscurely and in riddle called *aenigma:* another while by
common proverb or Adage called *paremia:* then by merry scoff called *ironia:*
then by bitter taunt called *sarcasmus:* then by periphrase or circumlocution
when all might be said in a word or two: then by incredible comparison
giving credit, as by your *hyperbole,* and many other ways seeking to inveigle
and appassionate the mind: which thing made the grave judges *Aeropagites*
(as I find written) to forbid all manner of figurative speeches to be used before
them in their consistory of justice, as mere illusions to the mind, and
wresters of upright judgment, saying that to allow such manner of foreign
and colored talk to make the judges affectioned, were all one as if the
carpenter before he began to square his timber would make his square
crooked: in so much as the straight and upright mind of a judge is the very
rule of justice till it be perverted by affection. This no doubt is true and was
by them gravely considered: but in this case because our maker or poet is
appointed not for a judge, but rather for a pleader, and that of pleasant and
lovely causes and nothing perilous, such as be those for the trial of life, limb,
or livelihood; and before judges neither sour nor severe, but in the ear of
princely dames, young ladies, gentlewomen and courtiers, being all for the
most part either meek of nature, or of pleasant humor, and that all his abuses
tend but to dispose the hearers to mirth and solace by pleasant conveyance
and efficacy of speech, they are not in truth to be accompted vices but for
virtues in the poetical science very commendable. On the other side, such
trespasses in speech (whereof there be many) as give dolor and disliking to the
ear and mind, by any foul indecency or disproportion of sound, situation, or
sense, they be called and not without cause, the vicious parts or rather
heresies of language: wherefore the matter resteth much in the definition and
acceptance of this word [*decorum*], for whatsoever is so cannot justly be
misliked. In which respect it may come to pass that what the grammarian
setteth down for a viciosity in speech may become a virtue and no vice;
contrari-wise his commended figure may fall into a reproachful fault, the
best and most assured remedy whereof is generally to follow the saying of

Bias: *ne quid nimis.*[3] So as in keeping measure, and not exceeding nor showing any defect in the use of his figures, he cannot lightly do amiss, if he have besides (as that must needs be) a special regard to all circumstances of the person, place, time, cause, and purpose he hath in hand, which being well observed it easily avoideth all the recited inconveniences, and maketh now and then very vice go for a formal virtue in the exercise of this art.

In What Cases the Artificiall Is More Commended Than the Naturall and Contrariwise

We do allow our courtly poet to be a dissembler only in the subtleties of his art: that is, when he is most artificial, so to disguise and cloak it as it may not appear, nor seem to proceed from him by any study or trade of rules, but to be his natural: nor so evidently to be descried, as every lad that reads him shall say he is a good scholar, but will rather have him to know his art well, and little to use it.

And yet peradventure in all points it may not be so taken, but in such only as may discover his grossness or his ignorance by some scholarly affectation, which thing is very irksome to all men to good training, and specially to courtiers. And yet for all that our maker may not be in all cases restrained, but that he may both use and also manifest his art to his great praise, and need no more be ashamed thereof than a shoemaker to have made a cleanly shoe, or a carpenter to have built a fair house. Therefore to discuss and make this point somewhat clearer, to weet, where art ought to appear and where not, and when the natural is more commendable than the artificial in any human action or workmanship, we will examine it further by this distinction.

In some cases we say art is an aid and coadjutor to nature, and a furtherer of her actions to good effect, or peradventure a means to supply her wants, by reenforcing the causes wherein she is impotent and defective—as doth the art of physic, by helping the natural concoction, retention, distribution, expulsion, and other virtues in a weak and unhealthy body. Or as the good gardener seasons his soil by sundry sorts of compost: as muck or marl,[4] clay or sand, and many times by blood, or lees[5] of oil or wine, or stale,[6] or perchance with more costly drugs; and waters his plants, and weeds his herbs and flowers, and prunes his branches, and unleaves his boughs to let in the sun. And twenty other ways cherisheth them, and cureth their infirmities,

3. Erasmus *Adagia*, 1.6.96. Bias was an Ionian philosopher, one of the so-called seven wise men of Greece. His advice was: "nothing in excess."
4. *marl*: soil of clay mixed with lime.
5. *lees*: sediment, dregs.
6. *stale*: urine.

and so makes that never, or very seldom any of them miscarry, but bring forth their flowers and fruits in season. And in both these cases it is no small praise for the physician and gardener to be called good and cunning artificers.

In another respect art is not only an aid and coadjutor to nature in all her actions, but an alterer of them, and in some sort a surmounter of her skill, so as by means of it her own effects shall appear more beautiful or strange and miraculous, as in both cases before remembered.[7] The physician, by the cordials he will give his patient, shall be able not only to restore the decayed spirits of man and render him health, but also to prolong the term of his life many years over and above the stint of his first and natural constitution. And the gardener by his art will not only make an herb, or flower, or fruit, come forth in his season without impediment, but also will embellish the same in virtue, shape, odor, and taste, that nature of her self would never have done: as to make the single gillyflower, or marigold, or daisy, double; and the white rose, red, yellow, or carnation; a bitter melon, sweet; a sweet apple, sour; a plum or cherry without a stone; a pear without core or kernel; a gourd or cucumber like to a horn or any other figure he will. Any of which things nature could not do without man's help and art. These actions also are most singular when they be most artificial.

In another respect, we say art is neither an aider nor a surmounter, but only a bare imitator of nature's works, following and counterfeiting her actions and effects, as the marmoset doth many countenances and gestures of man, of which sort are the arts of painting and carving, whereof one represents the natural by light and color and shadow in the superficial or flat, the other in a body massive expressing the full and empty, even, extant, rabbeted,[8] hollow, or whatsoever other figure and passion of quantity. So also the alchemist counterfeits gold, silver, and all other metals, the lapidary pearls and precious stones by glass and other substances falsified and sophisticated by art. These men also be praised for their craft, and their credit is nothing impaired to say that their conclusions and effects are very artificial. Finally, in another respect art is, as it were, an encounterer and contrary to nature, producing effects neither like to hers, nor by participation with her

7. Puttenham suggests that in the ideal relationship between art and nature, art complements nature. In The Temple of Venus episode of *The Faerie Queen*, Spenser describes this relationship in which art creates what nature lacks:

> *For all that nature by her mother wit*
> *Could frame in earth, and forme of substance base,*
> *Was there, and all that nature did omit,*
> *Art playing second natures part, supplyed it.*

(IV.x.21)

8. *rabbeted:* grooved or channeled.

operations, nor by imitation of her patterns, but makes things and produceth effects altogether strange and diverse, and of such form and quality (nature always supplying stuff) as she never would nor could have done of her self: as the carpenter that builds a house, the joiner that makes a table or a bedstead, the tailor a garment, the smith a lock or a key, and a number of like; in which case the workman gaineth reputation by his art, and praise when it is best expressed and most apparent and most studiously. Man also in all his actions that be not altogether natural, but are gotten by study and discipline or exercise, as to dance by measures, to sing by note, to play on the lute, and suchlike, it is a praise to be said an artificial dancer, singer, and player on instruments, because they be not exactly known or done, but by rules and precepts or teaching of schoolmasters. But in such actions as be so natural and proper to man, as he may become excellent therein without any art or imitation at all (custom and exercise excepted, which are requisite to every action not numbered among the vital or animal), and wherein nature should seem to do amiss, and man suffer reproach to be found destitute of them: in those to show himself rather artificial than natural, were no less to be laughed at than for one that can see well enough to use a pair of spectacles, or not to hear but by a trunk put to his ear, nor feel without a pair of annealed gloves which things indeed help an infirm sense, but annoy the perfect, and therefore, showing a disability natural, move [one] rather to scorn the commendation and to pity sooner than to praise. But what else is language, and utterance, and discourse, and persuasion, and argument in man, than the virtues of a well-constituted body and mind, little less natural than his very sensual actions, saving that the one is perfected by nature at once, the other not without exercise and iteration? Peradventure also it will be granted, that a man sees better and discerns more brimly[9] his colors, and hears and feels more exactly by use and often hearing and feeling and seeing, and though it be better to see with spectacles than not to see at all, yet is their praise not equal nor in any man's judgment comparable. No more is that which a poet makes by art and precepts rather than by natural instinct. And that which he doth by long meditation rather than by a sudden inspiration, or with great pleasure and facility than hardly (and as they are wont to say) in spite of Nature or Minerva, than which nothing can be more irksome or ridiculous.

And yet I am not ignorant that there be arts and methods both to speak and to persuade and also to dispute, and by which the natural is in some sort relieved, as th'eye by his spectacle, I say relieved in his imperfection, but not made more perfect than the natural. In which respect I call those arts of grammar, logic, and rhetoric not bare imitations, as the painter or carver's

9. *brimly*: clearly, distinctly.

craft and work in a foreign subject—viz a lively portrait in his table or wood—but by long and studious observation rather a repetition or reminiscence natural, reduced into perfection, and made prompt by use and exercise. And so whatsoever a man speaks or persuades, he doth it not by imitation artificially, but by observation naturally (though one follow another) because it is both the same and the like that nature doth suggest. But if a popinjay speak, she doth it by imitation of man's voice artificially and not naturally, being the like but not the same that nature doth suggest to man. But now, because our maker or poet is to play many parts and not one alone, as first to devise his plat[10] or subject, then to fashion his poem, thirdly to use his metrical proportions, and last of all to utter with pleasure and delight, which rests in his manner of language and style as hath been said, whereof the many moods and strange phrases are called figures, it is not altogether with him as with the craftsman, nor altogether otherwise than with the craftsman. For in that he useth his metrical proportions by appointed and harmonical measures and distances, he is like the carpenter or joiner; for, borrowing their timber and stuff of nature, they appoint and order it by art otherwise than nature would do, and work effects in appearance contrary to hers. Also in that which the poet speaks or reports of another man's tale or doings, as Homer of *Priamus* or *Ulysses*, he is as the painter or carver that work by imitation and representation in a foreign subject. In that he speaks figuratively, or argues subtly, or persuades copiously and vehemently, he doth as the cunning gardener that, using nature as a coadjutor, furthers her conclusions and many times makes her effects more absolute and strange. But for that in our maker or poet which rests only in devices and issues from an excellent, sharp, and quick invention, helped by a clear and bright phantasy and imagination, he is not as the painter to counterfeit the natural by the like effects and not the same, nor as the gardener aiding nature to work both the same and the like, nor as the carpenter to work effects utterly unlike, but even as nature herself working by her own peculiar virtue and proper instinct and not by example or meditation or exercise as all other artificers do, is then most admired when he is most natural and least artificial. And in the feats of his language and utterance, because they hold as well of nature to be suggested and uttered as by art to be polished and reformed. Therefore shall our poet receive praise for both, but more by knowing of his art than by unseasonable using it, and be more commended for his natural eloquence than for his artificial, and more for his artificial well dissembled, than for the same overmuch affected or indiscreetly betrayed, as many makers and orators do.

10. *plat or subject:* outline, plan.

Education

Educations was at the heart and center of the Renaissance program for transforming society, for humanists believed that only if individuals were pointed in the right direction and encouraged to develop their talents to the full would it be possible to re-create in the contemporary world the virtues and values of antiquity. Even before the Renaissance began, the schools of rhetoric in the city-states of northern Italy had been developing the concept that the health of any political community depended not upon its institutions but on the public spirit of its citizens, and that a man's worth or *virtù* was to be measured not by birth or wealth but by commitment to the common good. It was the Florentine humanists, led by Petrarch, who put this concept in a Renaissance context. Convinced that ancient Greece and Rome had been in every way superior to all other societies, they argued that an intensive study of classical literature and culture would provide an ideal education for the future citizens of their own day.

As Renaissance influences extended beyond Italy into northern and western Europe, so did this belief in the value of a classical education. But the northern humanists placed greater emphasis than their Italian counterparts on their Christian inheritance, and Erasmus led the way in producing editions of the Bible and the early fathers that made full use of the techniques devised by earlier Renaissance scholars to establish authentic texts of classical authors. It was the Christian humanists of Europe beyond the Alps who took the lead in propagating ideas about education that were designed to do for the sixteenth century what St. Thomas Aquinas had done for the thirteenth—namely, to unify into one consistent whole the secular and Christian elements that had been transmitted from the antique world to their own day.

Sir Thomas Elyot: *The Boke Named the Governour*

The Boke Named the Governour was the first treatise on education to be written in English. Hitherto it had been taken for granted that learned works should be in Latin, the *lingua franca* of the European intelligentsia, and even the distinguished Spanish humanist Juan Luis Vives, who advocated the use of the vernacular in teaching, used Latin to propagate his views. It was not incapacity that persuaded Elyot to write in English. Although he apparently received no formal education, he acquired a good knowledge of both Greek and Latin in the household of his father, a distinguished judge, and in 1538 he published a Latin-English dictionary that quickly established itself as a standard work of reference, far superior to anything else in the field. Elyot chose English deliberately, not merely because he wanted to appeal to the widest possible audience but also to demonstrate that the vernacular of his own day was a worthy instrument for the discussion of philosophical and kindred themes. Greek and Latin were admittedly richer, but Elyot took care to introduce new words into his *Boke*, in order to fill the more obvious gaps and thereby give his native language the flexibility and range in which it was deficient. As Henry VIII correctly observed, Elyot's purpose was "to augment our English tongue, whereby men should as well express more abundantly the thing that they conceived in their hearts . . . having words apt for the purpose: as also to interpret out of Greek, Latin, or any other tongue into English as sufficiently as out of any one of the said tongues into another."

Elyot took Plato's *Republic* as his model, and in common with Renaissance humanists as a whole, he subscribed to Plato's belief that education and politics were intimately connected. Elyot was convinced that institutions of government by themselves were insufficient to guarantee the well-being of the community, since they could be corrupted or turned to evil ends by wicked rulers. The only ultimate safeguard consisted in inculcating among members of the political elite a love of virtue and an instinctive desire to attain it. There was no reason in principle why *virtù*—in the sense of a commitment to the public good—should be confined to the existing upper levels of society, which in England meant the aristocracy and gentry. Elyot owed his practical experience of central government to Cardinal Wolsey, a man of low birth who had risen by sheer ability to be the King's chief minister, and even before Wolsey fell from power Elyot had established good relations with his successor, Thomas Cromwell, who was another parvenu. Yet as the following extracts show, Elyot assumed that the nobility and gentry would, in normal circumstances, be the men who ruled England, under the sovereign. His *Boke* was therefore aimed at them, for if only he could persuade them to take their duties with appropriate seriousness and make the public good their overriding aim he would bring England close to that ideal of a res publica or, as he termed it, a "public weal," which he believed to be the best of all forms of government.

Elyot was also undoubtedly hoping to influence the King himself, for Henry VIII was not devoid of humanist knowledge or inclinations. Power corrupted him, and the high hopes aroused at the beginning of his reign were destined never to be fulfilled, but his favorable reaction to Elyot's *Boke* showed that he approved of *virtù* in theory even if he rarely applied it in practice. Shortly after the publication of the *Boke* in 1531 Henry chose Elyot, whom he had recently knighted, as his ambassador to the Emperor Charles V. Elyot was instructed to win Charles's approval for Henry's plan to divorce his wife, Catherine of Aragon (who was the Emperor's aunt), and although he was unsuccessful in his mission he did not thereby forfeit the King's approval. In 1536 he was again sent off on embassy to Charles, and when, on his return, he embarked on the formidable task of compiling a Latin-English dictionary, Henry buoyed up his occasionally flagging spirits and spurred him on with the loan of books from the royal library.

Elyot died in 1546, but by that time *The Boke Named the Governour* had been through four editions, and more followed in the course of the sixteenth century. Elyot contributed a great deal to the process whereby the ideal of a "gentleman" came to include knowledge of the classics as well as the Bible, and also implied commitment to the common good. In addition, Elyot gave Englishmen a pride in their own language, and a significantly extended vocabulary. If by the time of Shakespeare English was well on the way to becoming a "classical" language in its own right, a suitable medium for interpreting the whole range of human experience and aspirations, this was due in no small part to Sir Thomas Elyot.

The Proheme of Thomas Elyot, Knight, unto the Most Noble and Victorious Prince, King Henry the Eight, King of England and France, Defender of the True Faith, and Lord of Ireland

. . . Taking comfort and boldness, partly of Your Grace's most benevolent inclination toward the universal weal of your subjects, partly inflamed with zeal, I have now enterprised to describe in our vulgar tongue the form of a just public weal: which matter I have gathered as well of the sayings of most noble authors (Greeks and Latins) as by mine own experience, I being continually trained in some daily affairs of the public weal of this your most noble realm, almost from my childhood. . . . And forasmuch as this present book treateth of the education of them that hereafter may be deemed worthy to be governors of the public weal under Your Highness (which Plato affirmeth to be the first and chief part of a public weal; Solomon saying also "where governors be not, the people shall fall into ruin"),[1] I therefore have named it *The Governour* and do now dedicate it unto Your Highness.

"The Signification of a Public Weal"

Elyot counted Sir Thomas More among his friends, even though he was twenty years younger than the author of *Utopia*. After More's eclipse he was careful to play down the connection, even though there is some evidence that he worked behind the scenes to try and secure More's rehabilitation, but there is no reason to assume that he ever approved of More's vision of the perfect commonwealth. The Utopians lived in a state not far removed from communism, and were free from hierarchies, but Elyot regarded such a system as unnatural. Degrees and estates were part of the God-given order of things and applied to the whole of creation. They were the sinews of the body politic, the means whereby the differing aptitudes and aspirations of its members were harmonized and made to yield their full potential. Furthermore they

1. Proverbs 11:14. The Douai Bible of 1609–10 gives "where there is no governor, the people shall fall." This comes closer than the King James Bible to Elyot's rendering.

were a guarantee of order, that greatest of all blessings, and without them there was every likelihood of a collapse into chaos. This was a traditional view but one that Elyot expressed with great force and conviction. In Book V of *The Faerie Queene*, Spenser describes an action that makes the same point as Elyot's argument. A mighty giant is rousing the commoners to near rebellion with his promise to re-distribute all things on earth, to level mountains and valleys and equalize the differences between rulers and subjects, rich and poor. Opposing him, Sir Artegall, the champion of justice, attempts to prove that these efforts would upset the divine plan of the universe, for God

> . . . *maketh Kings to sit in soverainty;*
> *He maketh subjects to their powre obay;*
> *He pulleth downe, he setteth up on hy;*
> *He gives to this, from that he takes away.*
> *For all we have is his: what he list doe, he may.*
>
> (V. ii. 41)

Ultimately, Artegall uses his squire, the iron man Talus, to destroy the giant and quell the "mutining" and "civil faction" that are the inevitable result of such schemes. And similar views can also be found in Shakespeare's plays. Although we cannot prove that Shakespeare actually read Elyot, the great speech from *Troilus and Cressida* that begins "Take but degree away . . ." could be a paraphrase of some of the following passages from *The Boke Named the Governour*.

Book I. Part I. The Signification of a Public Weal, and Why It Is Called in Latin Respublica

A public weal is a body living, compact or made of sundry estates and degrees of men, which is disposed by the order of equity and governed by the rule and moderation of reason. . . . And they which do suppose it so to be called for that, that everything should be to all men in common, without discrepance [distinction] of any estate or condition, be thereto moved more by sensuality than by any good reason or inclination to humanity. And that shall soon appear unto them that will be satisfied either with authority or with natural order and example.

First, the proper and true signification of the words "public" and "common," which be borrowed of the Latin tongue for the insufficiency of our own language, shall sufficiently declare the blindness of them which have hitherto holden and maintained the said opinions. As I have said, "public" took his beginning of "people," which in Latin is *populus*, in which word is contained all the inhabitants of a realm or city, of what estate or condition soever they be.

Plebs in English is called the "commonalty," which signifieth only the multitude, wherein be contained the base and vulgar inhabitants not advanced to any honor or dignity. . . . And consequently there may appear like diversity to be in English between a public weal and a common weal as should be in Latin between *Res publica* and *Res plebeia*. And after that signification, if there should be a common weal, either the commoners only must be wealthy, and the gentle and noblemen needy and miserable; or else, excluding gentility, all men must be of one degree and sort, and a new name provided. Forasmuch as *plebs* in Latin, and "commoners" in English, be words only made for the discrepancy of degrees, whereof proceedeth order, which in things as well natural as supernatural hath ever had such a preeminence that thereby the incomprehensible majesty of God, as it were by bright leme [light] of a torch or candle, is declared to the blind inhabitants of this world. Moreover, take away order from all things, what should then remain? Certes, nothing finally, except some man would imagine eftsoons *Chaos*, which of some is expound a confuse mixture. Also, where there is any lack of order, needs must be perpetual conflict: and in things subject to Nature nothing of himself only may be nourished, but when he hath destroyed that wherewith he doth participate by the order of his creation, he himself of necessity must then perish, whereof ensueth universal dissolution.

But now to prove, by example of those things that be within the compass of man's knowledge, of what estimation order is, not only among men but also with God, albeit His wisdom, bounty, and magnificence can be with no tongue or pen sufficiently expressed; hath not He set degrees and estates in all His glorious works? First in His heavenly ministers, whom, as the Church affirmeth, He hath constituted to be in divers degrees called hierarchies. Also Christ saith by his evangelist that in the house of his father (which is God) be many mansions.[2]

But to treat of that which by natural understanding may be comprehended. Behold the four elements whereof the body of man is compact, how they be set in their places called spheres, higher or lower according to the sovereignty of their natures: that is to say, the fire, as the most pure element, having in it nothing that is corruptible, in his place is highest and above other elements. The air, which next to the fire is most pure in substance, is in the second sphere or place. The water, which is somewhat consolidate and

2. John 14:2.

approacheth to corruption, is next unto the earth. The earth, which is of substance gross and ponderous, is set of all elements most lowest.

Behold also the order that God hath put generally in all His creatures, beginning at the most inferior or base, and ascending upward. He made not only herbs to garnish the earth, but also trees of a more eminent stature than herbs, and yet in the one and the other be degrees of qualities—some pleasant to behold; some delicate or good in taste; other wholesome and medicinable; some commodious and necessary. Semblably in birds, beasts, and fishes: some be good for the sustenance of man; some bear things profitable to sundry uses; other be apt to occupation and labor. In diverse is strength and fierceness only; in many is both strength and commodity; some other serve for pleasure. None of them hath all these qualities. Few have the more part, or many—specially beauty, strength, and profit. But where any is found that hath many of the said properties, he is more set by than all the other, and by that estimation the order of his place and degree evidently appeareth. So that every kind of trees, herbs, birds, beasts, and fishes, beside their diversity of forms, have (as who saith) a peculiar disposition appropered [proper] unto them by God their creator. So that in everything is order, and without order may be nothing stable or permanent. And it may not be called order except it do contain in it degrees, high and base, according to the merit or estimation of the thing that is ordered.

Now to return to the estate of mankind, for whose use all the said creatures were ordained of God, and also excelleth them all by prerogative of knowledge and wisdom, it seemeth that in him should be no less providence of God declared than in the inferior creatures, but rather with a more perfect order and disposition. And therefore it appeareth that God giveth not to every man like gifts of grace, or of nature, but to some more, some less, as it liketh His divine majesty. Nor they be not in common (as fantastical fools would have all things), nor one man hath not all virtues and good qualities.

Notwithstanding, forasmuch as understanding is the most excellent gift that man can receive in his creation, whereby he doth approach most nigh unto the similitude of God (which understanding is the principal part of the soul), it is therefore congruent and according that as one excelleth another in that influence, as thereby being next to the similitude of his maker, so should the estate of his person be advanced in degree or place where understanding may profit; which is also distributed into sundry uses, faculties, and offices necessary for the living and governance of mankind. And like as the angels which be most fervent in contemplation be highest exalted in glory (after the opinion of holy doctors), and also the fire, which is the most pure of elements, is deputed to the highest sphere or place, so in this world they which excel other in this influence of understanding, and do employ it to the detaining of other within the bounds of reason, and show them how to provide for their necessary living; such ought to be set in a more high place than the residue, where they may see and also be seen; that by the beams of their excellent wit, showed through the glass of authority, other of inferior understanding may be directed to the way of virtue and commodious living.

And unto men of such virtue by very equity appertaineth honor, as their just reward and duty, which by other men's labors must also be maintained according to their merits, forasmuch as the said persons, excelling in knowledge whereby other be governed, be ministers for the only profit and commodity of them which have not equal understanding; where they which do exercise artificial science or corporal labor do not travail for their superiors only, but also for their own necessity. So the husbandman feedeth himself and the clothmaker. The clothmaker appareleth himself and the husband. They both succor other artificers; other artificers them; they and other artificers them that be governors. But they that be governors (as I before said) nothing do acquire by the said influence of knowledge for their own necessity, but do employ all the powers of their wits, and their diligence, to the only preservation of other their inferiors. Among which inferiors also behoveth to be a disposition and order according to reason: that is to say that the slothful or idle person do not participate with him that is industrious and taketh pain; whereby the fruits of his labors should be diminished, wherein should be none equality but thereof should proceed discourage and finally dissolution for lack of provision. Wherefore it can none other wise stand with reason but that the estate of the person in preeminence of living should be esteemed with his understanding, labor and policy, whereunto must be added an augmentation of honor and substance which not only impresseth a reverence, whereof proceedeth due obedience among subjects, but also inflameth men naturally inclined to idleness or sensual appetite to covet like fortune and for that cause to dispose them to study or occupation.

Now to conclude my first assertion or argument. Where all thing is common, there lacketh order; and where order lacketh, there all thing is odious and uncomely. And that have we in daily experience. For the pans and pots garnisheth well the kitchen, and yet should they be to the chamber none ornament. Also the beds, testers, and pillows beseemeth not the hall, no more than the carpets and cushions becometh the stable. Semblably, the potter and tinker, only perfect in their craft, shall little do in the ministration of justice. A ploughman or carter shall make but a feeble answer to an ambassador. Also a weaver or fuller should be an unmeet captain of an army, or in any other office of a governor. Wherefore, to conclude, it is only a public weal, where, like as God hath disposed the said influence of understanding, is also appointed degrees and places according to the excellency thereof; and thereto also would be substance convenient and necessary for the ornament of the same, which also impresseth a reverence and due obedience to the vulgar people or commonalty. And without that it can be no more said that there is a public weal than it may be affirmed that a house without his proper and necessary ornaments is well and sufficiently furnished.

"The Order of Learning"

Humanist writers on education frequently stressed the need to win the child to love of learning by treating him with kindness. Since education, in their view, was of such transcendent importance in shaping a man's character, it was essential to start the process at an early age and give it an impetus that would endure for a whole lifetime. They were only too aware that practice and theory widely diverged, and that many children were to be found, in Shakespeare's phrase, "creeping like snail unwillingly to school." Not all schoolmasters were endowed with the necessary qualities to inspire their pupils with a genuine love of learning, and many parents held the view that to spare the rod was to spoil the child. Little William Page in Shakespeare's *The Merry Wives of Windsor*, for instance, is warned that he could be breeched, or whipped, for failing to learn his lessons. But the humanists could cite classical authors in defense of their claim that love was far more effective in the long run than force. The *Institutio Oratoria* of Quintilian, rediscovered in 1417, made their case for them: hence their repeated references to it. Elyot's views, as expressed in the following extracts, show clear traces of the influence of Quintilian and provide a good example of the way in which the writings of classical authors afforded both a stimulus and a frame of reference for the solution of contemporary problems.

Since *The Boke Named the Governour* was directed towards the English nobility and gentry, it is hardly surprising to find Elyot primarily concerned with their attitude towards education. As Clerk of the Council under Wolsey, and subsequently as ambassador, he learned at firsthand how essential it was for the state to be served by men of learning. Yet old attitudes died hard, and Richard Pace, writing to John Colet, the founder of St. Paul's School, in 1517, recalled one particular Englishman of his acquaintance who declared that he would sooner see his son "hanged than be a bookworm. It is a gentleman's calling to be able to blow the horn, to hunt and hawk. He should leave learning to clodhoppers."[3] Such attitudes offended Elyot's sense of the proper ordering of things, for if those who had traditionally held sway over English society abdicated their responsibilities by refusing to give their sons an appropriate education for the service of the Renaissance state, they would merely open the way to men lower down the social scale. *Virtù* in the Renaissance sense of the term, was acquired by natural aptitude and learning rather than by birth or wealth, but if the children of the poor began taking over government it would destroy the existing hierarchy of estates and degrees and lead to anarchy. In Elyot's opinion, the very preservation of society demanded a commitment to education on the part of its traditional governors. He wrote his *Boke* in order to encourage them along this path and to guide their footsteps.

Book I, Part V. The Order of Learning that a Nobleman Should Be Trained in Before he Come to the Age of Seven Years

Some old authors hold opinion that before the age of seven years a child should not be instructed in letters. But those writers were either Greeks or Latins, among whom all doctrine and sciences were in their maternal tongues, by reason whereof they saved all that long time which at this day is spent in understanding perfectly the Greek or Latin. Wherefore it requireth now a longer time to the understanding of both. Therefore that infelicity of our time and country compelleth us to encroach somewhat upon the years of children, and specially of noblemen, that they may sooner attain to wisdom and gravity than private persons—considering, as I have said, their charge and example, which above all things is most to be esteemed.

Notwithstanding, I would not have them enforced by violence to learn, but . . . to be sweetly allured thereto with praises and such pretty gifts as children delight in. And their first letters to be painted or limned in a pleasant manner, wherein children of gentle courage have much delectation. And also there is no better allective [enticement] to noble wits than to induce them into a contention with their inferior companions—they sometime purposely suffering the more noble children to vanquish, and, as it were, giving to them place and sovereignty, though indeed the inferior children have more learning. But there can be nothing more convenient than by little and little to train and exercise them in speaking of Latin, informing them to know first the names in Latin of all things that cometh in sight and to name all the parts of their bodies; and giving them somewhat that they covet or desire, in most gentle manner to teach them to ask it again in Latin. And if by this means they may be induced to understand and speak Latin, it shall

3. *Calendar of Letters and Papers, Foreign and Domestic, of the Reign of Henry VIII*, ed. J. S. Brewer, Vol. 2 (1864). No. 3765.

afterwards be less grief to them, in a manner, to learn anything where they understand the language wherein it is written. . . .

And it shall be no reproach to a nobleman to instruct his own children, or at the leastways to examine them, by the way of dalliance or solace, considering that the Emperor Octavius Augustus disdained not to read the works of Cicero and Virgil to his children and nephews. And why should not noblemen rather so do than teach their children how at dice and cards they may cunningly lose and consume their own treasure and substance? Moreover, teaching representeth the authority of a prince: wherefore Dionysius, King of Sicily, when he was for tyranny expelled by his people, he came into Italy and there in a common school taught grammar. Wherewith when he was of his enemies upbraided and called a schoolmaster, he answered them that although Sicilians had exiled him, yet in despite of them all he reigned—noting thereby the authority that he had over his scholars. Also, when it was of him demanded what availed him Plato or philosophy, wherein he had been studious, he answered that they caused him to sustain adversity patiently and made his exile to be to him more facile and easy. Which courage and wisdom considered of his people, they eftsoons restored him unto his realm and estate royal; where, if he had procured against them hostility or wars, or had returned into Sicily with any violence, I suppose the people would have always resisted him and have kept him in perpetual exile, as the Romans did the proud king Tarquin, whose son ravished Lucrece.

But to return to my purpose, it shall be expedient that a nobleman's son in his infancy have with him continually only such as may accustom him by little and little to speak pure and elegant Latin. Semblably, the nurses and other women about him, if it be possible, to do the same: or at the leastway that they speak none English but that which is clean, polite, perfectly and articulately pronounced, omitting no letter or syllable, as foolish women oftentimes do of a wantonness, whereby divers noblemen and gentlemen's children (as I do at this day know) have attained corrupt and foul pronunciation.

This industry used in forming little infants, who shall doubt but that they (not lacking natural wit) shall be apt to receive learning when they come to more years? And in this wise may they be instructed, without any violence or enforcing; using the more part of the time until they come to the age of seven years in such disports as do appertain to children, wherein is no resemblance or similitude of vice.

Book I. Part X. What Order Should be in Learning, and Which Authors Should Be First Read

Now let us return to the order of learning apt for a gentleman. Wherein I am of the opinion . . . that I would have him learn Greek and Latin authors both at one time—or else to begin with Greek, as that it is hardest to come by, by reason of the diversity of tongues (which be five in number) and all must be known, or else unneth [scarcely] any poet can be well understood. And if a child do begin therein at seven years of age he may continually learn Greek authors three years and in the meantime use the Latin tongue as a familiar language—which in a nobleman's son may well come to pass, having none other persons to serve him or keeping him company but such as can speak Latin elegantly. And what doubt is there but so may he as soon speak good Latin as he may do pure French, which now is brought into as many rules and figures, and as long a grammar, as is Latin or Greek.

I will not contend who, among them that do write grammars of Greek (which now almost be innumerable), is the best, but that I refer to the discretion of a wise master. Always I would advise him not to detain the child too long in that tedious labors, either in the Greek or Latin grammar, for a gentle wit is therewith soon fatigate. Grammar being but an introduction to the understanding of authors, if it be made too long or exquisite to the learner it in a manner mortifieth his courage, and by that time he cometh to the most sweet and pleasant reading of old authors, the sparks of fervent desire of learning is extinct with the burden of grammar—like as a little fire is soon quenched with a great heap of small sticks, so that it can never come to the principal logs, where it should long burn in a great pleasant fire.

Now to follow my purpose: after a few and quick rules of grammar, immediately, or interlacing it therewith, would be read to the child Aesop's fables in Greek, in which argument children much do delight. And surely it is a much pleasant lesson, and also profitable, as well for that it is elegant and brief (and, notwithstanding, it hath much variety in words, and therewith much helpeth to the understanding of Greek), as also in those fables is included much moral and politic wisdom. Wherefore, in the teaching of them the master diligently must gather together those fables which may be most accommodate to the advancement of some virtue whereto he perceiveth the child inclined, or to the rebuke of some vice whereto he findeth his nature disposed. . . .

The next lesson would be some quick and merry dialogues, elect out of Lucian, which be without ribaldry or too much scorning—for either of them is exactly to be eschewed, specially for a nobleman; the one annoying the soul, the other his estimation concerning his gravity. The comedies of Aristophanes may be in the place of Lucian, and by reason that they be in metre they be the sooner learned by heart. I dare make none other comparison between them, for offending the friends of them both. But thus much I dare say, that it were better that a child should never read any part of Lucian than all Lucian.

I could rehearse divers other poets which for matter and eloquence be very necessary, but I fear me to be too long from noble Homer, from whom, as from a fountain, proceeded all eloquence and learning. For in his books be contained and most perfectly expressed not only the documents martial and discipline of arms, but also incomparable wisdoms, and instructions for politic governance of people, with the worthy commendation and laud of noble princes; wherewith the readers shall be so all inflamed that they most fervently shall desire and covet, by the imitation of their virtues, to acquire semblable glory. For the which occasion Aristotle, most sharpest-witted and excellent learned philosopher, as soon as he had received Alexander from King Philip his father, he before any other thing taught him the most noble works of Homer. Wherein Alexander found such sweetness and fruit that ever after he had Homer not only with him in all his journeys but also laid him under his pillow when he went to rest; and oftentimes would purposely wake some hours of the night, to take, as it were, his pastime with that most noble poet. . . . Therefore I now conclude that there is no lesson for a young gentleman to be compared with Homer, if he be plainly and substantially expounded and declared by the master.

Notwithstanding, forasmuch as the said works be very long and do require therefore a great time to be all learned and kenned, some Latin author would be therewith mixed, and specially Virgil, which in his work called *Eneidos* [*Aeneid*] is most like to Homer and almost the same Homer in Latin. Also, by the joining together of those authors, the one shall be the better understand by the other. And verily (as I before said) none one author serveth to so divers wits as doth Virgil. For there is not that affect or desire whereto any child's fantasy is disposed but in some of Virgil's works may be founden matter thereto apt and propice [suitable] . . . This noble Virgil, like to a good nurse, giveth to a child, if he will take it, everything apt for his wit and capacity; wherefore he is in the order of learning to be preferred before any other author Latin.

Book I. Part XI. The Most Commodious and Necessary Studies Succeeding Ordinately the Lessons of Poets

Demosthenes and Tully [i.e., Cicero], by the consent of all learned men, have preeminence and sovereignty over all orators; the one reigning in wonderful eloquence in the public weal of the Romans, who had the empire and dominion of all the world; the other, of no less estimation, in the city of Athens, which of long time was accounted the mother of sapience and the palace of music and all liberal sciences. Of which two orators may be attained not only eloquence, excellent and perfect, but also precepts of wisdom and gentle manners, with most commodious examples of all noble virtues and policy. Wherefore the master, in reading them, must well observe and express the parts and colors of rhetoric in them contained, according to the precepts of that art before learned.

The utility that a nobleman shall have by reading these orators is that when he shall happen to reason in council, or shall speak in a great audience, or to strange ambassadors of great princes, he shall not be constrained to speak words sudden and disordered, but shall bestow them aptly and in their places. Wherefore the most noble Emperor Octavius is highly commended, for that he never spake in the Senate or to the people of Rome but in an oration prepared and purposely made.

Also, to prepare the child to understanding of histories, which, being replenished with the names of countries and towns unknown to the reader do make the history tedious, or else the less pleasant; so if they be in any wise known, it increaseth an inexplicable delectation. It shall be therefore, and also for refreshing the wit, a convenient lesson to behold the old tables of Ptolemy, wherein all the world is painted, having first some introduction into the sphere. . . . And surely this lesson is both pleasant and necessary. For what pleasure is it in one hour to behold those realms, cities, seas, rivers, and mountains that uneth in an old man's life cannot be journeyed and pursued. What incredible delight is taken in beholding the diversities of people, beasts, fowls, fishes, trees, fruits, and herbs; to know the sundry manners and conditions of people, and the variety of their natures—and that in a warm study or parlor, without peril of the sea or danger of long and painful journeys. I cannot tell what more pleasure should happen to a gentle wit than to behold in his own house everything that within all the world is contained. . . .

Cosmography being substantially perceived, it is then time to induce a child to the reading of histories: but first to set him in a fervent courage, the master in the most pleasant and elegant wise expressing what incomparable delectation, utility, and commodity shall happen to emperors, kings, princes, and all other gentlemen by reading of histories. . . . It is best that he begin with Titus Livius, not only for his elegancy of writing, which floweth in him like a fountain of sweet milk, but also forasmuch as by reading that author he may know how the most noble city of Rome, of a small and poor beginning, by prowess and virtue, little and little came to the empire and dominion of all the world. Also in that city he may behold the form of a public weal: which, if the insolency and pride of Tarquin had not excluded kings out of the city, it had been the most noble and perfect of all other. . . .

Julius Caesar and Sallust, for their compendious writing—to the understanding whereof is required an exact and perfect judgment—and also for the exquisite order of battle and continuing of the history without any variety whereby the pain of study should be alleviate, they two would be reserved until he that shall read them shall see some experience in semblable matters. And then shall he find in them such pleasure and commodity as therewith a noble and gentle heart ought to be satisfied. . . .

In the learning of these authors a young gentleman shall be taught to note and mark not only the order and elegancy in declaration of the history, but also the occasion of the wars, the counsels and preparations on either part, the estimation of the captains, the manner and form of their governance, the continuance of the battle, the fortune and success of the whole affairs. Semblably . . . in other daily affairs: the estate of the public weal, if it be prosperous or in decay; what is the very occasion of the one or of the other; the form and manner of the governance thereof; the good and evil qualities of them that be rulers; the commodities and good sequel of virtue; the discommodities and evil conclusions of vicious license. Surely if a nobleman do thus seriously and diligently read histories, I dare affirm there is no study or science for him of equal commodity and pleasure, having regard to every time and age.

By the time that the child do come to seventeen years of age, to the intent his courage be bridled with reason, it were needful to read unto him some works of philosophy—specially that part that may inform him unto virtuous manners: which part of philosophy is called moral. Wherefore there would be read to him, for an introduction, two the first books of the work of Aristotle called *Ethicae*, wherein is contained the definitions and proper significations of every virtue—and that to be learned in Greek; for the translations that we yet have be but a rude and gross shadow of the eloquence and wisdom of Aristotle.

Forthwith would follow the work of Cicero called in Latin *De officiis*, whereunto yet is no proper English word to be given; but to provide for it some manner of exposition, it may be said in this form: "Of the Duties and Manners appertaining to Men." But above all other the works of Plato would be most studiously read, when the judgment of a man is come to perfection, and by the other studies is instructed in the form of speaking that philosophers used. Lord God, what incomparable sweetness of words and matter shall he find in the said works of Plato and Cicero; wherein is joined gravity with dilectation, excellent wisdom with divine eloquence, absolute virtue with pleasure incredible, and every place is so infarced [stuffed] with profitable counsel joined with honesty that those three books be almost sufficient to make a perfect and excellent governor.

The Proverbs of Solomon, with the Books of Ecclesiastes and Ecclesiasticus, be very good lessons. All the historical parts of the Bible be right necessary for to be read of a nobleman, after that he is mature in years. And the residue (with the New Testament) is to be reverently touched, as a celestial jewel or relic; having the chief interpreter of those books, true and constant faith. . . . It would not be forgotten that the little book of the most excellent Doctor Erasmus Roterodamus (which he wrote to Charles, now being emperor and then prince of Castile), which book is entitled *The Institution of a Christian Prince*, would be as familiar alway with gentlemen at all times and in every age as was Homer with the great king Alexander, or Xenophon with Scipio: for as all men may judge that have read that work of Erasmus, that there was never book written in Latin that in so little a portion contained of sentence, eloquence, and virtuous exhortation a more compendious abundance.

*Book I. Part XII. Why Gentlemen in this Present Time Be Not
Equal in Doctrine to the Ancient Noblemen*

Now will I somewhat declare of the chief causes why, in our time, noblemen be not as excellent in learning as they were in old time among the Romans and Greeks. Surely, as I have diligently marked in daily experience, the principal causes be these: the pride, avarice, and negligence of parents; and the lack or fewness of sufficient masters or teachers.

As I said, pride is the first cause of this inconvenience. For of those persons be some which, without shame, dare affirm that to a great gentleman it is a notable reproach to be well learned and to be called a great clerk: which name they account to be of so base estimation that they never have it in their mouths but when they speak anything in derision. . . . These persons that so much contemn learning, that they would that gentlemen's children should have no part, or very little thereof, but rather should spend their youth alway (I say not only in hunting and hawking, which, moderately used as solaces ought to be, I intend not to dispraise) but in those idle pastimes which, for the vice that is therein, the commandment of the prince and the universal consent of the people, expressed in statutes and laws, do prohibit: I mean playing at dice, and other games named unlawful. These persons, I say, should remember—or else now learn, if they never else heard it—that the noble Philip, King of Macedonia, who subdued all Greece, above all the good fortunes that ever he had, most rejoiced that his son Alexander was born in the time that Aristotle the philosopher flourished, by whose instruction he might attain to most excellent learning. Also the same Alexander oftentimes said that he was equally as much bounden to Aristotle as to his father, King Philip: for of his father he received life, but of Aristotle he received the way to live nobly. . . .

Verily, they be far from good reason, in mine opinion, which covet to have their children goodly in stature, strong, deliver [nimble], well singing: wherein trees, beasts, fishes, and birds be not only with them equal, but also far do exceed them. And cunning [knowledge], whereby only man excelleth all other creatures in earth, they reject and account unworthy to be in their children. What unkind appetite were it to desire to be father rather of a piece of flesh, that can only move and feel, than of a child that should have the perfect form of a man? . . .

Book I. Part XIII. The Second and Third Decay of Learning among Gentlemen

The third cause of this hindrance is negligence of parents, which I do specially note in this point. There have been divers, as well gentlemen as of the nobility, that, delighting to have their sons excellent in learning, have provided for them cunning masters, who substantially have taught them grammar and very well instructed them to speak Latin elegantly; whereof the parents have taken much delectation. But when they have had of grammar sufficient, and be comen to the age of fourteen years, and do approach or draw toward the estate of man, which age is called mature or ripe (wherein not only the said learning, continued by much experience, shall be perfectly digested and confirmed in perpetual remembrance, but also more serious learning contained in other liberal sciences, and also philosophy, would then be learned), the parents—that thing nothing regarding,[4] but being sufficed that their children can only speak Latin properly, or make verses without matter or sentence—they from thenceforth do suffer them to live in idleness; or else, putting them to service, do, as it were, banish them from all virtuous study or exercise of that which they before learned; so that we may behold divers young gentlemen who in their infancy and childhood were wondered at for their aptness to learning and prompt speaking of elegant Latin, which now, being men, not only have forgotten their congruity (as in the common word) and unneth can speak one whole sentence in true Latin, but, that wars is, hath all learning in derision, and in scorn thereof will, of wantonness, speak the most barbarously that they can imagine.

4. i.e., not taking into account the advantages of further learning.

Roger Ascham:
The Scholemaster

One of the most influential of the schemes of education devised by Renaissance humanists was that outlined by Juan Luis Vives in his treatise *On Education* in 1531. Other innovators preferred a more practical approach and set up schools in which to try out their ideas. Among the most famous of these was the Strasbourg "Gymnasium" founded by Johannes Sturm (Latinized as "Sturmius," 1507–89), who had established his reputation by producing an edition of Cicero. Strasbourg was the chosen home of the reformer Martin Bucer, and attracted visitors from all over Protestant Europe. These included Roger Ascham, who had already made a name for himself as one of the finest Greek scholars in England. Ascham was a close friend of Bucer, whom he had come to know when the reformer took refuge at Cambridge in the late 1540s, and it was through Bucer that he made contact with Sturm. Ascham and Sturm never seem to have met, but they kept up a regular correspondence and it was the example of Sturm that prompted Ascham to compose his own treatise on education a few years before his death in 1568. *The Scholemaster* was an immediate success. Published posthumously in 1570, it went through four editions in the next twelve years and provided for the late-Elizabethan and early-Stuart generations the same sort of stimulus that their fathers and grandfathers had found in Sir Thomas Elyot's *The Boke Named the Governour.*

Elyot and Ascham between them played a major part in transforming both the form and the substance of English education. A knowledge of the classics and the Bible came to be one of the hallmarks of a gentleman, and references that today would require elucidation through a footnote were for the next three centuries or so part of the common culture of the English-speaking world. Several of Shakespeare's earliest works reveal his debt to his grammar-school education. For example, Ovid's *Metamorphoses*, with its vivid descriptions of the rape and mutilation of Philomela by Tereus, influenced the presentation of similar actions in *Titus Andronicus* (1591), and Ovid's *Ars Amatoria* and *Amores* contributed to the eroticism of Shakespeare's long narrative poems *Venus and Adonis* (1593) and *The Rape of Lucrece* (1594).

"Making of Latins"

Ascham spent twenty years teaching Greek at Cambridge and thereby became aware how much his pupils had suffered at the hands of their schoolmasters, who all too frequently concentrated on the dry bones of grammar without relating them to the living body of classical literature, and terrorized their charges instead of spurring them on by kindness. Moreover, when he was just short of forty, Ascham married and in due course became the father of two boys. He now had the opportunity to put his theories into practice in his own home, and *The Scholemaster* was the fruit of this, as well as of his earlier experience.

There is no one thing that hath more either dulled the wits or taken away the will of children from learning than the care they have to satisfy their masters in making of Latins. For the scholar is commonly beat for the making when the master were more worthy to be beat for the mending, or rather marring, of the same, the master many times being as ignorant as the child what to say properly and fitly to the matter. . . .

There is a way, touched in the first book of Cicero *De Oratore*, which, wisely brought into schools, truly taught and constantly used, would not only take wholly away this butcherly fear in making of Latins but would also, with ease and pleasure and in short time—as I know by good experience— work a true choice and placing of words, a right ordering of sentences, an easy understanding of the tongue, a readiness to speak, a facility to write, a true judgment both of his own and other men's doings, what tongue soever he doth use.

The way is this. . . . Let the master read unto him the *Epistles* of Cicero, gathered together and chosen out by Sturmius for the capacity of children.

First let him teach the child, cheerfully and plainly, the cause and matter of the letter. Then let him construe it into English so oft as the child may easily carry away the understanding of it. Lastly, parse it over perfectly. This done thus, let the child by and by both construe and parse it over again, so that it may appear that the child doubteth in nothing that his master taught him before. After this, the child must take a paper book and, sitting in some place where no man shall prompt him, by himself, let him translate into English his former lesson. Then, showing it to his master, let the master take from him his Latin book and, pausing an hour at the least, then let the child translate his own English into Latin again in another paper book. When the child bringeth it turned into Latin, the master must compare it with Tully's [i.e., Cicero's] book and lay them both together. And where the child doth well, either in choosing or true placing of Tully's words, let the master praise him and say, "Here ye do well." For I assure you there is no such whetstone to sharpen a good wit and encourage a will to learning as is praise.

But if the child miss—either in forgetting a word, or in changing a good with a worse, or misordering the sentence—I would not have the master either frown or chide with him, if the child have done his diligence and used no truantship therein. For I know by good experience that a child shall take more profit of two faults gently warned of than of four things rightly hit. For then the master shall have good occasion to say unto him, "Tully would have used such a word, not this. Tully would have placed this word here, not there; would have used this case, this number, this person, this degree, this gender. He would have used this mood, this tense, this simple rather than this compound; this adverb here not there. He would have ended the sentence with this verb, not with that noun or participle, etc."

In these few lines I have wrapped up the most tedious part of grammar, and also the ground of almost all the rules that are so busily taught by the master, and so hardly learned by the scholar, in all common schools; which after this sort the master shall teach without all error, and the scholar shall learn without great pain—the master being led by so sure a guide, and the scholar being brought into so plain and easy a way. . . . For when the master shall compare Tully's book with his scholar's translation, let the master at the first lead and teach his scholar to join the rules of his grammar book with the examples of his present lesson, until the scholar by himself be able to fetch out of his grammar every rule for every example, so as the grammar book be ever in the scholar's hand, and also used of him as a dictionary for every present use. This is a lively and perfect way of teaching of rules: where the common way, used in common schools, to read the grammar alone, by itself, is tedious for the master, hard for the scholar, cold and uncomfortable for them both.

Let your scholar be never afraid to ask you any doubt, but use discreetly the best allurements ye can to encourage him to the same, lest his overmuch fearing of you drive him to seek some misorderly shift—as to seek to be helped by some other book, or to be prompted by some other scholar, and so go about to beguile you much and himself more.

With this way of good understanding the matter, plain construing, diligent parsing, daily translating, cheerful admonishing, and heedful amending of faults, never leaving behind just praise for well doing, I would have the scholar brought up withal, till he had read and translated over the first book of *Epistles* chosen out by Sturmius, with a good piece of comedy of Terence also. . . .

"Learning Should Be Taught Rather by Love Than Fear"

And speaking thus much of the wits of children for learning, the opportunity of the place and goodness of the matter might require to have here declared the most special notes of a good wit for learning in a child—after the manner and custom of a good horseman, who is skillful to know, and able to tell others, how by certain sure signs a man may choose a colt that is like to prove another day excellent for the saddle. And it is pity that commonly more care is had—yea, and that among very wise men—to find out rather a cunning man for their horse than a cunning man for their children. They say nay in word, but they do so in deed; for to the one they will gladly give a stipend of two hundred crowns by year, and loth to offer to the other two hundred shillings.[1] God, that sitteth in heaven, laugheth their choice to scorn and rewardeth their liberality as it should, for He suffereth them to have tame and well-ordered horse, but wild and unfortunate children. And therefore, in the end, they find more pleasure in their horse than comfort in their children. . . .

Some will say that children, of nature, love pastime and mislike learning, because in their kind the one is easy and pleasant, the other hard and wearisome. Which is an opinion not so true as some men ween, for the matter lieth not so much in the disposition of them that be young as in the order and manner of bringing up by them that be old, nor yet in the difference of learning and pastime. For beat a child if he dance not well, and cherish him though he learn not well, ye shall have him unwilling to go to dance, and glad to go to his book. Knock him always when he draweth his shaft ill, and favor him again though he fault at his book, ye shall have him very loth to be in the field and very willing to be in the school.[2] Yea. I say

1. A crown was worth five shillings.
2. *draweth his shaft ill* refers to archery. Popular in Tudor England, it was encouraged by the government, which needed a reserve of archers for use if war broke out. Ascham's *Toxophilus*, a treatise on archery, was widely read and admired.

more—and not of myself, but by the judgment of those from whom few wise men will gladly dissent—that if ever the nature of man be given at any time more than other to receive goodness, it is in innocency of young years, before that experience of evil have taken root in him. For the pure, clean wit of a sweet young babe is like the newest wax, most able to receive the best and fairest printing; and like a new, bright silver dish, never occupied, to receive and keep clean anything that is put into it. . . .

The godly counsels of Solomon and Jesus, the son of Sirach,[3] for sharp keeping-in and bridling of youth, are meant rather for fatherly correction than masterly beating; rather for manners than for learning; for other places than for schools. For God forbid but all evil touches, wantonness, lying, picking, sloth, will, stubbornness, and disobedience should be with sharp chastisement daily cut away.

This discipline was well-known and diligently used among the Grecians and old Romans, as doth appear in Aristophanes, Isocrates, and Plato, and also in the comedies of Plautus, where we see that children were under the rule of three persons, *Praeceptore, Paedagogo, Parente.* The schoolmaster taught him learning with all gentleness. The governor corrected his manners with much sharpness. The father held the stern of his whole obedience. And so he that used to teach did not commonly use to beat, but remitted that over to another man's charge. But what shall we say when now in our days the schoolmaster is used both for *Praeceptor* in learning and *Paedagogus* in manners? Surely I would he should not confound their offices, but discreetly use the duty of both, so that neither ill touches should be left unpunished nor gentleness in teaching anywise omitted. And he shall well do both if wisely he do appoint diversity of time and separate place for either purpose, using always such discreet moderation as the schoolhouse should be counted a sanctuary against fear, and very well learning a common pardon for ill doing, if the fault of itself be not overheinous.

And thus the children, kept up in God's fear and preserved by His grace, finding pain in ill doing and pleasure in well studying, should easily be brought to honesty of life and perfectness of learning—the only mark that good and wise fathers do wish and labor that their children should most busily and carefully shoot at. . . .

"Nobility Governed by Learning and Wisdom"

The humanists' insistence that *virtù* took no account of birth or wealth struck at the privileged position of the nobles and gentry in the Euro-

3. Jesus ben Sirach, who lived in Palestine c. 190 B.C. and wrote in Hebrew, was the author of the apocryphal Ecclesiasticus, which was included in the Greek Bible (the Septuagint) but excluded from the Hebrew version.

pean monarchies. Sir Thomas Elyot was alarmed at the prospect of the aristocracy losing its customary influence, so he wrote *The Boke Named the Governour* in order to persuade the traditional governing class of England to fit itself for new responsibilities. Ascham hammered home the same message, but in fact by the time he wrote the situation was already changing. In Elizabeth's reign the sons of nobles and gentry began to flock to the universities—previously the preserve of clerics— and equip themselves with a humanist education. By so doing they trained themselves for public life and ensured their continuing importance in the new world that was emerging out of the older feudal one.

They were set an example by Queen Elizabeth, who was herself the product of a humanist education, and, in her own inimitable way, something of a bluestocking. Ascham had been her tutor, and his eulogy of her is therefore based upon firsthand knowledge. Ascham's praise of "exercises and pastimes" is also based upon experience, for he was a keen archer and had produced a treatise upon the subject entitled *Toxophilus* which won him a pension from Henry VIII.

Our time is so far from that old discipline and obedience, as now not only young gentlemen but even very girls dare without all fear—though not without open shame—where they list, and how they list, marry themselves, in spite of father, mother, God, good order, and all. The cause of this evil is that youth is least looked unto when they stand most need of good keep and regard. It availeth not to see them well taught in young years, and after, when they come to lust and youthful days, to give them license to live as they lust themselves. For if ye suffer the eye of a young gentleman once to be entangled with vain sights, and the ear to be corrupted with fond or filthy talk, the mind shall quickly fall sick and soon vomit and cast up all the wholesome doctrine that he received in childhood, though he were never so well brought up before. And being once englutted with vanity, he will straightway loath all learning and all good counsel to the same. And the parents, for all their great cost and charge, reap only in the end the fruit of grief and care.

This evil is not common to poor men, as God will have it, but proper to rich and great men's children, as they deserve it. Indeed, from seven to seventeen young gentlemen commonly be carefully enough brought up. But from seventeen to seven-and-twenty (the most dangerous time of all a man's life, and most slippery to stay well in) they have commonly the rein of all license in their own hand, and specially such as do live in the Court. And that which is most to be marveled at, commonly the wisest and also best men be found the fondest fathers in this behalf. And if some good father would seek some remedy herein, yet the mother (if the house hold of our lady) had rather—yea, and will too—have her son cunning and bold in making him to live trimly when he is young, than by learning and travel to be able to serve his Prince and his country both wisely in peace and stoutly in war when he is old.

The fault is in yourselves, ye noblemen's sons, and therefore ye deserve the greater blame, that commonly the meaner men's children come to be the wisest councillors and greatest doers in the weighty affairs of this realm. And why? For God will have it so, of His providence, because ye will have it no otherwise, by your negligence. And God is a good God and wisest in all His doings, that will place virtue and displace vice in those kingdoms where He doth govern. For He knoweth that nobility without virtue and wisdom is blood indeed, but blood truly, without bones and sinews, and so of itself, without the other, very weak to bear the burden of weighty affairs. . . .

Nobility governed by learning and wisdom is indeed most like a fair ship, having tide and wind at will, under the rule of a skilful master; when, contrariwise, a ship—carried, yea, with the highest tide and greatest wind— lacking a skilful master, most commonly doth either sink itself upon sands or break itself upon rocks. And even so, how many have been either drowned in vain pleasure or overwhelmed by stout wilfulness, the histories of England be able to afford overmany examples unto us. Therefore, ye great and noble men's children, if ye will have rightfully that praise, and enjoy surely that place, which your fathers have and elders had and left unto you, ye must keep it as they gat it, and that is by the only way of virtue, wisdom, and worthiness. . . .

Erasmus, the honor of learning of all our time, said wisely that experience is the common schoolhouse of fools and ill men. Men of wit and honesty be otherwise instructed. For there be that keep them out of fire, and yet was never burned; that beware of water, and yet was never nigh drowning; that hate harlots, and was never at the stews [i.e., brothels]; that abhor falsehood, and never brake promises themselves. . . . Learning therefore, ye wise fathers, and good bringing up, and not blind and dangerous experience, is the next and readiest way that must lead your children first to wisdom and then to worthiness (if ever ye purpose they shall come there).

And to say all in short, though I lack authority to give counsel, yet I lack not goodwill to wish that the youth in England, specially gentlemen, and namely nobility, should be by good bringing up so grounded in judgment of learning, so founded in love of honesty, as when they should be called forth to the execution of great affairs in service of their Prince and country they might be able to use and to order all experiences (were they good, were they bad), and that according to the square, and rule and line of wisdom, learning, and virtue.

And I do not mean by all this my talk that young gentlemen should always be poring on a book, and by using good studies should lose honest pleasure and haunt no good pastime. I mean nothing less. For it is well known that I both like and love, and have always and do yet still use, all exercises and pastimes that be fit for my nature and ability. . . . Therefore, to ride comely; to run fair at the tilt or ring; to play at all weapons; to shoot fair in bow, or surely in gun; to vault lustily; to run; to leap; to wrestle; to swim; to dance comely; to sing and play of instruments cunningly; to hawk; to hunt; to play at tennis; and all pastimes generally which be joined with labor, used in open place and on the daylight, containing either some fit exercise for war or some pleasant pastime for peace, be not only comely and decent but also very necessary for a courtly gentleman to use. . . .

To join learning with comely exercises, Count Baldassare Castiglione, in his book *Cortegiano*, doth trimly teach. Which book, advisedly read and diligently followed but one year at home in England would do a young gentleman more good, I wis, than three years travel abroad spent in Italy. And I marvel this book is no more read in the Court than it is, seeing it is so well translated into English by a worthy gentleman, Sir Th. Hoby, who was many ways well furnished with learning and very expert in knowledge of divers tongues.

And beside good precepts in books in all kinds of tongues, this Court also never lacked many fair examples for young gentlemen to follow. . . . There is one example for all the gentlemen of the Court to follow that may well satisfy them, or nothing will serve them, nor no example move them to goodness and learning. It is your shame—I speak to you all, you young gentlemen of England—that one maid should go beyond you all, in excellency of learning and knowledge of divers tongues. Point forth six of the best given gentlemen of this Court, and all they together show not so much good will, spend not so much time, bestow not so many hours daily, orderly and constantly for the increase of learning and knowledge, as doth the Queen's Majesty herself. Yea, I believe that beside her perfect readiness in Latin, Italian, French, and Spanish, she readeth here now at Windsor more Greek every day than some prebendary of this Church doth read Latin in a whole week. And that which is most praiseworthy of all, within the walls of her privy chamber she hath obtained that excellency of learning, to understand, speak and write both wittily with head and fair with hand, as scarce one or two rare wits in both the universities have in many years reached unto. Amongst all the benefits that God hath blessed me withal, next the knowledge of Christ's true religion I count this the greatest: that it pleased God to call me to be one poor minister in setting forward these excellent gifts of learning in this most excellent Prince. Whose only example, if the rest of our nobility would follow, then might England be for learning and wisdom in nobility a spectacle to all the world beside. . . .

Take heed therefore, ye great ones in the Court. Yea, though ye be the greatest of all, take heed how ye live. For as you great ones use to do, so all mean men love to do. You be indeed makers or marrers of all men's manners within the realm. For though God hath placed you to be chief in making of laws, to bear greatest authority, to command all others, yet God doth order that all your laws, all your authority, all your commandments, do not half so much with mean men as doth your example and manner of living. And for example, even in the greatest matter, if you yourselves do serve God gladly and orderly for conscience' sake, not coldly and sometime for manner' sake, you carry all the Court with you, and the whole realm beside, earnestly and orderly to do the same. If you do otherwise you be the only authors of all misorders in religion, not only to the Court but to all England beside. Infinite shall be made cold by your example that never were hurt by reading of books.

"Italy Now Is Not That Italy That It Was Wont to Be"

English humanists were ambivalent in their attitude towards Italy. It was esteemed as the former capital of the Roman empire, honored as the birthplace of the Renaissance, and held in high regard for its music, manners, swordsmanship, and even its cuisine. But it was also regarded with suspicion as the seat of the Pope, whom most Englishmen believed to be Antichrist, and there was general agreement among them that whatever Renaissance scholars might teach about the need to acquire virtue, contemporary Italy was the home of vice. In *The Unfortunate Traveler, or The Life of Jack Wilton* (1593), a mixture of adventure story and jestbook, Thomas Nashe presents a complete catalogue of Italian horrors: rapes and robberies, plagues and poisonings, torments, depravity, revenge, and murder. Similar events also characterize the sensational tales that often became the source material for the plots of English tragedies. Some of these tragedies, such as Webster's *The White Devil* (1612), were based on historical events; others, such as Shakespeare's *Othello*, were based on fictional material.

Nashe's little book reflected the popular literary image of Italy—and contributed to it—rather than any firsthand experience. Nashe never seems to have visited Venice, Florence, Rome, and Bologna, the locations of his story. As for Ascham, he spent a mere nine days in Italy, but what he saw of Venice convinced him that the city lacked "all service of God in spirit and truth." Since, in his eyes, "an Italianate Englishman is the devil incarnate," Ascham determined to improve the standards of English education, so that his fellow countrymen would no longer have to put their souls at risk by venturing south of the Alps.

Sir Richard Sackville[4] . . . was most earnest with me to have me say my mind also, what I thought concerning the fancy that many young gentlemen of England have to travel abroad—and namely to lead a long life in Italy . . . "Sir," quoth I, "I take going thither and living there, for a young gentleman that doth not go under the keep and guard of such a man as both by wisdom can, and authority dare, rule him, to be marvellous dangerous." And why I said so then, I will declare at large now: which I said then privately and write now openly not because I do contemn either the knowledge of strange and diverse tongues—and namely the Italian tongue, which next the Greek and Latin tongue I like and love above all other—or else because I do despise the learning that is gotten, or the experience that is gathered, in strange countries, or for any private malice that I bear to Italy. Which country, and in it namely Rome, I have always specially honored, because time was when Italy and Rome have been, to the great good of us that now live, the best breeders and bringers-up of the worthiest men, not only for wise speaking but also for well doing in all civil affairs, that ever was in the world.

But now that time is gone, and though the place remain, yet the old and present manners do differ as far as black and white, as virtue and vice. Virtue once made that country mistress over all the world. Vice now maketh that country slave to them that before were glad to serve it. . . . For sin by lust and vanity hath and doth breed up everywhere common contempt of God's word, private contention in many families, open factions in every city; and so, making themselves bond to vanity and vice at home, they are content to bear the yoke of serving strangers abroad. Italy now is not that Italy that it was wont to be, and therefore now not so fit a place as some do count it for young men to fetch either wisdom or honesty from thence. For surely they will make but bad scholars that be so ill masters to themselves. . . .

I was once in Italy myself, but I thank God my abode there was but nine days. And yet I saw in that little time, in one city, more liberty to sin than ever I heard tell of in our noble city of London in nine year. I saw it was there as free to sin, not only without all punishment but also without any man's marking, as it is free in the city of London to choose without all blame whether a man lust to wear shoe or pantocle [slipper]. And good cause why.

4. Sir Richard Sackville (d. 1566), known as "Fill-sack," made a fortune for himself as one of the government's financial officers. He was a friend of Ascham, who was entrusted by him with the education of his grandson, Robert Sackville, second Earl of Dorset.

For being unlike in truth of religion they must needs be unlike in honesty of living. For blessed be Christ, in our city of London commonly the commandments of God be more diligently taught, and the service of God more reverently used—and that daily, in many private men's houses—than they be in Italy once a week in their common churches; where masking ceremonies to delight the eye, and vain sounds to please the ear, do quite thrust out of the churches all service of God in spirit and truth. Yea, the Lord Mayor of London, being but a civil officer, is commonly for his time more diligent in punishing sin—the bent enemy against God and good order—than all the bloody Inquisitors in Italy be in seven year. For their care and charge is not to punish sin, not to amend manners, not to purge doctrine, but only to watch and oversee that Christ's true religion set no sure footing where the Pope hath any jurisdiction. . . .

Our "Italians" bring home with them other faults from Italy, though not so great as this of religion yet a great deal greater than many good men can well bear. For commonly they come home common contemners of marriage and ready persuaders of all other to the same. Not because they love virginity, nor yet because they hate pretty young virgins; but being free in Italy to go whithersoever lust will carry them, they do not like that law and honesty should be such a bar to their like liberty at home in England. And yet they be the greatest makers of love, the daily dalliers with such pleasant words, with such smiling and secret countenances, with such signs, tokens, wagers purposed to be lost before they were purposed to be made, with bargains of wearing colors, flowers, and herbs to breed occasion of often meeting of him and her, and bolder talking of this and that, etc. And although I have seen some, innocent of all ill and staid in all honesty, that have used these things without all harm, without all suspicion of harm, yet these knacks were brought first into England by them that learned them in Italy. . . .

"Books . . . Most Worthy for a Man, the Lover of Learning and Honesty"

A good student would bend himself to read diligently over Tully, and with him also at the same time as diligently Plato and Xenophon with his books of philosophy, Isocrates and Demosthenes with his orations, and Aristotle with his rhetorics—which five of all other be those whom Tully best loved and specially followed . . . These books be not many, nor long, nor rude in speech, nor mean in matter; but next the majesty of God's holy word most worthy for a man, the lover of learning and honesty, to spend his life in. . . .
In tragedies (the goodliest argument of all, and for the use either of a learned preacher or a civil gentleman more profitable than Homer, Pindar, Virgil,

and Horace—yea, comparable in my opinion with the doctrine of Aristotle, Plato and Xenophon) the Grecians Sophocles and Euripides far overmatch our Seneca in Latin . . . although Seneca's elocution and verse be very commendable for his time . . . In histories, and namely in Livy, the like diligence of imitation could bring excellent learning and breed staid judgment in taking any like matter in hand. Only Livy were a sufficient task for one man's study, to compare him first with his fellow for all respects, Dion. Halicarnassus, who both lived in one time, took both one history in hand to write, deserved both like praise of learning and eloquence; then with Polybius, that wise writer whom Livy professeth to follow. . . . Lastly with Thucydides, to whose imitation Livy is curiously bent. . . .

The Latin tongue, concerning any part of pureness of it, from the spring to the decay of the same, did not endure much longer than is the life of a well-aged man. . . . Of this short time of any pureness of the Latin tongue, for the first forty year of it and all the time before, we have no piece of learning left save Plautus and Terence, with a little rude, unperfect pamphlet of the elder Cato. And as for Plautus, except the schoolmaster be able to make wise and ware choice, first in propriety of words, then in framing of phrases and sentences, and chiefly in choice of honesty of matter, your scholar were better to play than learn all that is in him. But surely, if judgment for the tongue and direction for the manners be wisely joined with the diligent reading of Plautus, then truly Plautus, for that pureness of the Latin tongue in Rome when Rome did most flourish in well doing (and so thereby in well speaking also), is such a plentiful storehouse for common eloquence in mean matters and all private men's affairs as the Latin tongue, for that respect, hath not the like again. When I remember the worthy time of Rome wherein Plautus did live I must needs honor the talk of that time which we see Plautus doth use.

Terence is also a storehouse of the same tongue for another time, following soon after, and although he be not so full and plentiful as Plautus is for multitude of matters and diversity of words, yet his words be chosen so purely, placed so orderly, and all his stuff so neatly packed up and wittily compassed in every place, as by all men's judgment he is counted the cunninger workman, and to have his shop, for the room that is in it, more finely appointed and trimlier ordered than Plautus is. . . .

"Our Rude, Beggarly Rhyming"

The meter and verse of Plautus and Terence be very mean and not to be followed—which is not their reproach but the fault of the time wherein they wrote, when no kind of poetry in the Latin tongue was brought to perfection. . . . This matter maketh me gladly remember my sweet time spent at Cambridge, and the pleasant talk which I had oft with Mr. Cheke and Mr. Watson[5] of this fault, not only in the old Latin poets but also in our new English rhymers at this day. They wished, as Virgil and Horace were not wedded to follow the faults of former fathers (a shrewd marriage in greater matters), but by a right imitation of the perfect Grecians had brought poetry to perfectness also in the Latin tongue, that we Englishmen likewise would acknowledge and understand rightfully our rude, beggarly rhyming, brought first into Italy by Goths and Huns—when all good verses, and all good learning too, were destroyed by them—and after carried into France and Germany, and at last received into England by men of excellent wit indeed but of small learning and less judgment in that behalf.

But now, when men know the difference and have the examples both of the best and of the worst, surely to follow rather the Goths in rhyming than the Greeks in true versification were even to eat acorns with swine when we may freely eat wheat bread amongst men. Indeed Chaucer . . . my Lord of Surrey, Mr. Wyatt . . .[6] and other gentlemen, in translating . . . have gone as far (to their great praise) as the copy they followed could carry them. But if such good wits and forward diligence had been directed to follow the best examples, and not have been carried by time and custom to content themselves with that barbarous and rude rhyming, amongst their other worthy praises which they have justly deserved this had not been the least, to be counted amongst men of learning and skill more like unto the Grecians than unto the Gothians in handling of their verse. . . .

For as the worthiest poets in Athens and Rome were more careful to satisfy the judgment of one learned than rash in pleasing the humor of a rude multitude, even so if men in England now had the like reverend regard to learning, skill, and judgment, and durst not presume to write except they came with the like learning, and also did use like diligence in searching out not only just measure in every meter (as every ignorant person may easily do)

5. Sir John Cheke (1514–57) was a pioneer in the establishment of Greek studies at Cambridge. Among his pupils at St. John's College was William Cecil, afterwards Lord Burghley and Elizabeth's principal minister, who married Cheke's sister. Another pupil was Ascham, who succeeded Cheke as Public Orator of the university. Cheke was tutor to Henry VIII's son, the future Edward VI, and in 1553, the last year of Edward's reign, was appointed Secretary of State.

Cheke was a committed Protestant, in contrast to Thomas Watson, another distinguished fellow of St. John's, who wrote a tragedy called *Absalom* and became Bishop of Lincoln under the Catholic Mary Tudor.

6. Henry Howard, Earl of Surrey (1517?–47), and Sir Thomas Wyatt (1503?–42), as well as being distinguished poets in their own right, also had a profound knowledge of classical and Italian literature. Surrey was commended by Ascham for being "the first of all Englishmen in translating the fourth book of Virgil," and Puttenham praised him and Wyatt as "novices newly crept out of the schools of Dante, Ariosto, and Petrarch [who] greatly polished our rude and homely manner of vulgar poesy."

but also true quantity in every foot and syllable (as only the learned shall be able to do, and as the Greeks and Romans were wont to do), surely then, rash, ignorant heads which now can easily reckon up fourteen syllables and easily stumble on every rhyme, either durst not, for lack of such learning, or else would not, in avoiding such labor, be so busy as everywhere they be, and shops in London should not be so full of lewd and rude rhymes as commonly they are.

But now the ripest of tongue be readiest to write, and many daily in setting out books and ballads make great show of blossoms and buds, in whom is neither root of learning nor fruit of wisdom at all. Some that make Chaucer in English and Petrarch in Italian their gods in verses, and yet be not able to make true difference what is a fault and what is a just praise in those two worthy wits, will much mislike this my writing. But . . . this misliking of rhyming beginneth not now of any newfangle singularity, but hath been long disliked of many—and that of men of greatest learning and deepest judgment. And such that defend it do so either for lack of knowledge what is best, or else of very envy that any should perform that in learning whereunto they, as I said before, either for ignorance cannot, or for idleness will not, labor to attain unto.

England
and Her History

The Renaissance humanists took great pride in their achievement. As they saw it, they had pierced through the "darkness" of what they christened the "Middle Ages" and brought the world of antiquity into the full light of day. They did not do this simply out of love of learning for its own sake. They were convinced that the classical world had reached a peak of perfection from which mankind had subsequently declined, and that by recovering it they were providing a model for future progress. Yet in the course of analyzing the social, political, and cultural structures of ancient Greece and Rome, they became aware of the extent to which all societies were a compound of past and present, of good and bad. While retaining their veneration for antiquity, they increasingly applied their critical faculties and techniques to the world in which they lived, and brought under close scrutiny for the first time the legal, political, and societal systems of the postmedieval European states.

Sir Thomas Smith:
De Republica Anglorum

Sir Thomas Smith, born in 1513, was one of the most distinguished of the English humanists. He acquired his knowledge and love of Greek at Cambridge University, and took a leading part in the campaign to reform the pronunciation of the language that created bitter divisions among the academic community. He was also an accomplished lawyer, having been awarded his doctorate in civil (or Roman) law at the University of Padua, which was a major center of legal studies. After his return to England in 1544 he was appointed Professor of Civil Law at Cambridge, but four years later he was called out of academic life into government, as Secretary of State in the administration that Protector Somerset formed in the name of the young King Edward VI. He received his reward in the shape of a knighthood, but his ardent Protestantism, which made him particularly acceptable in Edward's reign, put an end to his career under Edward's successor, the Roman Catholic Mary Tudor.

Not until the accession of Elizabeth did Sir Thomas return to public life. He was elected to the House of Commons in Elizabeth's first Parliament, and in 1562 the Queen sent him on embassy to France, where he witnessed the opening stages of the Wars of Religion. After his return he was readmitted to the Privy Council, which governed England under the sovereign, and then sent back to France again in 1572 to discuss a possible marriage between Elizabeth and the Duc d'Alençon, brother to King Henry III. The discussion came to nothing, but Elizabeth showed her satisfaction with Sir Thomas by appointing him

Secretary of State. From 1572 until his death five years later he was at the heart of Elizabethan government and in frequent attendance upon the Queen.

Sir Thomas Smith's distinction as a scholar and his political career would have earned him a place in the reference books, but he has a further claim as the author of one of the earliest and most accomplished accounts of the English constitution. He composed the *De Republica Anglorum* during his first spell as ambassador to France, and a letter which he wrote at the time explains his motives: "Because in my absence I feel a yearning for our commonwealth, I have put together three books here at Toulouse describing it . . . and in these I have set forth almost the whole of its form, especially those points in which it differs from the others. But it differs in almost all, with the consequence that the work has grown larger than I expected. I have written it, moreover, in the language of our own country, in a style midway between the historical and the philosophical, giving it the shape in which I imagined that Aristotle wrote of the many Greek commonwealths. . . . I have furnished fruitful argument for those who would debate after the fashion of philosophers on single topics and raise nice points as to justice and injustice, and whether what is held yonder in England as law be the better, or what is held here and in those regions which are administered in accordance with the Roman Law. For all things almost are different, and I have set them forth on both sides in rough general outline."

Smith realized that constitutions do not exist in a vacuum. He therefore gave an account of the main features of Elizabethan society, which is one of the most valuable sections of his book, though in fact it derives in large part from William Harrison's *Description of England* that was incorporated into Raphael Holinshed's *Chronicles*, published in 1577. The *De Republica* did not appear in print until 1583, but it immediately established itself as a classic of its kind and its continuing popularity was attested by frequent reprints over the course of the next hundred years.

In the extract that follows, Smith traces the distinctions of class as determined by birth, education, and wealth, and proclaimed by such symbols as coats of arms. The significance of such matters to Elizabethan men and women is demonstrated by the Shakespeare family, for in 1596 "Shakespeare the Player" revived his father's earlier application to the College of Heralds for a coat of arms. As a former bailiff of his town, a magistrate and an alderman, Shakespeare senior, abetted by his son in London, was hoping for confirmation that his family had made the crucial breakthrough from yeoman status to the rank of gentleman.

In his plays, Shakespeare reveals his familiarity with the social structure of his native country. In *Henry VI, Part Two* Alexander Iden takes pride in being "an esquire of Kent," while in *Henry IV, Part Two*, Justice Shallow—a former classmate of Falstaff in the days when they were students at the Inns of Court—describes himself as "a poor esquire of this country, and one of the King's justices of the peace." In *As You Like It,* Shakespeare uses the pastoral convention to contrast various social and economic strata. Corin, for instance, a hired shepherd who owns neither field nor flock, speaks with dignity of his industry, honesty, and self-reliance:

> I am a true laborer: I earn that I eat, get that I wear, owe no man hate, envy no man's happiness, glad of other men's good, content with my harm, and the greatest of my pride is to see my ewes graze and my lambs suck. (III.ii)

Although Shakespeare was aware of social distinctions, he was also aware that birth, wealth, and rank do not define the essential human nature of those who possess them; in *All's Well That Ends Well* (1602) the King remarks that titles held by those without virtue are "a dropsied honour. Good alone / Is good . . . not by title" (II.iii.). The point is treated delightfully in *The Winter's Tale,* when two shepherds, father and son, are ennobled for their part in raising a princess who was abandoned as an infant. As the son explains:

> I was a gentleman born before my father; for the king's son took me by the hand, and called me brother; and then the two kings called my father brother; and then the prince, my brother, and the princess, my sister, called my father father; and so we wept; and there was the first gentleman-like tears that ever we shed. (V.ii.)

Social advancement, which is here treated lightheartedly, became a matter for increasing concern as the Tudor period drew to a close. Elizabeth had been extremely reluctant to bestow peerages: even her chief minister, William Cecil, who gave her forty years of devoted service, was only raised to the lowest rung of the aristocratic ladder.

James I, by contrast, was lavish in granting titles, and quickly began the practice of selling honors to all those who were willing, and rich enough, to buy them. There was no shortage of demand, for a great deal of new wealth had been created through trade, finance, and the law. English society had never been rigid, but the rate of change now increased rapidly and led to fears that persons of inferior status, who had hitherto been content to defer to their perceived superiors, would no longer be so compliant. As Hamlet explained to Horatio, "The age is grown so picked that the toe of the peasant comes so near the heel of the courtier, he galls his kibe" (*Hamlet*, V.i.)—in other words, the peasant apes the manners of the courtier so effectively that the distinction between them is in danger of disappearing altogether.

The disintegration of the social fabric is treated far more harshly by such playwrights as Philip Massinger in *A New Way to Pay Old Debts* (1621), Thomas Middleton in *A Chaste Maid in Cheapside* (1611) and Chapman, Marston, and Jonson in *Eastward Ho* (1605). These plays, and others like them—the so-called "city comedies"—satirize merchants who are ambitious to become gentlemen, and nobles who live by corrupt values. Even the Italianate revenge tragedies comment on the changes in English life that enabled the sons of farmers to "wash their hands and come up gentlemen" (*The Revenger's Tragedy* II.i.).

Sir Thomas Smith was writing at an early stage in this process, and although he observed that "gentlemen . . . be made good cheap in England" he did not seem particularly alarmed. A degree of fluidity was essential if the social structure was not to become dangerously divorced from economic realities, and Smith assumed that the requisite changes could be accommodated within the existing system. To this extent he reflects traditional attitudes that subsequent generations were to call into question.

Of Gentlemen

Gentlemen be those whom their blood and race doth make noble and known . . . or (in fewer words) old riches or prowess remaining in one stock . . . Yet such is the nature of all human things, and so the world is subject to mutability, that it doth many times fail: but when it doth, the prince and commonwealth have the same power that their predecessors had, and as the husbandman hath to plant a new tree where the old faileth, so hath the prince to honor virtue where he doth find it, to make gentlemen, esquires, knights, barons, earls, marquises, and dukes where he seeth virtue able to bear that honor, or merits and deserves it, and so it hath always been used amongst us. But ordinarily the King doth only make knights and create barons or higher degrees; for as for gentlemen, they be made good cheap in England. For whosoever studieth the laws of the realm, who studieth in the universities, who professeth liberal sciences, and to be short, who can live idly and without manual labor, and will bear the port, charge, and countenance of a gentleman, he shall be called *master*—for that is the title which men give to esquires and other gentlemen—and shall be taken for a gentleman. . . . And if need be, a king of heralds shall also give him (for money) arms newly made and invented, the title whereof shall pretend to have been found by the said herald in perusing and viewing of old registers, where his ancestors in times past had been recorded to bear the same.

Of Citizens and Burgesses

Next to gentlemen be appointed citizens and burgesses, such as not only be free and received as officers within the cities, but also be of some substance to bear the charges. But these citizens and burgesses be to serve the commonwealth in their cities and boroughs or in corporate towns where they dwell. Generally in the shires they be of none account, save only in the common assembly of the realm to make laws, which is called the Parliament. The ancient cities appoint four, and each borough two, to have voices in it, and to give their consent or dissent in the name of the city or borough for which they be appointed.

Of Yeomen

Those whom we call yeomen, next unto the nobility, knights, and squires have the greatest charge and doings in the commonwealth—or rather are more travailed to serve in it than all the rest, as shall appear hereafter. I call him a yeoman . . . which is a freeman, born English, and may dispend of his own free land in yearly revenue to the sum of forty shillings sterling. This maketh (if the just value were taken now to the proportion of monies) six pounds of our current money at this present.[1]

This sort of people confess themselves to be no gentlemen, but give the honor to all which be or take upon them to be gentlemen. And yet they have a certain preeminence and more estimation than laborers and artificers, and commonly live wealthily, keep good houses, and do their business and travail to acquire riches. These be, for the most part, farmers unto gentlemen,

1. Twenty shillings equaled one pound sterling. Smith's distinction between the nominal and the real value of money reflects the impact of the rapid inflation that affected all European states in the sixteenth century.

which with grazing, frequenting of markets, and keeping servants not idle as the gentleman doth but such as get both their own living and part of their master's, by these means do come to such wealth that they are able and daily do buy the lands of unthrifty gentlemen, and after setting their sons to the school at the universities, to the law of the realm, or otherwise leaving them sufficient lands whereon they may live without labor, do make their said sons by those means gentlemen.

These be not called *masters*, for that, as I said, pertaineth to gentlemen only. But to their surnames, men add *goodman:* as if the surname be Luter, Finch, White, Browne, they are called Goodman Luter, Goodman White, Goodman Finch, Goodman Browne amongst their neighbors. I mean not in matters of importance or in law; but in matters of law and for distinction, if one were a knight they would write him (for example sake) Sir John Finch, knight. So, if he be an esquire, John Finch, esquire, or gentleman. If he be no gentleman, John Finch, yeoman. For amongst the gentlemen, they which claim no higher degree, and yet to be exempted out of the number of the lowest sort thereof, be written *esquires.* So amongst the husbandmen laborers, lowest and rascal sort of the people, such as be exempted out of the number of the rascability of the popular be called and written *yeomen*, as in the degree next to gentlemen. . . . These are they which in the old world gat that honor to England; not that either for wit, conduction, or for power they are, or were ever to be, compared to the gentlemen, but because they be so many in number, so obedient at the lord's call, so strong of body, so hard to endure pain, so courageous to adventure with their lord or captain.

Of the Fourth Sort of Men, Which Do Not Rule

The fourth sort or class amongst us is of those . . . day laborers, poor husbandmen, yea merchants or retailers which have no free land; copyholders,[2] and all artificers, such as tailors, shoemakers, carpenters, brickmakers, masons, etc. These have no voice nor authority in our commonwealth, and no account is made of them but only to be ruled, not to rule other. And yet they be not altogether neglected, for in cities and corporate towns, for default of yeomen, inquests and juries are empanelled of such manner of people. And in villages they be commonly made churchwardens, aleconners[3] and many times constables, which office toucheth more the commonwealth, and at the first was not employed upon such low and base persons.

2. A copyholder held his land from the lord of the manor, and the conditions of his tenure (of which he was given a copy) were recorded on the roll of the manorial court.

3. Aleconners were responsible for testing ales and ensuring that they met the prescribed standards of strength.

William Camden:
Britannia

By turning to the past as a guide to present conduct, the Renaissance humanists transformed history from a diversion into a necessity. But it had to be "real" history and not the compound of folk memories, myths, and legends that constituted so many medieval chronicles. They therefore invented methods by which to test evidence, to weigh it as judges did, and to sift out the grains of truth it contained. In so doing they virtually created history as an academic discipline.

The Renaissance was not, however, the only influence tending in this direction. The discovery of a sea route to India and then of a entire new world across the Atlantic transformed geographical studies and created an enormous demand for accurate maps. These were useful tools also for the historian, who was concerned to establish the facts about his own county or country and replace speculation with well-founded deduction. Patriotism was another factor that encouraged the writing of history. English patriotism had long roots, but it had been stimulated by the Hundred Years' War against France and by the increasing awareness—made explicit in Fortescue, for instance—that the English had a great deal of which to be proud. They had preserved a high degree of political liberty at a time when it was disappearing from large parts of Europe; they had secured their persons and their property under the protection of the common law, which was a native growth; and in the course of the sixteenth century they had thrown off the shackles of the Papacy and emerged as an "elect nation," chosen by God for His transcendent purposes.

William Camden, born in 1551, was from all these points of view the archetypal English historian. His natural interest in "antiquities" was encouraged by Sir Philip Sidney, a fellow student at Oxford, and a teaching post at Westminster School gave him time, during the holidays, to travel around England, amassing information as he went. He did this at first simply for his own delight. The idea that he should conduct a systematic survey of the whole kingdom only took shape in 1577 after his meeting with the great geographer Abraham Ortelius. Camden was not the first into the field, for John Leland, appointed to the specially created post of "King's Antiquary" by Henry VIII, had also traveled widely throughout England in the 1530s and 1540s, as he recorded in his *Itinerary.* But Leland, though an assiduous collector of information, was "unscientific" when it came to assessing it, and his prose style was at best utilitarian. Camden's *Britannia,* which was published in 1586 with a dedication to William Cecil, Lord Burghley, was a far more comprehensive and distinguished piece of work than the *Itinerary,* and it made Camden famous.

In 1575 Camden began teaching at Westminster School, of which he was subsequently appointed headmaster. Among his pupils was Ben Jonson, who later became one of his close friends, despite the fact that he was some twenty years younger than his mentor. Jonson freely acknowledged his gratitude to Camden, for, in his own words, "I am none of those that can suffer the benefits conferred upon my youth to perish with my age." Jonson also credited his teacher for "all that I am in the arts," and that was high praise indeed, for Jonson was among the most well-read of Renaissance poets and playwrights. He dedicated his first major success in the theater, *Every Man in His Humor* (1598), to Camden; praised the historian's learning, knowledge, and modesty in *Epigram XIIII*; and called him "the glory and light of our kingdom" in the *King's Entertainment at Welbeck* (1633). Jonson may also have had Camden in mind when he wrote *The New Inn,* for the eccentric Lord Frampul proudly declares: "I am he / Have measured all the shires of England over" (V.iv).

In 1598 Camden gave up teaching, after being appointed Clarenceux king of arms. His work as one of the principal heralds seems to have left him plenty of time to pursue his travels and enlarge and revise his *Britannia*—a never-ending task. He also wrote and published the *Annals* of Queen Elizabeth's reign and demonstrated his continuing commitment to historical studies by endowing a chair of history at Oxford shortly before his death in 1623.

Six editions of the *Britannia,* in its original Latin, were published during Camden's lifetime, of which the last, of 1607, contained maps by Saxton and Norden. There was also an English translation, made by

Philemon Holland under Camden's direction, which was published in 1610. It was no coincidence that Camden wrote *Britannia* in Latin, for it was addressed to the international scholarly community, as well as to Camden's fellow countrymen, and it was "classical" in both its range and its approach. What it said, in effect, was that Britain had come of age. Her past was as worthy of study in its own right as that of ancient Rome, her antiquities as reverend as anything that Italy or France had to offer. Camden's magnificent achievement stimulated the already-growing demand for English history that flowed over into poetry and drama. Michael Drayton's *Polyolbion* (1612; 1622), a loving topographical description of England in some thirty thousand lines of verse, was inspired by Camden, who was a personal friend and placed his manuscripts and books at Drayton's disposal.

Preface

I hope it shall be no discredit if I now use again, by way of preface, the same words, with a few more, that I used twenty-four years since in the first edition of this work. Abraham Ortelius, the worthy restorer of ancient geography, arriving here in England about thirty-four years past, dealt earnestly with me that I would illustrate this isle of Britain—or, as he said, that I would restore antiquity to Britain and Britain to his [i.e., its] antiquity.[1] Which was, as I understood, that I would renew ancientry, enlighten obscurity, clear doubts, and recall home verity by way of recovery, which the negligence of writers and credulity of the common sort had in a manner proscribed and utterly banished from amongst us. A painful matter, I assure you, and more than difficult; wherein what toil is to be taken, as no man thinketh, so no man believeth but he that hath made the trial. Nevertheless, how much the difficulty discouraged me from it, so much the glory of my country encouraged me to undertake it. So while at one and the same time I was fearful to undergo the burden and yet desirous to do some service to my country, I found two different affections, fear and boldness, I know not why, conjoined in me.

Notwithstanding, by the most gracious direction of the Almighty, taking industry for my comfort, I adventured upon it, and with all my study, care, cogitation, continual meditation, pain, and travail I employed myself there-

---

1. Abraham Ortelius (1527–98) was a native of Antwerp and shared with his friend Mercator the reputation of being the greatest geographer of his day—the Ptolemy of the early modern world. He traveled widely through Europe and was in England in 1577, when presumably he meet Camden. His *Theatrum Orbis Terrarum* was, in effect, the first modern atlas.

unto when I had any spare time. I made search after the etymology of Britain and the first inhabitants timorously; neither, in so doubtful a matter, have I affirmed aught confidently. For I am not ignorant that the first originals of nations are obscure, by reason of their profound antiquity, as things which are seen very deep and far remote; like as the courses, the reaches, the confluents, and the outlets of great rivers are well-known, yet their first fountains and heads lie commonly unknown. I have succinctly run over the Romans' government in Britain, and the inundation of foreign people thereinto; what they were, and from whence they came. I have traced out the ancient divisions of these kingdoms. I have summarily specified the states and judicial courts of the same.

In the several counties I have compendiously set down the limits (and yet not exactly by perch and pole,[2] to breed questions) what is the nature of the soil; which were the places of greatest antiquity; who have been the Dukes, Marquesses, Earls, Viscounts, Barons; and some of the most signal and ancient families therein—for who can particulate all? . . . I have in no wise neglected such things as are most material to search and sift out the truth. I have attained to some skill of the most ancient British and English-Saxon tongues. I have travailed all over England for the most part. I have conferred with most skilful observers in each country [i.e., county]. I have studiously read over our own country writers, old and new; all Greek and Latin authors which have once made mention of Britain. I have had conference with learned men in other parts of Christendom. I have been diligent in the records of this realm. I have looked into most libraries, registers, and memorials of churches, cities and corporations. I have pored upon many an old roll and evidence, and produced their testimony (as beyond all exception) when the cause required, in their own words (although barbarous they be), that honor and verity might in no wise be impeached.

For all this I may be censured [as] unadvised and scant modest, who being but of the lowest form in the school of antiquity, where I might well have lurked in obscurity, have adventured as a scribbler upon the stage in this learned age, amidst diversities of relishes both in wit and judgment. But to tell the truth unfeignedly, the love of my country (which compriseth all love in it, and hath endeared me unto it), the glory of the British name, [and] the advice of some judicious friends hath so overmastered my modesty and (willed I, nilled I) hath enforced me against my own judgment to undergo this burden too heavy for me, and so thrust me forth into the world's view. For I see judgments, prejudices, censures, reprehensions, obtrectations,

---

2. Perches and poles were measuring rods.

detractions, affronts, and confronts, as it were in battle array to environ me on every side. Some there are which wholly contemn and avile this study of antiquity as a back-looking curiosity; whose authority, as I do not utterly vilify, so I do not overprice or admire their judgment.

Neither am I destitute of reasons whereby I might approve this my purpose to well-bred and well-meaning men which tender the glory of their native country, and moreover could give them to understand that in the studies of antiquity (which is always accompanied with dignity, and hath a certain resemblance with eternity) there is a sweet food of the mind, well befitting such as are of honest and noble disposition. If any there be which are desirous to be strangers in their own soil and foreigners in their own city, they may so continue, and therein flatter themselves. For such like I have not written these lines nor taken these pains. . . .

Many haply will insult over me for that I have adventured to hunt after the originals of names by conjectures; who if they proceed on to reject all conjectures, I fear me a great part of liberal learning and humane knowledge will be utterly cast out into banishment. For the edge of our understanding is so blunt that we are of necessity enforced to prosecute many matters in all professions conjecturally. . . . But if these men may be induced to attribute aught to conjecture, I doubt not but my modesty and moderation in conjecturing may withal purchase my pardon. Plato, in his *Cratilus*, commandeth that we recall the originals of names to the barbarous tongues (for so he called all but Greek), as being the most ancient.[3] I thereupon, in etymologies and my conjectures, have made recourse to the British or Welsh tongue (so they now call it), as being the same which the primitive and most ancient inhabitants of this land used, and to the English-Saxon tongue which our progenitors, the English, spake. He commandeth that the name be consonant to the nature of the thing, and the nature thereof to the name. If they be herein dissonant, I admit them not. . . . As for obscure etymologies, farfetched, hardly wrested, and which may be drawn diversely, I have vouchsafed them no place in this work. . . .

Some will blame me for that I have omitted this or that town and castle— as though I purposed to mention any but such as were most notorious and mentioned by ancient authors! Neither verily were it worth the labor once to name them, whenas beside the naked name there is nothing memorable. Truly it was my project and purpose to seek, rake out, and free from darkness such places as Caesar, Tacitus, Ptolemy, Antonine the Emperor, *Notitia Provinciarum*,[4] and other antique writers have specified and time hath

3. Plato, *Cratilus*, 423d.
4. This is presumably the *Notitia Dignitatum et Administrationum in Partibus Orientis et Occidentis* drawn up in about A.D. 395. It listed all the major military and civil offices in the Roman Empire at the time of its division into a western and an eastern section.

overcast with mist and darkness by extinguishing, altering, and corrupting their old true names. In searching and seeking after these, as I will not avouch uncertainties, so I do not conceal probabilities. That I have not found out every one, although I have sought after them with painful and chargeable enquiry, let it be no imputation to me, as it is not to a spadiard[5] that worketh in mines, who, while he findeth and followesth the main veins, seeth not the hidden small fillets. . . . Another age and other men may daily find out more. It is enough for me to have begun, and I have gained as much as I look for if I shall draw others into this argument, whether they will undertake a new work or amend this.

There are certain, as I hear, who take it impatiently that I have mentioned some of the most famous monasteries and their founders. I am sorry to hear it, and with their good favor will say thus much: they may take it as impatiently, and peradventure would have us forget, that our ancestors were, and we are, of the Christian profession; whenas there are not extant any other more conspicuous and certain monuments of their piety and zealous devotion toward God. Neither were there any other seed-gardens from whence Christian religion and good learning were propagated over this isle, howbeit in corrupt ages some weeds grew out overrankly.

Mathematicians will accuse me as though I had wholly missed the mark in the cosmographical dimensions of longitude and latitude. Yet hear me, I pray you. I have carefully conferred the local tables, new and old, manuscript and printed. . . . In the latitude they do not vary much from Ptolemy, but agree well together. . . . Therefore I have relied upon them. But in the longitude there is no accord, no consent at all. What should I then do? Whenas therefore the modern navigators have observed that there is no variation of the compass at the isles of Azores, I have thence begun with them the account of longitude, as from the first meridian, which yet I have not precisely measured.

As for obscurity, fables, extravagant digressions, I trust there is no cause to sue out my pardon. There will be no obscurity but to them which have not sipped the first elements of antiquity and our histories. Upon fables I have in no wise relied, and that I might not digress extravagantly I have had often recourse to the title of my book (as Pliny adviseth)[6] and eftsoons demanded of myself why I took pen in hand. Many have found a defect in this work that maps were not adjoined, which do allure the eyes by pleasant portraiture and are the best directions in geographical studies, especially when the light of learning is adjoined to the speechless delineations. Yet my ability could not

5. *Spadiard* was a name given to a Cornish tin miner.
6. The Younger Pliny, *Letters*, Book 5, Letter 6.

compass it; which . . . is now performed out of the labors of Christopher Saxton and John Norden, most skilful chorographers.[7]

But lest I should run at random in my preface: To accomplish this work, the whole main of my industry hath been employed for many years with a firm, settled study of the truth, and sincere antique faithfulness to the glory of God and my country. I have done dishonor to no nation; have descanted upon no man's name. I have impaired no man's reputation. I have impeached no man's credit—no, not Geoffrey of Monmouth, whose *History* (which I would gladly support) is held suspected among the judicious.[8] Neither have I assumed upon myself any persuasion of knowledge, but only that I have been desirous to know much. And so I right willingly acknowledge that I may err much. Neither will I soothe and smooth my errors. Who, shooting all day long, doth always hit the mark? Many matters in these studies are raked under deceitful ashes. There may be some escapes from memory, for who doth so comprehend particularities in the treasury of his memory that he can utter them at his pleasure? There may be mistakings in regard of my unskilfulness, for who is so skilful that, struggling with time in the foggy dark sea of antiquity, may not run upon rocks? It may be that I have been misled by the credit of authors and others whom I took to be most true and worthy of credit. Neither is there verily (as Pliny saith)[9] any easier slipping from truth than when a grave author warranteth an untruth. Others may be more skilful and more exactly observe the particularities of the places where they are conversant. If they, or any other whosoever, will advertise me wherein I am mistaken, I will amend it with manifold thanks. If I have, unwitting, omitted aught, I will supply it. If I have not fully explicated any point, upon their better information I will more clear it, if it proceed from good meaning and not from a spirit of contradiction and quarrelling, which do not befit such as are well-bred and affect the truth.

7. Christopher Saxton (*flor.* 1570s–1590s) was one of the finest mapmakers of his day. His collection of maps of every English county, published in 1597 and dedicated to Queen Elizabeth, was a source of inspiration for all subsequent English cartographers. John Norden (1548?–1625) compiled the first complete series of geographical and historical surveys of English counties. He executed maps of Hampshire, Hertfordshire, Kent, Middlesex, Surrey, and Sussex for the 1607 edition of Camden's *Britannia*.

8. Geoffrey of Monmouth (d. 1155), Bishop of St. Asaph in Wales, was the author of the *Historia Regum Britanniae*, which became one of the most popular books in medieval England. British history, according to Geoffrey's highly unreliable account, began with the arrival and settlement in this country of Brutus, the great-grandson of Aeneas of Troy, and culminated in the reign of (the largely mythical) King Arthur, when the prophet Merlin flourished. Geoffrey also records the foundation of Leicester by King Leir and the subsequent division of his kingdom between two ungrateful daughters. Geoffrey's *History* retained its popularity throughout the Tudor period. Holinshed used it as one of the sources of his *Chronicles*; the poet William Warner for his *Albion's England*, published in 1586; and Michael Drayton for his *Polyolbion*, published in the reign of James I.

9. The Elder Pliny, *Natural History*, book 5, 12.

Meanwhile, let your kind courtesy, my industry, the common love of our common mother our native country, [and] the ancient honor of the British name, obtain so much upon their entreaty that I may utter my judgment without prejudice to others; that I may proceed in that course that others have formerly done in the like argument; and that you would pardon my errors upon my acknowledgment; which may be as well hoped as requested from good, indifferent, and reasonable men. . . . As for myself and this work, I do most humbly submit it to the censure of the godly, honest, and learned, with all respective reverence; of whom, if it be not approved, I hope in regard of my professed love to our native country that it may be excused. Farewell.

Monarchy
in Action

❦

Englial sovereigns, as Fortescue had made plain (see part V), were not absolute monarchs. For one thing, they were expected to rule according to law, and at their coronation they made a solemn promise to do so (see page 140). Furthermore, they were expected to take cognizance of the wishes of their people by summoning Parliament at frequent intervals.

Parliament consisted of two Houses. The upper chamber, the House of Lords, was composed of the bishops—the lords spiritual—and the holders of hereditary peerages—the lords temporal. The lower chamber, the House of Commons, consisted of some 470 members, of whom 90 were "Knights of the Shire," representing the English and Welsh counties. The remainder were nominally "burgesses," though the greater part were country gentry, and they were elected by some two hundred boroughs that had acquired the right to be represented either through prescription or by the grant of a royal charter. The two Houses, taken together, were a microcosm of the "political nation," that minority of the population that, on account of its status and wealth, dominated political life. Yet members did not take a narrow view of their responsibilities, as was shown by their concern for such matters as the promotion and regulation of trade, and the creation of a comprehensive system of poor relief. They believed that they represented all the people, not just a section, and although their attitude was paternalist it was not always or necessarily selfish.

Parliament's two main functions were to make statutes, binding on the common-law courts, and to vote money to the royal government. Although members were imbued with a strong sense of loyalty to the crown, they were also responsive to the attitudes of their constituents, and for this reason their reaction to government policy was never entirely predictable.

Elizabeth I
and Parliament

Elizabeth's success in achieving a good working relationship with the two Houses derived in large part from the close watch she kept on proceedings when Parliament was in session—which happened for a few weeks approximately every three years. Those of her ministers who were peers sat in the upper House and helped to guide its deliberations. The rest secured election to the Commons, and there they acted as the Queen's eyes and ears, informing her of what was taking place, and carrying out her instructions about how to manage business.

At first glance, it might seem that the Queen would have been well advised to emulate her fellow monarchs on the Continent and dispense with Parliament. But laws that had the approval of her people, and money grants that were voluntarily offered (at least in appearance), were far easier to enforce and to collect than would otherwise have been the case. An obstreperous Parliament was worse than no Parliament at all, from the crown's point of view, but a cooperative Parliament was a demonstration of unity and strength and an invaluable means of communication between the sovereign and her subjects. Generally speaking, Elizabethan Parliaments were cooperative, particularly in the second half of the reign when England was at war with Spain. Members of Parliament—which, where money grants were concerned, meant principally the House of Commons—responded to the Queen's appeals for aid, because she was the embodiment of their unique brand of Protestantism and also the symbolic champion of English resistance to the Pope (whom they regarded as Antichrist) and his agent, King Philip II of Spain.

Nevertheless, the crown finances, already crippled by the long period of inflation in the sixteenth century, were brought close to collapse by the additional strain of war, and Elizabeth and her ministers exploited every available device to raise money. Among other things the crown sold patents of monopoly that gave the patentee the sole right to trade in or manufacture a particular commodity. The royal Exchequer benefited not simply from the lump sum payment but also from a continuing share of the profits, while the patentee enjoyed what was, in effect, a license to coin money. It was the consumers who suffered, and this meant the people as a whole. As they saw it, their Queen, who was supposed to promote their welfare, was exploiting them—or at any rate allowing her officers and courtiers to do so.

Elizabeth and her successor, James I, both professed their dislike of monopolies and monopolists, yet they could not afford to dispense with them, and the souring of relations between crown and people that became increasingly apparent in the closing decade of the Queen's reign continued under the first Stuart. An infamous expression of this breed of patent-holders, the rapacious Sir Giles Mompesson, served as a model for the heartless *arriviste* in Philip Massinger's *A New Way to Pay Old Debts*. Parliament's anger was so intense that in 1621, despite his powerful allies among King James's courtiers, Mompesson was stripped of his knighthood, fined ten thousand pounds, and sentenced to banishment. The continuing zeal for reform on the part of Parliament led to accusations of corruption against the Lord Chancellor, Viscount St. Alban, better known as Francis Bacon. Bacon acknowledged his guilt and was dismissed from the King's service—the first minister to be toppled in this way since the turbulent years of the fifteenth century that ushered in the Wars of the Roses.

Elizabeth managed to contain popular anger, at least in the short run. She frequently professed her care for her subjects' welfare, and stressed the bonds of affection that united crown and people. Her popular image was enhanced by poets and playwrights, who proclaimed her beauty, wit, intelligence, and chastity in their verses. Whether as "Cynthia" (a name used by Lyly, Raleigh, and Jonson); or "Gloriana" and "Belphoebe" (names used by Spenser); or "Eliza" (used by Spenser and Thomas Dekker); or "Astraea" (used by George Peele and Sir John Davies), Elizabeth had her praises sung. Peele's *The Arraignment of Paris* (1581) is an example of this combination of flattery and genuine admiration that was focused on the Queen. In this Court entertainment, the quarrel among the goddesses Juno, Pallas Athena, and Venus is resolved by giving the prize into "the Queen's own hands." As "Zabeta," a votary of Diana, Elizabeth is judged unmatched "for wisdom, princely state, and peerless beauty."

Elizabeth, in short, benefited from the "Gloriana" cult that she carefully encouraged. But she also made her own inimitable contribution to it. In the following speech, which she delivered to members of Parliament at the close of her reign, she acknowledged her obligations towards her people and professed her desire to rule only with their loves. It was a classic statement of the humanist view of the ruler's duty, and it shows how the practice of monarchy, at least under Elizabeth, reflected the principles put forward in the advice books to princes. It also shows how, in the words of her godson, Sir John Harington, she succeeded in "converting her reign, through the perpetual love-tricks that passed between her and her people, into a kind of romance."

The Queen Addresses the Members of the Commons, 30 November 1601.

In the afternoon, about three of the clock, some seven score of the House met at the great chamber before the Council Chamber in Whitehall. At length the Queen came into the Council Chamber, where, sitting under the cloth of state at the upper end, the Speaker with all the company came in, and after three low reverences made, [he delivered his speech]. . . . And after three low reverences made, he with the rest kneeled down, and Her Majesty began thus to answer herself, *viz.* . . . .

Mr. Speaker, you give me thanks, but I doubt me I have more cause to thank you all than you me; and I charge you to thank them of the House of Commons from me, for had I not received a knowledge from you, I might have fallen into the lap of an error only for lack of true information. Since I was Queen, yet did I never put my pen to any grant but that upon pretext and semblance made unto me that it was both good and beneficial to the subjects in general. . . . But the contrary being found by experience, I am exceeding beholden to such subjects as would move the same at first. . . . and I take it exceeding grateful from them, because it gives us to know that no respects or interests had moved them other than the minds they bear to suffer no diminution of our honor and our subjects' love unto us. The zeal of which affection tending to ease my people and knit their hearts unto me, I embrace with a princely care; for above all earthly treasure I esteem my people's love, more than which I desire not to merit. . . . I have ever used to set the last judgment day before mine eyes, and so to rule as I shall be judged to answer before a Higher Judge. To whose judgment seat I do appeal, that never thought was cherished in my heart that tended not to my people's good. . . . And though you have had and may have many princes more mighty and wise sitting in this seat, yet you never had or shall have any that will be more careful and loving. . . . And so I commit you all to your best fortunes and further counsels. And I pray you, Mr. Controller, Mr. Secretary, and you of my Council, that before these gentlemen depart into their countries [i.e., counties] you bring them all to kiss my hand.

The Courtier in Action:
The Earl of Essex

Unlike her cousin, Mary, Queen of Scots, who allowed her personal passions to destroy her, Queen Elizabeth kept a tight rein on her emotions and never let them cloud her political judgment. She was not, however, without feelings. For much of her reign she was romantically attached to Robert Dudley, Earl of Leicester, but in the late 1580s she began showing marked attention to Leicester's stepson, Robert Devereux, second Earl of Essex, who was thirty years her junior. In May 1587 one observer noted that when the Queen went out she often had "nobody with her but my Lord of Essex; and at night my Lord is at cards, or one game or another with her, that he cometh not to his own lodging till birds sing in the morning." Leicester did not resent Essex's good fortune. On the contrary, he helped advance his stepson's career in order to counteract the influence of his rival, Sir Walter Raleigh, and the ill feeling between Raleigh and the old favorite was thereby extended to the new one as well.

Essex was in many respects the archetypal Renaissance hero, a man of action with a humanist education and a passionate desire for honor and glory. He had close links with Sir Philip Sidney, who was in love with his sister, Penelope Devereux—the "Stella" of Sidney's magnificent sonnet sequence *Astrophel and Stella*. Sidney was a member of the Leicester circle that wanted Elizabeth to take a much more committed part in the struggle to defend European Protestantism against the counterattack of a revived Roman Catholicism spearheaded by Spain. In 1585 Leicester persuaded the reluctant Queen to let him lead an English expeditionary force to aid the Dutch in their revolt against

Spain, and Sidney and Essex went with him. Sidney, mortally wounded at the battle of Zutphen, but he bequeathed his sword to Essex, and a few years later the young Earl married Sidney's widow.

Essex chose to seek glory as a soldier. He distinguished himself in the fight at Zutphen, and in 1591 he added to his reputation by leading an army to France to fight for the Huguenot champion, Henry of Navarre. His fame seemed assured when in 1596 he commanded the expedition against Spain that captured and sacked Cadiz, and he returned home a popular hero. However, political advancement eluded him, for although the Queen was captivated by his panache she preferred more sober qualities in those who formed her government. William Cecil had been her close adviser for many years, and as he grew old she turned increasingly to his son, Robert Cecil, who advocated a cautious and pragmatic policy rather than grand gestures in the Essex style.

Although Essex continued to enjoy the Queen's favor, he felt, with good reason, that the Cecils and their adherents were gradually taking over the key positions in the state. When he tried to advance his own protégés, such as the rising lawyer Francis Bacon, he was conspicuously unsuccessful, and this made him even more suspicious and embittered. Essex House in the Strand became a center for all those who, for one reason and another, were disaffected with the Elizabethan regime. They included Essex's friend Henry Wriothesley, third Earl of Southampton, who was already well-known as a lover of poetry and the patron of men of letters—among them Shakespeare, who dedicated *Venus and Adonis* to him. Southampton accompanied Essex on the Cadiz expedition and, on his return, married Essex's cousin, Elizabeth Vernon, who was one of the Queen's waiting women. The Queen strongly disapproved of the match, and ordered the imprisonment of the young couple. They were soon released but not restored to favor.

Meanwhile Essex had been quarreling with the Queen over who should be her deputy in Ireland. So angry did he become that he turned his back on her, telling her that the conditions she laid down for the appointment "were as crooked as her carcass." The enraged Queen struck him a blow on the ear, which had Essex reaching for his sword. The onlookers calmed him down and persuaded him to retire, but from then on the relationship between the two was tense and uncertain. In 1599 the Queen appointed Essex to command the army that she was sending to Ireland to suppress the revolt that had broken out there. The crowds thronged the streets to cheer Essex on his way, and it was certain that if he returned successful he would evoke even greater displays of enthusiasm: as Shakespeare wrote in *Henry V*:

Were now the general of our gracious empress,
As in good time he may, from Ireland coming,
Bringing rebellion broached on his sword,
How many would the peaceful city quit
To welcome him!

(V. Chorus)

However, Essex did not return in triumph. While he and his men were bogged down in Ireland, his rivals and enemies were securing their power at home. Despite the Queen's explicit instructions that he was to stay in Ireland until recalled, he abandoned his command and returned home to plead his cause in person. The Queen received him kindly when he burst in on her, unexpected, in her bedchamber at Nonsuch Palace, but she could not overlook or forgive his flagrant disobedience and breach of trust. Essex was stripped of his offices and pensions and confined to house arrest. In a last desperate gambler's throw he and his fellow malcontents planned an armed uprising to "free" the Queen from her evil advisers and open the way to their own accession to power. Southampton prepared the ground by paying for a performance of Shakespeare's *Richard II* at the Globe Theatre: the story of a monarch whose arrogance and unwise choice of counselors led to his deposition had an obvious and relevant political message. The performance took place on Saturday 7 February 1601, and on the following day Essex rode into the city at the head of several hundred men, calling on the inhabitants to rise up and join him. There was no response, and the frustrated Earl had little choice but to return to Essex House and await the inevitable. After a formal trial in Westminster Hall, Essex met his death on the block. Southampton was also sentenced to death, but reprieved.

The following extracts begin with a letter from Essex to Bacon about his efforts to obtain for him the post of Solicitor General. It gives a remarkable insight into the relationship between the favorite and his sovereign, and demonstrates not only the pressures that someone as single-minded as Essex could exert upon the Queen, but also Elizabeth's strength of character and her determination not to let her mind be swayed by her heart. Lady Bacon was perhaps correct in believing that "though the Earl showed great affection, yet he marred all with violent courses."

Essex to Bacon, 26 March 1594

I have received your letter, and since I have had opportunity to deal freely with the Queen. I have dealt confidently with her, as of a matter wherein I did more labor to overcome her delays than I did fear her denial. I told her how much you were thrown down with the correction she had already given you; that she might in that point hold herself already satisfied. . . . I find the Queen very reserved, staying herself from giving any kind of hope, yet not passionate against you till I grew passionate for you. Then she said that none thought you fit for the place but my Lord Treasurer and myself: "Marry! The others must, some of them, say so before us, for fear of flattery." I told her the most and wisest of her Council had delivered their opinions, and preferred you before all men for that place. . . . Yet if they had been never for you, but contrarily against you, I thought that my credit, joined with the approbation and mediation of her greatest Councillors, might prevail in greater matter than this, and urged her that though she could not signify her mind to others, I might have a secret promise; wherein I should receive great comfort, as in the contrary great unkindness. She said she neither was persuaded, nor would hear of it till Easter, when she might advise with her Council (who were now all absent); and therefore in passion bade me go to bed if I would talk of nothing else. Wherefore in passion I went away, saying while I was with her I could not but solicit for the cause and the man I so much affected, and therefore I would retire myself till I might be more graciously heard. And so we parted. Tomorrow I will go hence of purpose, and on Thursday I will write an expostulating letter to her. That night, or upon the Friday morning, I will be here again and follow on the same course, stirring a discontentment in her, etc.

Letter of Bacon to Essex, 4 October 1596

The next letter, from Bacon to Essex, assumes a degree of learning in the recipient that could not have been taken for granted in a pre- Renaissance aristocrat. But its particular fascination comes from its insight into the character not only of Essex but also of the Queen. The appraisal of Elizabeth's character, and the recommendations to Essex of ways to project himself positively, display Bacon's acute deductive powers, his talent at drawing subtle inferences, and his careful attention to specific instances. Much of what he deferentially suggests to Essex reminds one of the dialogue Shakespeare wrote for the conspirators in *Julius Caesar* when they dissect Antony, or for Menenius, the practical man of the world, when he gives advice to Coriolanus.

Bacon brings out Elizabeth's love of peace, her fear of incurring additional expenses by a more aggressive foreign policy, her distrust of ambitious courtiers who made war their occupation and sought their reputation in the cannon's mouth, and above all her deep suspicion of those who cultivated "popularity." Elizabeth was well versed in ancient history and knew how much of a threat was implied to her government by a successful soldier with a mass following. Bacon, as befitted a protégé, had to phrase his letter to Essex carefully and imply more than he stated openly. Nevertheless, the basic message comes through clearly: a warning to the Earl that unless he changed course, or at least appeared to do so, he was heading for a dangerous confrontation. It was advice that Essex would have done well to heed.

I humbly desire your lordship, before you give access to my poor advice, to look about, even jealously a little if you will, and to consider: first, whether I have not reason to think that your fortune comprehendeth mine? Next, whether I shift my counsel and do not *constare mihi?*[1]—for I am persuaded there are some would give you the same counsel now which I shall, but that they should derogate from that which they have said heretofore. Thirdly, whether you have taken hurt at any time by my careful and devoted counsel? For although I remember well your lordship once told me that you having submitted, upon my well-meant motion, at Nonsuch[2] (the place where you renewed a treaty with Her Majesty of obsequious kindness), she had taken advantage of it, yet I suppose you do since believe that it did much attemper a cold, malignant humor then growing upon Her Majesty towards your lordship, and hath done you good in consequence. And for my being against it, now lately, that you should not estrange yourself, although I give place to none in true gratulation, yet neither do I repent me of safe counsel; neither do I judge of the whole play by the first act. But whether I counsel you the best, or for the best, duty bindeth me to offer to you my wishes. I said to your lordship last time, *Martha, Martha, attendis ad plurima, unum sufficit.*[3] Win the Queen. If this be not the beginning of any other course, I see no end. And I will not now speak of favor of affection, but of other correspondence and agreeableness. Which, whensoever it shall be conjoined with the other of affection, I durst wager my life (let them make what *prosopopoeias*

1. stand firm in my opinions.
2. Nonsuch Palace in Surrey, built by Henry VIII, was a favorite residence of Queen Elizabeth. Nothing of any significance now remains of it.
3. "Martha, Martha, thou art careful and troubled about many things, but one thing is needful." Luke 10:41–42.

[i.e., interpretations] they will of Her Majesty's nature) that in you she will come to the question of *Quid fiet homini quem rex vult honorare?*[4]

But how is it now? A man of a nature not to be ruled; that hath the advantage of my affection, and knoweth it; of an estate not grounded to his greatness; of a popular reputation; of a military dependence. I demand whether there can be a more dangerous image than this represented to any monarch living—much more to a lady, and of Her Majesty's apprehension? And is it not more evident than demonstration itself that whilst this impression continueth in Her Majesty's breast you can find no other condition than inventions to keep your estate bare and low; crossing and disgracing your actions; extenuating and blasting of your merit; carping with contempt at your nature and fashions; breeding, nourishing, and fortifying such instruments as are most factious against you; repulses and scorns of your friends and dependants that are true and steadfast; winning and inveigling away from you such as are flexible and wavering; thrusting you into odious employments and offices, to supplant your reputation; abusing you and feeding you with dalliances and demonstrations to divert you from descending into the serious consideration of your own case; yea, and percase venturing you in perilous and desperate enterprises.

Herein it may please your lordship to understand me. For I mean nothing less than that these things should be plotted and intended as in Her Majesty's royal mind towards you. I know the excellency of her nature too well. But I say, wheresoever the formerly described impression is taken in any king's breast towards a subject, these other recited inconveniences must, of necessity of politic consequence, follow—in respect of such instruments as are never failing about princes; which spy into their humors and conceits and second them; and not only second them, but in seconding increase them; yea, and many times, without their knowledge, pursue them further than themselves would.

Your lordship will ask the question wherewith the Athenians were wont to interrupt their orators when they exaggerated their dangers: *Quid igitur agendum est?*[5] I will tell your lordship *quae mihi nunc in mentem veniunt;*[6] supposing nevertheless that yourself, out of your own wisdom, upon the case with this plainness and liberty represented to you, will find out better expedients and remedies. I wish a cure applied to every of the five former impressions, which I will take not in order but as I think they are of weight.

For the removing the impression of your nature to be *opiniastre* and not

---

4. "What shall be done unto the man whom the king delighteth to honor?" Esther 6:6.
5. What therefore is to be done?
6. what thoughts now come into my mind.

rulable: first, and above all things, I wish that all matters past, which cannot be revoked, your lordship would turn altogether upon insatisfaction, and not upon your nature or proper disposition. This string you cannot upon every apt occasion harp upon too much. Next, whereas I have noted you to fly and avoid (in some respect justly) the resemblance or imitation of my Lord of Leicester and my Lord Chancellor Hatton, yet I am persuaded (howsoever I wish your lordship as distant as you are from them in points of favor, integrity, magnanimity, and merit) that it will do you much good between the Queen and you to allege them, as oft as you find occasion, for authors and patterns; for I do not know a readier mean to make Her Majesty think you are in your right way. Thirdly, when at any time your lordship upon occasion happen in speeches to do Her Majesty right—for there is no such matter as flattery amongst you all—I fear you handle it *magis in speciem adornatis verbis quam ut sentire videaris,*[7] so that a man may read formality in your countenance; whereas your lordship should do it familiarly *et oratione fida.*[8]

Fourthly, your lordship should never be without some particulars afoot, which you should seem to pursue with earnestness and affection; and then let them fall, upon taking knowledge of Her Majesty's opposition and dislike. Of which the weightiest sort may be if your lordship offer to labor in the behalf of some that you favor for some of the places now void, choosing such a subject as you think Her Majesty is like to oppose unto. And if you will say that this is *conjunctum cum aliena injuria*[9] I will not answer *Haec non aliter constabunt;*[10] but I say commendation from so good a mouth doth not hurt a man, though you prevail not. A less-weighty sort of particulars may be the pretence of some journeys, which, at Her Majesty's request, your lordship might relinquish: as if you would pretend a journey to see your living and estate towards Wales, or the like; for as for great foreign journeys of employment and service, it standeth not with your gravity to play or stratagem with them. And the lightest sort of particulars, which yet are not to be neglected, are in your habits, apparel, wearings, gestures, and the like.

The impression of greatest prejudice next is that of a military dependence. Wherein I cannot sufficiently wonder at your lordship's course, that you say the wars are your occupation, and go on in that course; whereas, if I might have advised your lordship, you should have left that person at Plymouth[11]—more than when in counsel, or in commending fit persons for service for wars, it had been in season. And here, my lord, I pray mistake me

7. rather in a flowery style of speaking than as if you really felt it.
8. with words that inspire confidence.
9. liable to do harm to another person.
10. there is no other way.
11. The Cadiz expedition of June 1596 sailed from Plymouth.

not. I am not to play now the part of a gown-man, that would frame you best to mine own turn. [12] I know what I owe you. I am infinitely glad of this last journey, now it is past;[13] the rather because you may make so honorable a full point for a time. You have property good enough in that greatness. There is none can, of many years, ascend near you in competition. Besides, the disposing of the places and affairs both, concerning the wars, you increasing in other greatness, will of themselves flow to you, which will preserve that dependence in full measure. It is a thing that of all things I would have you retain—the times considered, and the necessity of the service; for other reason I know none. But I say, keep it in substance, but abolish it in shows to the Queen. For Her Majesty loveth peace. Next, she loveth not charge. Thirdly, that kind of dependence maketh a suspected greatness. Therefore, *quod instat agamus.* [14] Let that be a sleeping honor a while, and cure the Queen's mind in that point.

Therefore again, whereas I heard your lordship designing to yourself the Earl Marshal's place, or the place of Master of the Ordnance, I did not in my mind so well like of either, because of their affinity with a martial greatness. But of the places now void, in my judgment and discretion I would name you to the place of Lord Privy Seal. For first, it is the third person of the great officers of the crown. Next, it hath a kind of superintendence over the Secretary . . .[15] And it is a fine honor, quiet place, and worth a thousand pounds by year. And my Lord Admiral's father had it, who was a martial man; and it fits a favorite to carry Her Majesty's image in seal, who beareth it best expressed in heart. But my chief reason is that which I first alleged: to divert Her Majesty from this impression of a martial greatness. In concurrence whereof, if your lordship shall not remit anything of your former diligence at the Star Chamber;[16] if you shall continue such intelligences as are worth the cherishing; if you shall pretend to be as bookish and contemplative as ever you were: all these courses have both their advantages and uses in themselves otherwise, and serve exceedingly aptly to this purpose. Whereunto I add one expedient more, stronger than all the rest, and, for my own confident opinion, void of any prejudice or danger of diminution of your greatness: and that is the bringing in of some martial man to be of the Council; dealing directly with Her Majesty in it, as for her service and your better assistance; choosing nevertheless some person that may be known not to come in against you by any former division. . . . And if your lordship see

12. Bacon was himself a "gown-man" or lawyer.
13. This refers to the Cadiz expedition.
14. let us do what needs to be done.
15. Sir Robert Cecil, Essex's rival, had been appointed Secretary of State in July 1596.
16. As a Privy Councillor, Essex was automatically a judge of the prerogative Court of Star Chamber.

deeplier into it than I do, that you would not have it done in effect; yet in my opinion you may serve your turn by the pretence of it, and stay it nevertheless.

The third impression is of a popular reputation; which, because it is a good thing in itself, being obtained as your lordship obtaineth it—that is *bonis artibus*[17]—and besides, well governed, is one of the best flowers of your greatness, both present and to come, it would be handled tenderly. The only way is to quench it *verbis* and not *rebus*,[18] and therefore to take all occasions to the Queen to speak against popularity and popular courses vehemently, and to tax it in all others, but nevertheless to go on in your honorable commonwealth courses as you do. And therefore I will not advise you to cure this by dealing in monopolies or any oppressions. Only, if in Parliament your lordship be forward for treasure, in respect of the wars, it becometh your person well. And if Her Majesty object "popularity" to you at any time, I would say to her, "A Parliament will show that," and so feed her with expectation.

The fourth impression, of the inequality between your estate of means and your greatness of respects, is not to be neglected. For believe it, my lord, that till Her Majesty find you careful of your estate, she will not only think you more like to continue chargeable to her, but also have a conceit that you have higher imaginations. The remedies are: first, to profess it in all speeches to her. Next, in such suits wherein both honor, gift and profit may be taken, to communicate freely with Her Majesty, by way of inducing her to grant, that it will be this benefit to you. Lastly, to be plain with your lordship (for the gentlemen are such as I am beholding to), nothing can make the Queen, or the world, think so much that you are come to a provident care of your estate, as the altering of some of your officers. . . .

For the fifth and last, which is of the advantage of a favorite: as, severed from the rest, it cannot hurt; so, joined with them, it maketh Her Majesty more fearful and shadowy, as not knowing her own strength. The only remedy to this is to give way to some other favorite, as in particular you shall find Her Majesty inclined—so as the subject hath no ill nor dangerous aspect towards yourself. For otherwise, whosoever shall tell me that you may not have singular use of a favorite at your devotion, I will say he understandeth not the Queen's affection nor your lordship's condition.

17. in an honest manner.
18. in words and not substance.

The Trial of Robert, Earl of Essex, and Henry, Earl of Southampton, before the Lords at Westminster, for High Treason: 43 Eliz. Feb. 19, A.D. 1601

Essex's trial, as is clear from the following extracts, was a carefully conceived and elaborately executed piece of theater. As peers of the realm Essex and Southampton had the right to be judged by their fellow peers, and a court, specially constituted for this purpose, was set up in Westminster Hall, normally the home of the common-law courts, where all major state trials took place. The High Steward, as presiding officer, sat under a canopy that symbolized the royal authority, and was flanked by other symbols in the shape of the principal herald, the King-at-Arms, and the Gentleman Usher of the White Rod. The two earls were accused of high treason as defined by statute in 1352 that made it a capital offense to plot the king's death or levy war against him or adhere to his enemies. The accusation that the earls had "popish" recusants and "atheists" as their accomplices had little substance but shows the emotive power of such terms. Essex was particularly concerned to rebut these charges and emphasize his Protestant commitment. He was too proud to throw himself upon the Queen's mercy, as did Southampton, even though this might have saved his neck. It was entirely in character that he should have preferred a swift and dramatic exit from this world to a life without fame, honor, and glory. His acknowledgment that "I owe God a death" (which echoes Falstaff's) displays the Stoic acceptance of fate and the awareness of God's omnipotence that were inculcated by a Christian humanist training.

A spacious court was made in Westminster Hall, where the Lord Treasurer, Lord Buckhurst, sat, as High Steward of England, under a canopy of state; where sat also about the table the earls, barons, and judges of the land, according to their degrees. . . . These seated all in the court next the bar, before the High Steward, seven sergeants at arms came in with maces before the High Steward and laid them down before him in the court. The King-at-Arms stood on the one side of the High Steward by his chair of estate, and one of Her Majesty's gentlemen ushers, with his white rod in his hand, on the other side. The Clerk of the Crown and his assistants sat before him, to read the common indictments and examinations. The Captain of the Guard (Sir Walter Raleigh) and forty of the Queen's Guard were there to attend the service. Then . . . proclamation was made by a sergeant at arms that the

Lieutenant of the Tower of London should return his precept and bring forth his prisoners, Robert, Earl of Essex, and Henry, Earl of Southampton.

Then the Lord High Constable of the Tower, the Lieutenant of the Tower, and the gentleman porter, who carried the axe before the prisoners, came first in; and the prisoners followed and made their appearance at the bar, the gentleman porter with the axe standing before them, with the axe's edge from them. And so the Lieutenant delivered his precept into the court. The two earls which were prisoners kissed one another's hands and embraced each other. . . . Then they were called to hold up their hands at the bar, which they did. And then the Clerk of the Crown read the indictments. . . . After which, the Clerk of the Crown asked them whether they were guilty or not guilty. They pleaded Not Guilty, and for their trials they put themselves upon God and their peers. They spake this severally. Then my Lord Steward, in a few words, gave the peers a charge, requiring them to have a due regard of their consciences.

Then Sergeant Yelverton opened the evidence . . . and said as followeth: "May it please your grace" (speaking to the High Steward), "about the 8th of February last, my lord of Essex (there prisoner at the bar) went about with armed men very rebelliously to disinherit the Queen of her crown and dignity; which when it came to Her Majesty's ear, she, of her abounding mercy, sent to see if it were possible to stop rebellion. And who did she send? She sent (my lord) no worse persons than my Lord Keeper, my Lord Chief Justice of England, the Earl of Worcester, and Sir William Knollys, all which went in Her Majesty's name and commanded the earls and their adherents very strictly to dissolve their assemblies and to lay down their arms. But he knowing it, very treacherously imprisoned the said lords and Councillors by Her Majesty so sent, and altogether refused Her Majesty's authority. And divers of their confederates cried out, 'Kill them! Kill them!,' thereby putting Her Majesty's Council in fear of their lives. . . .

"Good my lord, I beseech your grace, and you my lords that are the peers, to understand that if any man do but intend the death of the king, it is death by the law; for he is the head of the commonwealth, and all his subjects, as members, ought to obey and stand with him. But as for this rebellion, being duly considered it contains in it many branches of treason, which are and will be directly proved; which being found to be so, my lords who are their peers are to find them guilty. Hereof need to be made no doubt, for it is more manifest than the sedition of Catiline to the city of Rome, and consequently England is in no less danger; for as Catiline entertained the most seditious persons about all Rome to join with him in his conspiracy, so the Earl of Essex had none but papists, recusants, and atheists for his adjutors and abettors in their capital rebellion against the whole estate of England.

"My lord, I much wonder that his heart could forget all the princely advancements given him by Her Majesty, and be so suddenly beflinted as to turn them all to rebellious ends. But it seems this overweighing a man's conceit, and an aspiring mind to wished honor, is like the crocodile, which is ever growing as long as he liveth. Your lordships know in what sort they went into the City, with armor and weapons, and how they returned to Essex House again . . . which makes me wonder they do not blush to be so forward to stand upon their trials without confession, when their intended treasons are in all men's judgments palpable. . . . My hope is that God, of His mercy, that hath revealed their treasons, will not suffer the rest of his or any others to the hurt of the state or prejudice to Her Majesty's most royal person, whom I pray God long to preserve from the hands of her enemies."

"Amen!" cried the Earl of Essex and the Earl of Southampton, "and God confound their souls that ever wished otherwise to her sacred person". . . .

SOUTHAMPTON: "I beseech your lordship and the rest thus much: that for my own part I did never know the laws. Now to show the causes that made me adventure so far as I did: the first occasion that made me adventure into these courses was the affinity between my lord of Essex and me, I being of his blood and marrying his kinswoman, so that for his sake I should have hazarded my life. But what I have, by my forwardness, offended in act, I am altogether ignorant; but in thought I am assured never. And if through my ignorance in the law I have offended, yet I humbly submit myself to Her Majesty, and from the bottom of my heart do beg her gracious pardon, if it please her. . . . For if any foolish speeches have passed, I protest, as I shall be saved, that they were never purposed by me, nor understood to be so purposed by me, to the hurt of Her Majesty's person". . . .

Then the Clerk of the Crown, speaking first to the Earl of Essex, said "Robert, Earl of Essex, you have been arraigned and indicted of high treason. . . . The peers here, who have heard the evidence and your answer in your defense, have found you Guilty. Now what can you say for yourself why you should not have judgment of death?"

ESSEX: "I only say this. That since I have committed that which hath brought me within the compass of the law, I may be counted the law's traitor in offending the law, for which I am willing to die, and will as willingly go thereto as ever did any. But I beseech your lordship and the rest of the lords here to have consideration of what I have formerly spoken, and do me the right as to think me a Christian, and that I have a soul to save, and that I know it is no time to jest. Lying and counterfeiting my soul abhorreth, for I am not desperate nor void of grace now to speak falsely. I do not speak to save my life, for that I see were vain. I owe God a death, which shall be welcome, how soon soever it pleaseth Her Majesty. And to satisfy the opinion of the world that my conscience is free from atheism and popery, howsoever I have been in this action misled to transgress the points of the law in the course and defense of private matters . . . yet I will live and die in the faith and true religion which here I have professed."

Then the Clerk of the Crown demanded of Henry, Earl of Southampton, what he could say for himself why judgment of death should not be pronounced against him.

SOUTHAMPTON: "My lords, I must say for my part, as I have said before, that since the ignorance of the law hath made me incur the danger of the law, I humbly submit myself to Her Majesty's mercy. . . . I know I have offended her, yet if it please her to be merciful unto me, I may live, and by my service deserve my life. I have spent the best part of my patrimony in Her Majesty's service, with danger of my life, as your lordships know. If there were any that could challenge me that I have ever heretofore committed or intended treason or any other thing prejudicial to Her Majesty or estate, God let me never inherit His kingdom, neither would I desire mercy. But since the law hath cast me, I do submit myself to death. And yet I will not despair of Her Majesty's mercy, for that I know she is merciful; and if she please to extend it, I shall with all humility receive it."

LORD STEWARD: "My Lord of Essex, the Queen's Majesty hath bestowed many favors on your predecessors and yourself. I would wish therefore that you likewise would submit yourself to Her Majesty's mercy, acknowledging your offenses and reconciling yourself inwardly to Her Majesty by laying open all matters that were intended to prejudice Her Majesty, and the actors thereof. And thereby no doubt you shall find Her Majesty merciful."

ESSEX: "My lord, you have made an honorable motion. Do but send to me at the time of my death, and you shall see how penitent and humble I will be towards Her Majesty, both in acknowledging her exceeding favors to my ancestors, and to myself. Whereby I doubt not but the penitent suffering of my death and sprinkling of my blood will quench the evil-conceited thoughts of Her Majesty against me. And I do most humbly desire Her Majesty that my death may put a period to my offenses committed, and be no more remembered by Her Highness. If I had ever perceived any of my followers to have harbored an evil thought against Her Majesty, I would have been the first that should have punished the same, in being his executioner. And therefore I beseech you, my good lord, mistake me not, nor think me so proud, that I will not crave Her Majesty's mercy. For I protest, kneeling upon the very knee of my heart, I do crave Her Majesty's mercy with all humility. Yet I had rather die than live in misery". . . .

Then the Lord High Steward gave judgment as followeth: "You must go to the place from whence you came, and there remain during Her Majesty's pleasure. From thence to be drawn on a hurdle through London streets, and so to the place of execution, where you shall be hanged, bowelled, and quartered; your head and quarters to be disposed of at Her Majesty's pleasure. And so God have mercy on your souls."

ESSEX: "My lord, I am not a whit dismayed to receive this sentence, for I protest death is as welcome to me as life, and I shall die as cheerful a death upon such a testimony as ever did man. And I think it fit my poor quarters, that have done Her Majesty true service in divers parts of the world, should be sacrificed and disposed of at Her Majesty's pleasure, whereunto with all willingness of heart I have submitted myself.

"But one thing I beg of you, my lords that have free access to Her Majesty's person, humbly to beseech Her Majesty to grant me that during the short time I shall live I may have the same preacher to comfort me that hath been with me since my troubles began. For as he that hath been long sick is most desirous of the physician which hath been and is best acquainted with the constitution of his body, so do I most wish to have the comfort and spiritual physic from the preacher which hath been and is acquainted with the inward griefs and secret affections of my soul". . . .

The Earl of Southampton obtained a reprieve, but the Earl of Essex was ordered for execution.

On the 15th of February 1601, which was the day appointed for his execution, [three divines] were sent unto him early in the morning to administer Christian consolation to his soul. In presence of these men he gave thanks to Almighty God, from the bottom of his heart, that his designs, which were so dangerous to the state, succeeded not. He told them he had now looked thoroughly and seriously into his sin, and was heartily sorry he had so obstinately defended an unjust cause at the bar. He thanked the Queen she had granted he should not be publicly executed, lest his mind, which was now settled and composed, might be disturbed by the acclamations of the people; protesting that he had now learned how vain a thing the blast of popular favor and applause was. He acknowledged how worthy he was to be spewed out (these were his words) by the commonwealth for the wickedness of his enterprise, which he likened to a leprosy spread far and near, that had infected many.

The Queen, in the meantime, wavered in her mind. One [moment] while relenting, she sent her command . . . that he should not be executed. But then remembering his perverse obstinacy, that he scorned to ask her pardon and had declared openly that his life would be the Queen's destruction, she soon after sent a fresh command that he should be put to death.

Then he was brought forth, between the divines, to a scaffold erected within the courtyard of the Tower, near which sat [a number of peers]. There were present also some of the aldermen of London, and Sir Walter Raleigh, who, if we may believe himself, came with an intent to make answer if anything should be objected against him by the Earl at his death; but others thought he came to feed his eyes with a sight of the Earl's sufferings, and to satiate his hatred with his blood. But being admonished not to press upon the Earl at his death, which is the part rather of ignoble brutes, he withdrew himself further off, and beheld his execution out of the Armoury.

The Earl, as soon as he was come upon the scaffold, uncovered his head, acknowledged that many and great had been the sins of his youth, for which, with most fervent prayer, he begged pardon of the eternal majesty of God through Christ his mediator; especially for this last sin, which he termed a bloody, crying and contagious sin, wherewith so many had been seduced to sin against God, their prince, and country. He besought the Queen and her ministers to forgive him, praying for her long life and prosperous estate, protesting withal that he never intended to lay violent hands on her person. He gave God thanks that he had never been atheist or papist, but had placed all his hope and confidence in the merits of Christ.

He prayed God to strengthen his mind against the terrors of death; desiring the standers-by to join with him in a short prayer, which with broken sighs and fervent affection of inward devotion he presently uttered. Afterwards, the executioner asking forgiveness, he forgave him. He recited the Apostles' Creed, and then, laying himself down, placed his neck upon the block. And having repeated the first verse of the Fifty-first Psalm, he said, "In humility and obedience I prostrate myself to my deserved punishment. Thou, O God, have mercy on thy prostrate servant. Into thy hands, O Lord, I commend my spirit."

His head was taken off at the third stroke; but the first took away all sense and motion.

Sources

The Arte of English Poesie, ed. Gladys Dodge Willcock and Alice Walker, 1936.

Ascham, Roger. *The Scholemaster*, ed. John E. B. Mayor, 1863.

Bacon, Francis. *The Works of*, ed. James Spedding, 1862.

Bodin, J. *The Six Bookes of a Commonweale . . . out of the French and Latin Copies, done into English, by Richard Knolles*, 1606.

Camden, William. *Britain, or a Chorographical Description of the Most Flourishing Kingdoms, England, Scotland and Ireland, and the Islands adjoining, out of the depth of Antiquity: Beautified with Maps of the several Shires of England. . . .* Translated newly into English by Philemon Holland, Doctor in Physic. Finally, revised, amended, and enlarged with sundry Additions by the said Author, London, 1610.

Castiglione, Baldassare. *The Book of the Courtier* translated by Sir Thomas Hoby, 1928.

Certain Sermons or Homilies Appointed to be Read in Churches in the Time of Queen Elizabeth . . . , 1844.

Coke, Edward. *The Reports of . . .* in English, 1738.

A Complete Collection of State Trials and Proceedings for High Treason and Other Crimes and Misdemeanors, ed. William Cobbett, 1809.

The Coronation Order of King James I, ed. J. Wickham Legg, 1902.

Dee, Dr. John. *The Mathematicall Praeface to the Elements of Geometrie of Euclid of Megara*, 1570 with an introduction by Allen G. Debus, 1975.

DuLaurens, André. *A Discourse of the Preservation of the Sight; of Melancholic Disease; of Rheumes, and of Old Age*. Translated by Richard Surphet, London, 1599.

Duplessis-Mornay, Philippe. *A Defence of Liberty against Tyrants. A translation of the Vindiciae Contra Tyrannos* by "Junius Brutus" (first published 1689), with an historical introduction by Harold J. Laski, 1924.

Elizabeth I. "Address to the Members of Commons, 30 November 1601" from *The Tudor Constitutions*, ed. J. R. Elton, 1982.

Elyot, Sir Thomas. *The Boke Named the Governour*, Everyman's Library, n.d.

Fortescue, Sir John. *De laudibus legum Angliae*, ed. by A. Amos, 1825.

————. *The Governance of England otherwise called The Difference between an Absolute and a Limited Monarchy*, ed. Charles Plummer, 1885.

Hooker, Richard. *The Works of That Learned and Judicious Divine arranged by the Rev. John Keble*, 1888.

James I. Political Works of, ed. Charles Howard McIlwain, 1918.

Machiavelli, Niccolò. *The Prince reprinted from the translation of Edward Dacres Published in 1640* with an introduction by W. E. C. Baynes, 1929.

Montaigne, Michel de. *The Essays of . . . Done into English by John Florio Anno 1603,* 1892.

Scot, Reginald. *The Discoverie of Witchcraft. . .* Introduced by Hugh Ross Williamson, 1964.

Smith, Sir Thomas. *De Republica Anglorum. A Discourse on the Commonwealth of England,* ed. L. Alston, 1906.

The Thirty-Nine Articles of the Church of England, ed. Edgar C. S. Gibson, 1897.

Wilson, Thomas. *The Arte of Rhetorique,* ed. Thomas J. Derrick, 1982.

Index